CONTENTS

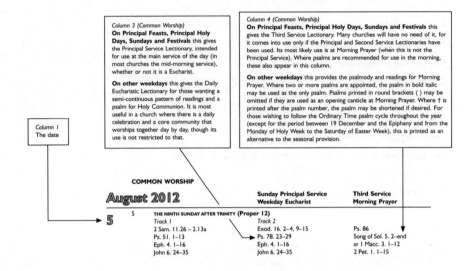

Column 1
The date

Column 3 (Common Worship)
On Principal Feasts, Principal Holy Days, Sundays and Festivals this gives the Principal Service Lectionary, intended for use at the main service of the day (in most churches the mid-morning service), whether or not it is a Eucharist.

On other weekdays this gives the Daily Eucharistic Lectionary for those wanting a semi-continuous pattern of readings and a psalm for Holy Communion. It is most useful in a church where there is a daily celebration and a core community that worships together day by day, though its use is not restricted to that.

Column 4 (Common Worship)
On Principal Feasts, Principal Holy Days, Sundays and Festivals this gives the Third Service Lectionary. Many churches will have no need of it, for it comes into use only if the Principal and Second Service Lectionaries have been used. Its most likely use is at Morning Prayer (when this is not the Principal Service). Where psalms are recommended for use in the morning, these also appear in this column.

On other weekdays this provides the psalmody and readings for Morning Prayer. Where two or more psalms are appointed, the psalm in bold italic may be used as the only psalm. Psalms printed in round brackets ( ) may be omitted if they are used as an opening canticle at Morning Prayer. Where † is printed after the psalm number, the psalm may be shortened if desired. For those wishing to follow the Ordinary Time psalm cycle throughout the year (except for the period between 19 December and the Epiphany and from the Monday of Holy Week to the Saturday of Easter Week), this is printed as an alternative to the seasonal provision.

COMMON WORSHIP

August 2012		Sunday Principal Service Weekday Eucharist	Third Service Morning Prayer
5	S	THE NINTH SUNDAY AFTER TRINITY (Proper 12)	
		Track 1 *Track 2*	
		2 Sam. 11.26 – 2.13a Exod. 16. 2–4, 9–15	Ps. 86
		Ps. 51. 1–13 Ps. 78. 23–29	Song of Sol. 5. 2–end
		Eph. 4. 1–16 Eph. 4. 1–16	or 1 Macc. 3. 1–12
		John 6. 24–35 John 6. 24–35	2 Pet. 1. 1–15
	G		
6 DEL 18	M	THE TRANSFIGURATION OF OUR LORD	
		Dan. 7. 9–10, 13–14	MP: Ps. 27; 150
		Ps. 97	Ecclus. 48. 1–10
		2 Pet. 1. 16–19	or 1 Kings 19. 1–16
	ꟻ	Luke 9. 28–36	1 John 3. 1–3
7	Tu	John Mason Neale, Priest, Hymn Writer, 1866	
		Jer. 30. 1–2, 12–15, 18–22	Ps. **48**; 52
		Ps. 102. 16–21	1 Sam. 20. 1–17
		Matt. 14. 22– end or 15. 1–2, 10–14	Acts 1. 15–end
	G		

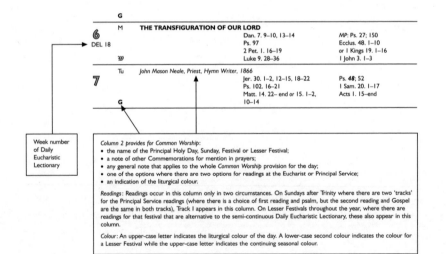

Week number of Daily Eucharistic Lectionary

Column 2 provides for Common Worship:
- the name of the Principal Holy Day, Sunday, Festival or Lesser Festival;
- a note of other Commemorations for mention in prayers;
- any general note that applies to the whole *Common Worship* provision for the day;
- one of the options where there are two options for readings at the Eucharist or Principal Service;
- an indication of the liturgical colour.

Readings: Readings occur in this column only in two circumstances. On Sundays after Trinity where there are two 'tracks' for the Principal Service readings (where there is a choice of first reading and psalm, but the second reading and Gospel are the same in both tracks), Track I appears in this column. On Lesser Festivals throughout the year, where there are readings for that festival that are alternative to the semi-continuous Daily Eucharistic Lectionary, these also appear in this column.

Colour: An upper-case letter indicates the liturgical colour of the day. A lower-case second colour indicates the colour for a Lesser Festival while the upper-case letter indicates the continuing seasonal colour.

LECTIONARY

Column 5 (Common Worship)
On Principal Feasts, Principal Holy Days, Sundays and Festivals this gives the Second Service Lectionary, intended for use when a second set of readings is required. Its most likely use is in the evening, when the Principal Service Lectionary has been used in the morning. Sometimes it might be used at an evening Eucharist. Where the second reading is not a Gospel reading, an alternative to meet this need is provided. Where psalms are recommended for use in the evening, these also appear in this column.

On other weekdays this provides the psalmody and readings for Evening Prayer. Where two or more psalms are provided, the psalm in bold italic may be used as the only psalm. Psalms printed in round brackets ( ) may be omitted if they are used as an opening canticle at Evening Prayer. Where † is printed after the psalm number, the psalm may be shortened if desired. For those wishing to follow the Ordinary Time psalm cycle throughout the year (except for the period between 19 December and the Epiphany and from the Monday of Holy Week to the Saturday of Easter Week), this is printed as an alternative to the seasonal provision.

Column 7 (Book of Common Prayer)
This provides the readings for Morning Prayer, together with psalm provision where it varies from the BCP monthly cycle.

A letter to indicate liturgical colour in this column indicates a change of colour before Evening Prayer. The symbol in bold lower case, **ct**, indicates that the Collect at Evening Prayer should be that of the following day.

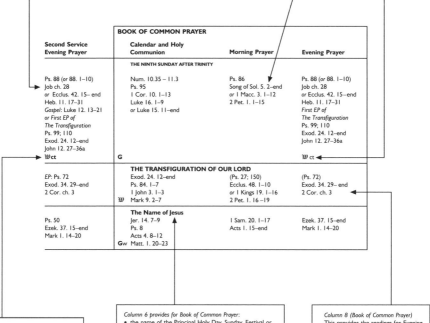

BOOK OF COMMON PRAYER

Second Service Evening Prayer	Calendar and Holy Communion	Morning Prayer	Evening Prayer
	THE NINTH SUNDAY AFTER TRINITY		
Ps. 88 (*or* 88. 1–10)	Num. 10.35 – 11.3	Ps. 86	Ps. 88 (*or* 88. 1–10)
Job ch. 28	Ps. 95	Song of Sol. 5. 2–end	Job ch. 28
or Ecclus. 42. 15– end	1 Cor. 10. 1–13	*or* 1 Macc. 3. 1–12	*or* Ecclus. 42. 15–end
Heb. 11. 17–31	Luke 16. 1–9	2 Pet. 1. 1–15	Heb. 11. 17–31
Gospel: Luke 12. 13–21	*or* Luke 15. 11–end		*First EP of*
or First EP of			*The Transfiguration*
The Transfiguration			Ps. 99; 110
Ps. 99; 110			Exod. 24. 12–end
Exod. 24. 12–end			John 12. 27–36a
John 12. 27–36a			
W **ct**	G		W **ct**
	THE TRANSFIGURATION OF OUR LORD		
EP: Ps. 72	Exod. 24. 12–end	(Ps. 27; 150)	(Ps. 72)
Exod. 34. 29–end	Ps. 84. 1–7	Ecclus. 48. 1–10	Exod. 34. 29– end
2 Cor. ch. 3	1 John 3. 1–3	*or* 1 Kings 19. 1–16	2 Cor. ch. 3
	W Mark 9. 2–7	2 Pet. 1. 16–19	
	The Name of Jesus		
Ps. 50	Jer. 14. 7–9	1 Sam. 20. 1–17	Ezek. 37. 15–end
Ezek. 37. 15–end	Ps. 8	Acts 1. 15–end	Mark 1. 14–20
Mark 1. 14–20	Acts 4. 8–12		
	Gw Matt. 1. 20–23		

A letter to indicate liturgical colour in this column indicates a change of colour before Evening Prayer. The symbol in bold lower case, **ct**, indicates that the Collect at Evening Prayer should be that of the following day.

Column 6 provides for Book of Common Prayer:
- the name of the Principal Holy Day, Sunday, Festival or Lesser Festival;
- any general note that applies to the whole Prayer Book provision for the day and an indication of points at which users may wish to draw on *Common Worship* material on the opposite page where the BCP has no provision;
- the Lectionary for the Eucharist on any day for which provision is made;
- an indication of liturgical colour (see column 2).

Column 8 (Book of Common Prayer)
This provides the readings for Evening Prayer, together with psalm provision where it varies from the BCP monthly cycle.

Making Choices in *Common Worship*

Common Worship makes provision for a variety of pastoral and liturgical circumstances. It needs to, for it has to serve some church communities where Morning Prayer, Holy Communion and Evening Prayer are all celebrated every day, and yet be useful also in a church with only one service a week, and that service varying in form and time from week to week.

At the beginning of the year, some decisions in principle need to be taken.

In relation to the Calendar, a decision needs to be taken whether to keep The Epiphany on Friday 6 January or on Sunday 8 January, The Presentation of Christ (Candlemas) on Thursday 2 February or on Sunday 29 January and whether to keep the Feast of All Saints on Thursday 1 November or on Sunday 4 November.

In relation to the Lectionary, the initial choices every year to decide in relation to Sundays are:

● which of the services on a Principal Feast, Principal Holy Day, Sunday or Festival constitutes the 'Principal Service'; then use the Principal Service Lectionary (column 3) consistently for that service through the year;
● during the Sundays after Trinity, whether to use Track 1 of the Principal Service Lectionary (column 2), where the first reading stays over several weeks with one Old Testament book read semi-continuously, or Track 2 (column 3), where the first reading is chosen for its relationship to the Gospel reading of the day;
● which, if any, service on a Principal Feast, Principal Holy Day, Sunday or Festival constitutes the 'Second Service'; then use the Second Service Lectionary (column 5) consistently for that service through the year;
● which, if any, service on a Principal Feast, Principal Holy Day, Sunday or Festival constitutes the 'Third Service'; then use the Third Service Lectionary (column 4) consistently for that service through the year.

And in relation to weekdays:

● whether to use the Daily Eucharistic Lectionary (column 3) consistently for weekday celebrations of Holy Communion (with the exception of Principal Feasts, Principal Holy Days and Festivals) or to make some use of the Lesser Festival provision;
● whether to follow the first psalm provision in column 4 (morning) and column 5 (evening), where psalms during the seasons have a seasonal flavour but in ordinary time follow a sequential pattern; or to follow the alternative provision in the same columns, where psalms follow the sequential pattern throughout the year, except for the period between 19 December and The Epiphany and from the Monday of Holy Week to the Saturday of Easter Week; or to follow the psalm cycle in the Book of Common Prayer, where they are nearly always used 'in course'.
● whether to use the Additional Weekday Lectionary (which begins on page 92) for weekday services (other than Holy Communion). It provides a one-year cycle of two readings for each day (except for Sundays, Principal Feasts, Principal Holy Days, Festivals and during Holy Week). Since each of the readings is designed to 'stand alone' (that is, it is complete in itself and will make sense to the worshipper who has not attended on the previous day and who will not be present on the next day), it is intended particularly for use in those churches and cathedrals that attract occasional rather than regular congregations.

The flexibility of *Common Worship* is intended to enable the church and the minister to find the most helpful provision for them. But once a decision is made, it is advisable to stay with that decision through the year or at the very least through a complete season.

Book of Common Prayer

A separate Lectionary for the Book of Common Prayer is no longer issued. Provision is made on the right-hand pages of this Lectionary for BCP worship on all Sundays in the year, for the major festivals and for Morning and Evening Prayer. The Epistles and Gospels for Holy Communion are those of 1662, with the additions and variations of 1928, now authorized under the *Common Worship* overall provision. The Old Testament readings and psalms for these services, formerly appended to the Series One Holy Communion service, may be used but are not mandatory with the 1662 order.

Readings for Morning and Evening Prayer, which are the same as those for *Common Worship*, are set out in the BCP section for Sundays and weekdays. The special psalm provision of the BCP is given. Otherwise the Psalter is read in course daily through each month.

The Calendar observes BCP dates when these differ from those of *Common Worship*; for example, St Thomas on 21 December. Additional commemorations in the *Common Worship* Calendar are not included, but those who wish to observe them may use the *Collects and Post Communions in Traditional Language: Lesser Festivals, Common of the Saints, Special Occasions* (Church House Publishing).

The Lectionaries of 1871 and 1922, to be found in many copies of the BCP, are still authorized and may be used, but – with the exception of the psalms and readings for Holy Communion mentioned above – the Additional Alternative Lectionary (1961) is no longer authorized for public worship.

Although those who use the BCP, for private or public worship or both, are free to follow any of the authorized lectionaries, there is much to be said for common usage across the Church of England, so that the same passages are being read by all. It is of course appropriate that BCP readings should be taken from the Authorized or King James Version for harmony of style, with the daily recitation of the BCP Psalter.

The integrity of the BCP as the traditional source of worship in the Church of England is not in any way affected by the use of a common lectionary for the daily offices.

CERTAIN DAYS AND OCCASIONS COMMONLY OBSERVED

Plough Sunday may be observed on 8 January 2012.

The Week of Prayer for Christian Unity may be observed from 18 to 25 January 2012.

Education Sunday may be observed on 5 February 2012.

Rogation Sunday may be observed on 13 May 2012.

The Feast of Dedication is observed on the anniversary of the dedication or consecration of a church, or, when the actual date is unknown, on 7 October 2012. In CW, 28 October 2012 is an alternative date.

Ember Days. CW encourages the bishop to set the Ember Days in each diocese in the week before the ordinations, whereas in BCP the dates are fixed.

Days of Discipline and Self-Denial in CW are the weekdays of Lent and all Fridays in the year, except all Principal Feasts and festivals outside Lent and Fridays between Easter Day and Pentecost. The eves of Principal Feasts are also appropriately kept as days of discipline and self-denial in preparation for the feast.

Days of Fasting and Abstinence according to the BCP are the forty days of Lent, the Ember Days at the four seasons, the three Rogation Days, and all Fridays in the year except Christmas Day. The BCP also orders the observance of the Evens or Vigils before The Nativity of our Lord, The Purification of the Blessed Virgin Mary, The Annunciation of the Blessed Virgin Mary, Easter Day, Ascension Day, Pentecost, and before the following saints' days: Matthias, John the Baptist, Peter, James, Bartholomew, Matthew, Simon and Jude, Andrew, Thomas, and All Saints. (If any of these days falls on Monday, the Vigil is to be kept on the previous Saturday.)

KEY TO LITURGICAL COLOURS

Common Worship suggests appropriate liturgical colours. They are not mandatory, and traditional or local use may be followed.

For a detailed discussion of when colours may be used, see *Common Worship: Services and Prayers for the Church of England* (Church House Publishing), *New Handbook of Pastoral Liturgy* (SPCK) or *A Companion to Common Worship: Volume I* (SPCK).

W	White
ℤℤ	Gold or white
R	Red
P	Purple (may vary from 'Roman purple' to violet, with blue as an alternative; a Lent array of sackcloth may be used in Lent, and rose pink on The Third Sunday of Advent and Fourth Sunday of Lent)
G	Green

When a lower-case letter accompanies an upper-case letter, the lower-case letter indicates the liturgical colour appropriate to the Lesser Festival of that day, while the upper-case letter indicates the continuing seasonal colour.

PRINCIPAL FEASTS, HOLY DAYS AND FESTIVALS

Principal Feasts, and other Principal Holy Days (Ash Wednesday, Maundy Thursday, Good Friday), are printed in **LARGE BOLD CAPITALS** in the Lectionary.

There are no longer proper readings relating to the Holy Spirit on the six days after Pentecost. Instead they have been located on the nine days before Pentecost.

When Patronal and Dedication Festivals are kept as Principal Feasts, they may be transferred to the nearest Sunday, unless that day is already either a Principal Feast or The First Sunday of Advent, The Baptism of Christ, The First Sunday of Lent or Palm Sunday.

Festivals are printed in the Lectionary in SMALL BOLD CAPITALS.

For each day there is a full liturgical provision for the Holy Communion and for Morning and Evening Prayer. Most holy days that are in the category 'Festival' are provided with an optional First Evening Prayer. Its use is entirely at the discretion of the minister. Where it is used, the liturgical colour for the next day should be used at that First Evening Prayer, and this has been indicated in the provision on the following pages.

LESSER FESTIVALS AND COMMEMORATIONS

Lesser Festivals (printed in **bold roman** typeface) are observed at the level appropriate to a particular church. The readings and psalms for The Common of the Saints are listed on page 9. In addition, there are special readings appropriate to the Festival listed in the first column. The daily psalms and readings at Morning and Evening Prayer are not usually superseded by those for Lesser Festivals, but the readings and psalms for Holy Communion may on occasion be used at Morning or Evening Prayer.

Commemorations are printed in the Lectionary in *italic* typeface. They do not have collect, psalm or readings, but may be observed by mention in prayers of intercession and thanksgiving. For local reasons, or where there is an established tradition in the wider Church, they may be kept as Lesser Festivals using the appropriate material from The Common of the Saints. Equally, it may be desirable to observe some Lesser Festivals as Commemorations.

If a Lesser Festival or a Commemoration falls on a Principal Feast, Principal Holy Day, Sunday or Festival, it is not normally observed that year, although it may be celebrated, where there is sufficient reason, on the nearest available day. Lesser Festivals and Commemorations which, for this reason, would not be celebrated in 2011–12 are listed on pages 7–8, so that, if desired, they may be mentioned in prayers of intercession and thanksgiving.

LESSER FESTIVALS AND COMMEMORATIONS NOT OBSERVED IN 2011–12

The Lesser Festivals and Commemorations (shown in italics) listed below fall on a Sunday or during Holy Week or Easter Week this year, and are thus not observed in this lectionary.

Common Worship

2011

December

4　　*John of Damascus, Monk, Teacher, c. 749*
　　　Nicholas Ferrar, Deacon, Founder of the Little Gidding Community, 1637

2012

January

22　　*Vincent of Saragossa, Deacon, first Martyr of Spain, 304*

March

18　　*Cyril, Bishop of Jerusalem, Teacher, 386*
26　　*Harriet Monsell, Founder of the Community of St John the Baptist, Clewer, 1883*

April

1　　*Frederick Denison Maurice, Priest, Teacher, 1872*
9　　*Dietrich Bonhoeffer, Lutheran Pastor, Martyr, 1945*
10　　William Law, Priest, Spiritual Writer, 1761
　　　William of Ockham, Friar, Philosopher, Teacher, 1347
11　　*George Augustus Selwyn, first Bishop of New Zealand, 1878*
29　　Catherine of Siena, Teacher, 1380

May

20　　Alcuin of York, Deacon, Abbot of Tours, 804

June

3　　*The Martyrs of Uganda, 1885–87 and 1977*
17　　*Samuel and Henrietta Barnett, Social Reformers, 1913 and 1936*

July

1　　*Henry, John and Henry Venn the Younger, Priests, Evangelical Divines, 1797,*
　　　1813 and 1873
15　　Swithun, Bishop of Winchester, c. 862
　　　Bonaventure, Friar, Bishop, Teacher, 1274
29　　Mary, Martha and Lazarus, Companions of Our Lord

August

5　　Oswald, King of Northumbria, Martyr, 642

September

2　　*The Martyrs of Papua New Guinea, 1901 and 1942*
9　　*Charles Fuge Lowder, Priest, 1880*

8

16	Ninian, Bishop of Galloway, Apostle of the Picts, c. 432
	Edward Bouverie Pusey, Priest, Tractarian, 1882
30	*Jerome, Translator of the Scriptures, Teacher, 420*

November

11	Martin, Bishop of Tours, c. 397
18	Elizabeth of Hungary, Princess of Thuringia, Philanthropist, 1231
25	*Catherine of Alexandria, Martyr, 4th century*
	Isaac Watts, Hymn Writer, 1748

Book of Common Prayer

2012

January

| 8 | Lucian, Priest and Martyr, 290 |
| 22 | Vincent of Saragossa, Deacon, first Martyr of Spain, 304 |

February

| 5 | Agatha, Martyr in Sicily, 251 |

March

| 18 | Edward, King of the W. Saxons, 978 |

April

| 3 | Richard, Bishop of Chichester, 1253 |
| 4 | Ambrose, Bishop of Milan, 397 |

May

| 6 | John the Evangelist, ante Portam Latinam |
| 27 | The Venerable Bede, Monk at Jarrow, Scholar, Historian, 735 |

June

| 17 | Alban, first Martyr of Britain, c. 250 |

July

| 15 | Swithun, Bishop of Winchester, c. 862 |

September

| 30 | Jerome, Translator of the Scriptures, Teacher, 420 |

November

| 11 | Martin, Bishop of Tours, c. 397 |
| 25 | Catherine of Alexandria, Martyr, 4th century |

THE COMMON OF THE SAINTS

The Blessed Virgin Mary
Genesis 3. 8–15, 20; Isaiah 7. 10–14; Micah 5. 1–4
Psalms 45. 10–17; 113; 131
Acts 1. 12–14; Romans 8. 18–30; Galatians 4. 4–7
Luke 1. 26–38; Luke 1. 39–47; John 19. 25–27

Martyrs
2 Chronicles 24. 17–21; Isaiah 43. 1–7; Jeremiah 11. 18–20; Wisdom 4. 10–15
Psalms 3; 11; 31. 1–5; 44. 18–24; 126
Romans 8. 35–end; 2 Corinthians 4. 7–15; 2 Timothy 2. 3–7 [8–13]; Hebrews 11. 32–end; 1 Peter
4. 12–end; Revelation 12. 10–12a
Matthew 10. 16–22; Matthew 10. 28–39; Matthew 16. 24–26; John 12. 24–26; John 15. 18–21

Teachers of the Faith and Spiritual Writers
1 Kings 3. [6–10] 11–14; Proverbs 4. 1–9; Wisdom 7. 7–10, 15–16; Ecclesiasticus 39. 1–10
Psalms 19. 7–10; 34. 11–17; 37. 31–35; 119. 89–96; 119. 97–104
1 Corinthians 1. 18–25; 1 Corinthians 2. 1–10; 1 Corinthians 2. 9–end;
Ephesians 3. 8–12; 2 Timothy 4. 1–8; Titus 2. 1–8
Matthew 5. 13–19; Matthew 13. 52–end; Matthew 23. 8–12; Mark 4. 1–9; John 16. 12–15

Bishops and Other Pastors
1 Samuel 16. 1, 6–13; Isaiah 6. 1–8; Jeremiah 1. 4–10; Ezekiel 3. 16–21; Malachi 2. 5–7
Psalms 1; 15; 16. 5–end; 96; 110
Acts 20. 28–35; 1 Corinthians 4. 1–5; 2 Corinthians 4. 1–10 (or 1–2, 5–7); 2 Corinthians 5. 14–20;
1 Peter 5. 1–4
Matthew 11. 25–end; Matthew 24. 42–46; John 10. 11–16; John 15. 9–17; John 21. 15–17

Members of Religious Communities
1 Kings 19. 9–18; Proverbs 10. 27–end; Song of Solomon 8. 6–7; Isaiah 61.10 – 62.5; Hosea 2.
14–15, 19–20
Psalms 34. 1–8; 112. 1–9; 119. 57–64; 123; 131
Acts 4. 32–35; 2 Corinthians 10.17 – 11.2; Philippians 3. 7–14; 1 John 2. 15–17; Revelation 19. 1,
5–9
Matthew 11. 25–end; Matthew 19. 3–12; Matthew 19. 23–end; Luke 9. 57–end; Luke 12. 32–37

Missionaries
Isaiah 52. 7–10; Isaiah 61. 1–3a; Ezekiel 34. 11–16; Jonah 3. 1–5
Psalms 67; 87; 97; 100; 117
Acts 2. 14, 22–36; Acts 13. 46–49; Acts 16. 6–10; Acts 26. 19–23; Romans 15. 17–21;
2 Corinthians 5.11 – 6.2
Matthew 9. 35–end; Matthew 28. 16–end; Mark 16. 15–20; Luke 5. 1–11; Luke 10. 1–9

Any Saint
Genesis 12. 1–4; Proverbs 8. 1–11; Micah 6. 6–8; Ecclesiasticus 2. 7–13 [14–end]
Psalms 32; 33. 1–5; 119. 1–8; 139. 1–4 [5–12]; 145. 8–14
Ephesians 3. 14–19; Ephesians 6. 11–18; Hebrews 13. 7–8, 15–16; James 2. 14–17; 1 John 4. 7–16;
Revelation 21. [1–4] 5–7
Matthew 19. 16–21; Matthew 25. 1–13; Matthew 25. 14–30; John 15. 1–8; John 17. 20–end

SPECIAL OCCASIONS

The Guidance of the Holy Spirit
Proverbs 24. 3–7; Isaiah 30. 15–21; Wisdom 9. 13–17
Psalms 25. 1–9; 104. 26–33; 143. 8–10
Acts 15. 23–29; Romans 8. 22–27; 1 Corinthians 12. 4–13
Luke 14. 27–33; John 14. 23–26; John 16. 13–15

The Commemoration of the Faithful Departed
Lamentations 3. 17–26, 31–33 or Wisdom 3. 1–9
Psalm 23 or Psalm 27. 1–6, 16–end
Romans 5. 5–11 or 1 Peter 1. 3–9
John 5. 19–25 or John 6. 37–40

Rogation Days
Deuteronomy 8. 1–10; 1 Kings 8. 35–40; Job 28. 1–11
Psalms 104. 21–30; 107. 1–9; 121
Philippians 4. 4–7; 2 Thessalonians 3. 6–13; 1 John 5. 12–15
Matthew 6. 1–15; Mark 11. 22–24; Luke 11. 5–13

Harvest Thanksgiving
Year A
Deuteronomy 8. 7–18 or Deuteronomy 28. 1–14
Psalm 65
2 Corinthians 9. 6–end
Luke 12. 16–30 or Luke 17. 11–19

Year B
Joel 2. 21–27
Psalm 126
1 Timothy 2. 1–7 or 1 Timothy 6. 6–10
Matthew 6. 25–33

Year C
Deuteronomy 26. 1–11
Psalm 100
Philippians 4. 4–9 or Revelation 14. 14–18
John 6. 25–35

Mission and Evangelism
Isaiah 49. 1–6; Isaiah 52. 7–10; Micah 4. 1–5
Psalms 2; 46; 67
Acts 17. 12–end; 2 Corinthians 5.14 – 6.2; Ephesians 2. 13–end
Matthew 5. 13–16; Matthew 28. 16–end; John 17. 20–end

The Unity of the Church
Jeremiah 33. 6–9a; Ezekiel 36. 23–28; Zephaniah 3. 16–end
Psalms 100; 122; 133
Ephesians 4. 1–6; Colossians 3. 9–17; 1 John 4. 9–15
Matthew 18. 19–22; John 11. 45–52; John 17. 11b–23

The Peace of the World
Isaiah 9. 1–6; Isaiah 57. 15–19; Micah 4. 1–5
Psalms 40. 14–17; 72. 1–7; 85. 8–13
Philippians 4. 6–9; 1 Timothy 2. 1–6; James 3. 13–18
Matthew 5. 43–end; John 14. 23–29; John 15. 9–17

Social Justice and Responsibility
Isaiah 32. 15–end; Amos 5. 21–24; Amos 8. 4–7; Acts 5. 1–11
Psalms 31. 21–24; 85. 1–7; 146. 5–10
Colossians 3. 12–15; James 2. 1–4
Matthew 5. 1–12; Matthew 25. 31–end; Luke 16. 19–end

Ministry (including Ember Days)
Numbers 11. 16 17, 24 29; Numbers 27. 15–end; 1 Samuel 16. 1–13a
Isaiah 6. 1–8; Isaiah 61. 1–3; Jeremiah 1. 4–10
Psalms 40. 8–13; 84. 8–12; 89. 19–25; 101. 1–5, 7; 122
Acts 20. 28–35; 1 Corinthians 3. 3–11; Ephesians 4. 4–16; Philippians 3. 7–14
Luke 4. 16–21; Luke 12. 35–43; Luke 22. 24–27; John 4. 31–38; John 15. 5–17

In Time of Trouble
Genesis 9. 8–17; Job 1. 13–end; Isaiah 38. 6–11
Psalms 86. 1–7; 107. 4–15; 142. 1–7
Romans 3. 21–26; Romans 8. 18–25; 2 Corinthians 8. 1–5, 9
Mark 4. 35–end; Luke 12. 1–7; John 16. 31–end

For the Sovereign
Joshua 1. 1–9; Proverbs 8. 1–16
Psalms 20; 101; 121
Romans 13. 1–10; Revelation 21.22 – 22.4
Matthew 22. 16–22; Luke 22. 24–30

November 2011

			Sunday Principal Service / Weekday Eucharist	Third Service / Morning Prayer
27	S	THE FIRST SUNDAY OF ADVENT CW Year B begins	Isa. 64. 1–9 Ps. 80. 1–8, 18–20 (or 80. 1–8) 1 Cor. 1. 3–9 Mark 13. 24–end	Ps. 44 Isa. 2. 1–5 Luke 12. 35–48
	P			
28	M	Daily Eucharistic Lectionary Year 2 begins	Isa. 2. 1–5 Ps. 122 Matt. 8. 5–11	Ps. **50**; 54 alt. Ps. **1**; 2; 3 Isa. 25. 1–9 Matt. 12. 1–21
	P			
29	Tu		Isa. 11. 1–10 Ps. 72. 1–4, 18–19 Luke 10. 21–24	Ps. **80**; 82 alt. Ps. **5**; 6; (8) Isa. 26. 1–13 Matt. 12. 22–37
		Day of Intercession and Thanksgiving for the Missionary Work of the Church	Isa. 49. 1–6; Isa. 52. 7–10; Mic. 4. 1–5 Ps. 2; 46; 47 Acts 17. 12–end; 2 Cor. 5.14 – 6.2; Eph. 2. 13–end Matt. 5. 13–16; Matt. 28. 16–end; John 17. 20–end	
	P			
30	W	ANDREW THE APOSTLE	Isa. 52. 7–10 Ps. 19. 1–6 Rom. 10. 12–18 Matt. 4. 18–22	MP: Ps. 47; 147. 1–12 Ezek. 47. 1–12 or Ecclus. 14. 20–end John 12. 20–32
	R			

December 2011

1	Th	*Charles de Foucauld, Hermit in the Sahara, 1916*	Isa. 26. 1–6 Ps. 118. 18–27a Matt. 7. 21, 24–27	Ps. **42**; 43 alt. Ps. 14; **15**; 16 Isa. 28. 14–end Matt. 13. 1–23
	P			
2	F		Isa. 29. 17–end Ps. 27. 1–4, 16–17 Matt. 9. 27–31	Ps. **25**; 26 alt. Ps. 17; **19** Isa. 29. 1–14 Matt. 13. 24–43
	P			
3	Sa	*Francis Xavier, Missionary, Apostle of the Indies, 1552*	Isa. 30. 19–21, 23–26 Ps. 146. 4–9 Matt. 9.35 – 10.1, 6–8	Ps. **9**; (10) alt. Ps. 20; 21; **23** Isa. 29. 15–end Matt. 13. 44–end
	P			
4	S	THE SECOND SUNDAY OF ADVENT	Isa. 40. 1–11 Ps. 85. 1–2, 8–end (or 85. 8–end) 2 Pet. 3. 8–15a Mark 1. 1–8	Ps. 80 Baruch 5. 1–9 or Zeph. 3. 14–end Luke 1. 5–20
	P			
5	M		Isa. ch. 35 Ps. 85. 7–end Luke 5. 17–26	Ps. 44 alt. Ps. 27; **30** Isa. 30. 1–18 Matt. 14. 1–12
	P			
6	Tu	**Nicholas, Bishop of Myra, c. 326** Com. Bishop or also Isa. 61. 1–3 1 Tim. 6. 6–11	Isa. 40. 1–11 Ps. 96. 1, 10–end Matt. 18. 12–14	Ps. **56**; 57 alt. Ps. 32; **36** Isa. 30. 19–end Matt. 14. 13–end
	Pw	Mark 10. 13–16		

Second Service Evening Prayer		Calendar and Holy Communion	Morning Prayer	Evening Prayer
		THE FIRST SUNDAY OF ADVENT		
Ps. 25 (or 25. 1–9)		Advent 1 Collect until Christmas	Ps. 44	Ps. 9
Isa. 1. 1–20		Eve	Isa. 2. 1–5	Isa. 1. 1–20
Matt. 21. 1–13		Mic. 4. 1–4, 6–7	Luke 12. 35–48	Mark 13. 24–end
		Ps. 25. 1–9		
		Rom. 13. 8–14		
	P	Matt. 21. 1–13		
Ps. 70; **71**			Isa. 25. 1–9	Isa. 42. 18–end
alt. Ps. **4**; 7			Matt. 12. 1–21	Rev. ch. 19
Isa. 42. 18–end				
Rev. ch. 19	**P**			
Ps. **74**; 75			Isa. 26. 1–13	Isa. 43. 1–13
alt. Ps. **9**; 10†			Matt. 12. 22–37	Rev. ch. 20
Isa. 43. 1–13				
Rev. ch. 20				or First EP of Andrew
or First EP of Andrew the Apostle				the Apostle
Ps. 48				(Ps. 48)
Isa. 49. 1–9a				Isa. 49. 1–9a
1 Cor. 4. 9–16				1 Cor. 4. 9–16
R ct				**R ct**
		To celebrate the Day of Intercession and Thanksgiving for the Missionary Work of the Church, see *Common Worship* provision.		
	P			
		ANDREW THE APOSTLE		
EP: Ps. 87; 96		Zech. 8. 20–end	(Ps. 47; 147. 1–12)	(Ps. 87; 96)
Zech. 8. 20–end		Ps. 92. 1–5	Ezek. 47. 1–12	Isa. 52. 7–10
John 1. 35–42		Rom. 10. 9–end	or Ecclus. 14. 20–end	John 1. 35–42
	R	Matt. 4. 18–22	John 12. 20–32	
Ps. **40**; 46			Isa. 28. 14–end	Isa. 44. 1–8
alt. Ps. 18†			Matt. 13. 1–23	Rev. 21. 9–21
Isa. 44. 1–8				
Rev. 21. 9–21	**P**			
Ps. 16; **17**			Isa. 29. 1–14	Isa. 44. 9–23
alt. Ps. 22			Matt. 13. 24–43	Rev. 21.22 – 22.5
Isa. 44. 9–23				
Rev. 21.22 – 22.5	**P**			
Ps. **27**; 28			Isa. 29. 15–end	Isa. 44.24 – 45.13
alt. Ps. **24**; 25			Matt. 13. 44–end	Rev. 22. 6–end
Isa. 44.24 – 45.13				
Rev. 22. 6–end				
ct	**P**			**ct**
		THE SECOND SUNDAY OF ADVENT		
Ps. 40 (or 40. 12–end)		2 Kings 22. 8–10; 23. 1–3	Ps. 80	Ps. 40
1 Kings 22. 1–28		Ps. 50. 1–6	Baruch 5. 1–9	(or 40. 12–end)
Rom. 15. 4–13		Rom. 15. 4–13	or Zeph. 3. 14–end	1 Kings 22. 1–28
Gospel: Matt. 11. 2–11		Luke 21. 25–33	Luke 1. 5–20	2 Pet. 3. 8–15a
	P			
Ps. **144**; 146			Isa. 30. 1–18	Isa. 45. 14–end
alt. Ps. 26; **28**; 29			Matt. 14. 1–12	1 Thess. ch. 1
Isa. 45. 14–end				
1 Thess. ch. 1	**P**			
		Nicholas, Bishop of Myra, c. 326		
Ps. **11**; 12; 13		Com. Bishop	Isa. 30. 19–end	Isa. ch. 46
alt. Ps. 33			Matt. 14. 13–end	1 Thess. 2. 1–12
Isa. ch. 46				
1 Thess. 2. 1–12	**Pw**			

December 2011

		Sunday Principal Service / Weekday Eucharist	Third Service / Morning Prayer

7 W

Ambrose, Bishop of Milan, Teacher, 397
Ember Day*
Com. Teacher
also Isa. 41. 9b–13
Luke 22. 24–30

or Isa. 40. 25–end
Ps. 103. 8–13
Matt. 11. 28–end

Ps. *62*; 63
alt. Ps. 34
Isa. ch. 31

Pw

Matt. 15. 1–20

---

8 Th

The Conception of the Blessed Virgin Mary
Com. BVM

or Isa. 41. 13–20
Ps. 145. 1, 8–13
Matt. 11. 11–15

Ps. 53; *54*; 60
alt. Ps. 37†
Isa. ch. 32

Pw

Matt. 15. 21–28

---

9 F

Ember Day*

Isa. 48. 17–19
Ps. 1
Matt. 11. 16–19

Ps. 85; *86*
alt. Ps. 31
Isa. 33. 1–22

P

Matt. 15. 29–end

---

10 Sa

Ember Day*

Ecclus. 48. 1–4, 9–11
or 2 Kings 2. 9–12
Ps. 80. 1–4, 18–19
Matt. 17. 10–13

Ps. 145
alt. Ps. 41; *42*; 43
Isa. ch. 35

P

Matt. 16. 1–12

---

11 S

THE THIRD SUNDAY OF ADVENT

Isa. 61. 1–4, 8–end
Ps. 126
or Canticle: Magnificat
1 Thess. 5. 16–24

Ps. 50. 1–6, 62
Isa. ch. 12
Luke 1. 57–66

P

John 1. 6–8, 19–28

---

12 M

Num. 24. 2–7, 15–17
Ps. 25. 3–8
Matt. 21. 23–27

Ps. 40
alt. Ps. 44
Isa. 38. 1–8, 21–22

P

Matt. 16. 13–end

---

13 Tu

Lucy, Martyr at Syracuse, 304
Samuel Johnson, Moralist, 1784
Com. Martyr
also Wisd. 3. 1–7
2 Cor. 4. 6–15

or Zeph. 3. 1–2, 9–13
Ps. 34. 1–6, 21–22
Matt. 21. 28–32

Ps. *70*; 74
alt. Ps. *48*; 52
Isa. 38. 9–20

Pr

Matt. 17. 1–13

---

14 W

John of the Cross, Poet, Teacher, 1591
Com. Teacher
esp. 1 Cor. 2. 1–10
also John 14. 18–23

or Isa. 45. 6b–8, 18, 21b–end
Ps. 85. 7–end
Luke 7. 18b–23

Ps. *75*; 96
alt. Ps. 119. 57–80
Isa. ch. 39

Pw

Matt. 17. 14–21

---

15 Th

Isa. 54. 1–10
Ps. 30. 1–5, 11–end
Luke 7. 24–30

Ps. *76*; 97
alt. Ps. 56; *57*; (63†)
Zeph. 1.1 – 2.3

P

Matt. 17. 22–end

---

16 F

Isa. 56. 1–3a, 6–8
Ps. 67
John 5. 33–36

Ps. 77; *98*
alt. Ps. *51*; 54
Zeph. 3. 1–13

P

Matt. 18. 1–20

---

17 Sa

O Sapientia
Eglantyne Jebb, Social Reformer, Founder of 'Save the Children', 1928

Gen. 49. 2, 8–10
Ps. 72. 1–5, 18–19
Matt. 1. 1–17

Ps. 71
alt. Ps. 68
Zeph. 3. 14–end

P

Matt. 18. 21–end

---

*For Ember Day provision, see p. 11.

Second Service Evening Prayer	Calendar and Holy Communion	Morning Prayer	Evening Prayer
Ps. *10*; 14 *alt.* Ps. 119. 33–56 Isa. ch. 47 1 Thess. 2. 13–end	P	Isa. ch. 31 Matt. 15. 1–20	Isa. ch. 47 1 Thess. 2. 13–end
Ps. 73 *alt.* Ps. 39; *40* Isa. 48. 1–11 1 Thess. ch. 3	**The Conception of the Blessed Virgin Mary** Pw	Isa. ch. 32 Matt. 15. 21–28	Isa. 48. 1–11 1 Thess. ch. 3
Ps. 82; *90* *alt.* Ps. 35 Isa. 48. 12–end 1 Thess. 4. 1–12	P	Isa. 33. 1–22 Matt. 15. 29–end	Isa. 48. 12–end 1 Thess. 4. 1–12
Ps. 93; *94* *alt.* Ps. 45; *46* Isa. 49. 1–13 1 Thess. 4. 13–end ct	P	Isa. ch. 35 Matt. 16. 1–12	Isa. 49. 1–13 1 Thess. 4. 13–end ct
Ps. 68. 1–19 (*or* 68. 1–8) Mal. 3. 1–4; ch. 4 Phil. 4. 4–7 *Gospel:* Matt. 14. 1–12	THE THIRD SUNDAY OF ADVENT Isa. ch. 35 Ps. 80. 1–7 1 Cor. 4. 1–5 Matt. 11. 2–10 P	Ps. 62 Isa. ch. 12 Luke 1. 57–66	Ps. 68. 1–19 (*or* 68. 1–8) Mal. 3. 1–4; ch. 4 Matt. 14. 1–12
Ps. 25; *26* *alt.* Ps. *47*; 49 Isa. 49. 14–25 1 Thess. 5. 1–11	P	Isa. 38. 1–8, 21–22 Matt. 16. 13–end	Isa. 49. 14–25 1 Thess. 5. 1–11
Ps. *50*; 54 *alt.* Ps. 50 Isa. ch. 50 1 Thess. 5. 12–end	**Lucy, Martyr at Syracuse, 304** Com. Virgin Martyr Pr	Isa. 38. 9–20 Matt. 17. 1–13	Isa. ch. 50 1 Thess. 5. 12–end
Ps. 25; *82* *alt.* Ps. *59*; 60; (67) Isa. 51. 1–8 2 Thess. ch. 1	Ember Day Ember CEG P	Isa. ch. 39 Matt. 17. 14–21	Isa. 51. 1–8 2 Thess. ch. 1
Ps. 44 *alt.* Ps. 61; *62*; 64 Isa. 51. 9–16 2 Thess. ch. 2	 P	Zeph. 1.1 – 2.3 Matt. 17. 22–end	Isa. 51. 9–16 2 Thess. ch. 2
Ps. 49 *alt.* Ps. 38 Isa. 51. 17–end 2 Thess. ch. 3	O Sapientia Ember Day Ember CEG P	Zeph. 3. 1–13 Matt. 18. 1–20	Isa. 51. 17–end 2 Thess. ch. 3
Ps. 42; *43* *alt.* Ps. 65; *66* Isa. 52. 1–12 Jude ct	Ember Day Ember CEG P	Zeph. 3. 14–end Matt. 18. 21–end	Isa. 52. 1–12 Jude ct

December 2011

		Sunday Principal Service Weekday Eucharist	Third Service Morning Prayer
18	S THE FOURTH SUNDAY OF ADVENT	2 Sam. 7. 1–11, 16 Canticle: Magnificat or Ps. 89. 1–4, 19–26 (or 1–8) Rom. 16. 25–end	Ps. 144 Isa. 7. 10–16 Rom. 1. 1–7
	P	Luke 1. 26–38	
19	M	Judg. 13. 2–7, 24–end Ps. 71. 3–8	Ps. 144; *146* Mal. 1. 1, 6–end
	P	Luke 1. 5–25	Matt. 19. 1–12
20	Tu	Isa. 7. 10–14 Ps. 24. 1–6 Luke 1. 26–38	Ps. *46*; 95 Mal. 2. 1–16 Matt. 19. 13–15
	P		
21	W*	Zeph. 3. 14–18 Ps. 33. 1–4, 11–12, 20–end Luke 1. 39–45	Ps. *121*; 122; 123 Mal. 2.17 – 3.12 Matt. 19. 16–end
	P		
22	Th	I Sam. 1. 24–end Ps. 113	Ps. *124*; 125; 126; 127 Mal. 3.13 – 4.end
	P	Luke 1. 46–56	Matt. 23. 1–12
23	F	Mal. 3. 1–4; 4. 5–end Ps. 25. 3–9	Ps. 128; 129; *130*; 131 Nahum ch. 1
	P	Luke 1. 57–66	Matt. 23. 13–28
24	Sa CHRISTMAS EVE	Morning Eucharist 2 Sam. 7. 1–5, 8–11, 16 Ps. 89. 2, 19–27 Acts 13. 16–26 Luke 1. 67–79	Ps. *45*; 113 Obadiah Matt. 23. 29–end
	P		
25	S **CHRISTMAS DAY** *Any of the following sets of readings may be used on the evening of Christmas Eve and on Christmas Day. Set III should be used at some service during the celebration.*	I Isa. 9. 2–7 Ps. 96 Titus 2. 11–14 Luke 2. 1–14 [15–20] II Isa. 62. 6–end Ps. 97 Titus 3. 4–7 Luke 2. [1–7] 8–20 III Isa. 52. 7–10 Ps. 98 Heb. 1. 1–4 [5–12] John 1. 1–14	MP: Ps. *110*; 117 Isa. 62. 1–5 Matt. 1. 18–end
	)))		
26	M STEPHEN, DEACON, FIRST MARTYR	2 Chron. 24. 20–22 or Acts 7. 51–end Ps. 119. 161–168 Acts 7. 51–end or Gal. 2. 16b–20 Matt. 10. 17–22	MP: Ps. *13*; 31. 1–8; 150 Jer. 26. 12–15 Acts ch. 6
	R		
27	Tu JOHN, APOSTLE AND EVANGELIST	Exod. 33. 7–11a Ps. 117 I John ch. 1 John 21. 19b–end	MP: Ps. *21*; 147. 13–end Exod. 33. 12–end I John 2. 1–11
	W		

*Thomas the Apostle may be celebrated on 21 December instead of 3 July.

Second Service Evening Prayer		Calendar and Holy Communion	Morning Prayer	Evening Prayer
Ps. 113; [131] Zech. 2. 10–end Luke 1. 39–55	P	**THE FOURTH SUNDAY OF ADVENT** Isa. 40. 1–9 Ps. 145. 17–end Phil. 4. 4–7 John 1. 19–28	Ps. 144 Isa. 7. 10–16 Rom. 1. 1–7	Ps. 113; [131] Zech. 2. 10–end Luke 1. 39–55
Ps. 10; *57* Isa. 52.13 – 53.end 2 Pet. 1. 1–15	P		Mal. 1. 1, 6–end Matt. 19. 1–12	Isa. 52.13 – 53.end 2 Pet. 1. 1–15
Ps. *4*; 9 Isa. ch. 54 2 Pet. 1.16 – 2.3	P		Mal. 2. 1–16 Matt. 19. 13–15	Isa. ch. 54 2 Pet. 1.16 – 2.3 *or First EP of Thomas* (Ps. 27) Isa. ch. 35 Heb. 10.35 – 11.1 **R ct**
Ps. 80, *84* Isa. ch. 55 2 Pet. 2. 4–end	R	**THOMAS THE APOSTLE** Job 42. 1–6 Ps. 139. 1–11 Eph. 2. 19–end John 20. 24–end	(Ps. 92; 146) 2 Sam. 15. 17–21 *or* Ecclus. ch. 2 John 11. 1–16	(Ps. 139) Hab. 2. 1–4 1 Pet. 1. 3–12
Ps. 24; *48* Isa. 56. 1–8 2 Pet. ch. 3	P		Mal. 3.13 – 4.end Matt. 23. 1–12	Isa. ch. 56. 1–8 2 Pet. ch. 3
Ps. 89. 1–37 Isa. 63. 1–6 2 John	P		Nahum ch. 1 Matt. 23. 13–28	Isa. 63. 1–6 2 John
Ps. 85 Zech. ch. 2 Rev. 1. 1–8	P	**CHRISTMAS EVE** Collect (1) Christmas Eve (2) Advent 1 Mic. 5. 2–5a Ps. 24 Titus 3. 3–7 Luke 2. 1–14	Obadiah Matt. 23. 29–end	Zech. ch. 2 Rev. 1. 1–8
EP: Ps. 8 Isa. 65. 17–25 Phil. 2. 5–11 *or* Luke 2. 1–20 *if it has not been used at the principal service of the day*	𝕎	**CHRISTMAS DAY** Isa. 9. 2–7 Ps. 98 Heb. 1. 1–12 John 1. 1–14	Ps. 110; 117 Isa. 62. 1–5 Matt. 1. 18–end	Ps. 8 Isa. 65. 17–25 Phil. 2. 5–11 *or* Luke 2. 1–20
EP: Ps. 57; *86* Gen. 4. 1–10 Matt. 23. 34–end	R	**STEPHEN, DEACON, FIRST MARTYR** Collect (1) Stephen (2) Christmas 2 Chron. 24. 20–22 Ps. 119. 161–168 Acts 7. 55–end Matt. 23. 34–end	(Ps. 13; 31. 1–8; 150) Jer. 26. 12–15 Acts ch. 6	(Ps. 57; 86) Gen. 4. 1–10 Matt. 10. 17–22
EP: Ps. 97 Isa. 6. 1–8 1 John 5. 1–12	W	**JOHN, APOSTLE AND EVANGELIST** Collect (1) John (2) Christmas Exod. 33. 18–end Ps. 92. 11–end 1 John ch. 1 John 21. 19b–end	(Ps. 21; 147. 13–end) Exod. 33. 7–11a 1 John 2. 1–11	(Ps. 97) Isa. 6. 1–8 1 John 5. 1–12

December 2011

			Sunday Principal Service Weekday Eucharist	Third Service Morning Prayer

28   W   THE HOLY INNOCENTS

	Sunday Principal Service / Weekday Eucharist	Third Service / Morning Prayer
	Jer. 31. 15–17	MP: Ps. *36*; 146
	Ps. 124	Baruch 4. 21–27
	1 Cor. 1. 26–29	or Gen. 37. 13–20
	Matt. 2. 13–18	Matt. 18. 1–10

R

29   Th   **Thomas Becket, Archbishop of Canterbury, Martyr, 1170***

			Weekday Eucharist	Morning Prayer
	Com. Martyr	or	1 John 2. 3–11	Ps. *19*; 20
	esp. Matt. 10. 28–33		Ps. 96. 1	Jonah ch. 1
Wr	also Ecclus. 51. 1–8		Luke 2. 22–35	Col. 1. 1–14

30   F

	Weekday Eucharist	Morning Prayer
	1 John 2. 12–17	Ps. 111; 112; *113*
	Ps. 96. 7–10	Jonah ch. 2
W	Luke 2. 36–40	Col. 1. 15–23

31   Sa   *John Wyclif, Reformer, 1384*

	Weekday Eucharist	Morning Prayer
	1 John 2. 18–21	Ps. 102
	Ps. 96. 1, 11–end	Jonah chs 3 & 4
	John 1. 1–18	Col. 1.24 – 2.7

W

January 2012

1   S   THE NAMING AND CIRCUMCISION OF JESUS (or transferred to 2nd)
      or THE SECOND SUNDAY OF CHRISTMAS

	Sunday Principal Service	Third Service / Morning Prayer
	Num. 6. 22–end	MP: Ps. *103*; 150
	Ps. 8	Gen. 17. 1–13
	Gal. 4. 4–7	Rom. 2. 17–end
	Luke 2. 15–21	

    or, for The Second Sunday of Christmas:

	Sunday Principal Service	Third Service / Morning Prayer
	Isa. 61.10 – 62.3	Ps. 105. 1–11
	Ps. 148 (*or* 148. 7–end)	Isa. 63. 7–9
	Gal. 4. 4–7	Eph. 3. 5–12
W	Luke 2. 15–21	

2   M   **Basil the Great and Gregory of Nazianzus, Bishops, Teachers, 379 and 389**
    Seraphim, Monk of Sarov, Spiritual Guide, 1833; Vedanayagam Samuel Azariah, Bishop in South India,
    Evangelist, 1945

			Weekday Eucharist	Morning Prayer
	Com. Teacher	or	1 John 2. 22–28	Ps. 18. 1–30
	esp. 2 Tim. 4. 1–8		Ps. 98. 1–4	Ruth ch. 1
W	Matt. 5. 13–19		John 1. 19–28	Col. 2. 8–end

3   Tu

	Weekday Eucharist	Morning Prayer
	1 John 2.29 – 3.6	Ps. *127*; 128; 131
	Ps. 98. 2–7	Ruth ch. 2
W	John 1. 29–34	Col. 3. 1–11

4   W

	Weekday Eucharist	Morning Prayer
	1 John 3. 7–10	Ps. 89. 1–37
	Ps. 98. 1, 8–end	Ruth ch. 3
W	John 1. 35–42	Col. 3.12 – 4.1

5   Th

	Weekday Eucharist	Morning Prayer
	1 John 3. 11–21	Ps. 8; *48*
	Ps. 100	Ruth 4. 1–17
	John 1. 43–end	Col. 4. 2–end

W

*Thomas Becket may be celebrated on 7 July instead of 29 December.

Second Service Evening Prayer		Calendar and Holy Communion	Morning Prayer	Evening Prayer
		THE HOLY INNOCENTS		
EP: Ps. 123; *128*		Collect	(Ps. *36*; 146)	(Ps. 124; 128)
Isa. 49. 14–25		(1) Innocents	Baruch 4. 21–27	Isa. 49. 14–25
Mark 10. 13–16		(2) Christmas	or Gen. 37. 13–20	Mark 10. 13–16
		Jer. 31. 10–17	Matt. 18. 1–10	
		Ps. 123		
		Rev. 14. 1–5		
	R	Matt. 2. 13–18		
Ps. 131; *132*			Jonah ch. 1	Isa. 57. 15–end
Isa. 57. 15–end			Col. 1. 1–14	John 1. 1–18
John 1. 1–18	W			
Ps. *65*; 84			Jonah ch. 2	Isa. 59. 1–15a
Isa. 59. 1–15a			Col. 1. 15–23	John 1. 19–28
John 1. 19–28	W			
		Silvester, Bishop of Rome, 335		
Ps. *90*; 148		Com. Bishop	Jonah chs 3 & 4	Isa. 59. 15b–end
Isa. 59. 15b–end			Col. 1.24 – 2.7	John 1. 29–34
John 1. 29–34				or First EP of
or First EP of The				The Circumcision
Naming of Jesus				of Christ
Ps. 148				(Ps. 148)
Jer. 23. 1–6				Jer. 23. 1–6
Col. 2. 8–15				Col. 2. 8–15
ct	W			ct
		THE CIRCUMCISION OF CHRIST (or transferred to 2nd)		
EP: Ps. 115		Additional collect	Ps. 103; 150	Ps. 115
Deut. 30. [1–10] 11–end		Gen. 17. 3b–10	Gen. 17. 1–13	Deut. 30. [1–10]
Acts 3. 1–16		Ps. 98	Rom. 2. 17–end	11–20
		Rom. 4. 8–13		Acts 3. 1–16
		or Eph. 2. 11–18		
	W	Luke 2. 15–21		
		or, for The Sunday after Christmas Day:		
Ps. 132		Isa. 62. 10–12	Ps. 105. 1–11	Ps. 132
Isa. ch. 35		Ps. 45. 1–7	Isa. 63. 7–9	Isa. ch. 35
Col. 1. 9–20		Gal. 4. 1–7	Eph. 3. 5–12	1 John 1. 1–7
or Luke 2. 41–end	W	Matt. 1. 18–end		
Ps. 45; *46*			Ruth ch. 1	Isa. 60. 1–12
Isa. 60. 1–12			Col. 2. 8–end	John 1. 35–42
John 1. 35–42	W			
Ps. *2*; 110			Ruth ch. 2	Isa. 60. 13–end
Isa. 60. 13–end			Col. 3. 1–11	John 1. 43–end
John 1. 43–end	W			
Ps. 85; *87*			Ruth ch. 3	Isa. ch. 61
Isa. ch. 61			Col. 3.12 – 4.1	John 2. 1–12
John 2. 1–12	W			
First EP of The Epiphany			Ps. 8; 48	*First EP of The Epiphany*
Ps. 96; *97*			Ruth 4. 1–17	Ps. 96; 97
Isa. 49. 1–13			Col. 4. 2–end	Isa. 49. 1–13
John 4. 7–26				John 4. 7–26
℣ ct				℣ ct
or, if The Epiphany is				
celebrated on 8 January:				
Ps. 96; *97*				
Isa. ch. 62				
John 2. 13–end	W			

January 2012

			Sunday Principal Service Weekday Eucharist	Third Service Morning Prayer
6	F 郑	**THE EPIPHANY**	Isa. 60. 1–6 Ps. 72 (or 72. 10–15) Eph. 3. 1–12 Matt. 2. 1–12	MP: Ps. *132*; 113 Jer. 31. 7–14 John 1. 29–34
		or, if The Epiphany is celebrated on 8 January:	I John 5. 5–13 Ps. 147. 13–end Mark 1. 7–11	Ps. **46**; 147. 13–end Baruch 1.15 – 2.10 *or* Jer. 23. 1–8 Matt. 20. 1–16
	W			
7	Sa		I John 3.22 – 4.6 Ps. 2. 7–end Matt. 4. 12–17, 23–end	Ps. **99**; 147. 1–12 *alt.* Ps. **76**; 79 Baruch 1.15 – 2.10 *or* Jer. 23. 1–8 Matt. 20. 1–16
	W			
		or, if The Epiphany is celebrated on 8 January:	I John 5. 14–end Ps. 149. 1–5 John 2. 1–11	Ps. **99**; 147. 1–12 Baruch 2. 11–end *or* Jer. 30. 1–17 Matt. 20. 17–28
	W			
8	S 郑	<small>THE BAPTISM OF CHRIST (THE FIRST SUNDAY OF EPIPHANY)</small> *or transferred to 9 January if The Epiphany is celebrated today. (For The Epiphany, see provision on the 6th.)* Gen. 1. 1–5 Ps. 29 Acts 19. 1–7 Mark 1. 4–11		Ps. 89. 19–29 I Sam. 16. 1–3, 13 John 1. 29–34
9 DEL 1	M W	*For the Baptism of Christ, see provision for the 7th and 8th.* I Sam. 1. 1–8 Ps. 116. 10–15 Mark 1. 14–20		Ps. **2**; 110 *alt.* Ps. **80**; 82 Gen. 1. 1–19 Matt. 21. 1–17
10	Tu W	*William Laud, Archbishop of Canterbury, 1645* I Sam. 1. 9–20 Canticle: I Sam. 2. 1, 4–8 or Magnificat Mark 1. 21–28		Ps. 8; **9** *alt.* Ps. 87; **89. 1–18** Gen. 1.20 – 2.3 Matt. 21. 18–32
11	W W	*Mary Slessor, Missionary in West Africa, 1915* I Sam. 3. 1–10, 19–20 Ps. 40. 1–4, 7–10 Mark 1. 29–39		Ps. 19; **20** *alt.* Ps. 119. 105–128 Gen. 2. 4–end Matt. 21. 33–end
12	Th W	**Aelred of Hexham, Abbot of Rievaulx, 1167** *Benedict Biscop, Abbot of Wearmouth, Scholar, 689* Com. Religious *or* I Sam. 4. 1–11 *also Ecclus. 15. 1–6* Ps. 44. 10–15, 24–25 Mark 1. 40–end		Ps. 21; 24 *alt.* Ps. 90; **92** Gen. ch. 3 Matt. 22. 1–14
13	F W	**Hilary, Bishop of Poitiers, Teacher, 367** *Kentigern (Mungo), Missionary Bishop in Strathclyde and Cumbria, 603; George Fox, Founder of* *the Society of Friends (the Quakers), 1691* Com. Teacher *or* I Sam. 8. 4–7, 10–end *also* I John 2. 18–25 Ps. 89. 15–18 John 8. 25–32 Mark 2. 1–12		Ps. **67**; 72 *alt.* Ps. **88**; (95) Gen. 4. 1–16, 25–26 Matt. 22. 15–33
14	Sa W		I Sam. 9. 1–4, 17–19; 10. 1a Ps. 21. 1–6 Mark 2. 13–17	Ps. 29; **33** *alt.* Ps. 96; **97**; 100 Gen. 6. 1–10 Matt. 22. 34–end

Second Service Evening Prayer	Calendar and Holy Communion	Morning Prayer	Evening Prayer
	THE EPIPHANY		
EP: Ps. *98*; 100 Baruch 4.36 – 5.end or Isa. 60. 1–9 John 2. 1–11	Isa. 60. 1–9 Ps. 100 Eph. 3. 1–12 Matt. 2. 1–12	Ps. 132; 113 Jer. 31. 7–14 John 1. 29–34	Ps. 72; 98 Baruch 4.36 – 5.end or Isa. 60. 1–9 John 2. 1–11
Ps. 145 Isa. 63. 7–end 1 John ch. 3	℟		
Ps. 118 *alt.* Ps. 81; **84** Isa. 63. 7–end 1 John ch. 3 ct *or First EP of The Baptism* Ps. 36 Isa. ch. 61 Titus 2. 11–14; 3. 4–7 ℟ ct		Baruch 1.15 – 2.10 or Jer. 23. 1–8 Matt. 20. 1–16	Isa. 63. 7–end 1 John ch. 3
First EP of The Epiphany Ps. 96; 97 Isa. 49. 1–13 John 4. 7–26 ℟ ct	W *or* G		
	THE FIRST SUNDAY AFTER EPIPHANY To celebrate The Baptism of Christ, see *Common Worship* provision.		
Ps. 46 [47] Isa. 42. 1–9 Eph. 2. 1–10 *Gospel:* Matt. 3. 13–end	Zech. 8. 1–8 Ps. 72. 1–8 Rom. 12. 1–5 Luke 2. 41–end W *or* G	Ps. 89. 19–29 1 Sam. 16. 1–3, 13 John 1. 29–34	Ps. 46; 47 Isa. 42. 1–9 Eph. 2. 1–10
Ps. *34*; 36 *alt.* Ps. *85*; 86 Amos ch. 1 1 Cor. 1. 1–17	W *or* G	Gen. 1. 1–19 Matt. 21. 1–17	Amos ch. 1 1 Cor. 1. 1–17
Ps. *45*; 46 *alt.* Ps. 89. 19–end Amos ch. 2 1 Cor. 1. 18–end	W *or* G	Gen. 1.20 – 2.3 Matt. 21. 18–32	Amos ch. 2 1 Cor. 1. 18–end
Ps. *47*; 48 *alt.* Ps. *91*; 93 Amos ch. 3 1 Cor. ch. 2	W *or* G	Gen. 2. 4–end Matt. 21. 33–end	Amos ch. 3 1 Cor. ch. 2
Ps. *61*; 65 *alt.* Ps. 94 Amos ch. 4 1 Cor. ch. 3	W *or* G	Gen. ch. 3 Matt. 22. 1–14	Amos ch. 4 1 Cor. ch. 3
	Hilary, Bishop of Poitiers, Teacher, 367 Com. Doctor		
Ps. 68 *alt.* Ps. 102 Amos 5. 1–17 1 Cor. ch. 4	W *or* Gw	Gen. 4. 1–16, 25–26 Matt. 22. 15–33	Amos 5. 1–17 1 Cor. ch. 4
Ps. 84; *85* *alt.* Ps. 104 Amos 5. 18–end 1 Cor. ch. 5 ct	W *or* G	Gen. 6. 1–10 Matt. 22. 34–end	Amos 5. 18–end 1 Cor. ch. 5 ct

January 2012

		Sunday Principal Service Weekday Eucharist	Third Service Morning Prayer
15	S	THE SECOND SUNDAY OF EPIPHANY	
		I Sam. 3. 1–10 [11–20] Ps. 139. 1–5, 12–18 (or 139. 1–9) Rev. 5. 1–10	Ps. 145. 1–12 Isa. 62. 1–5 I Cor. 6. 11–end
	W	John 1. 43–end	
16 DEL 2	M	I Sam. 15. 16–23 Ps. 50. 8–10, 16–17, 24 Mark 2. 18–22	Ps. 145; *146* *alt.* Ps. *98*; 99; 101 Gen. 6.11 – 7.10
	W		Matt. 24. 1–14
17	Tu	**Antony of Egypt, Hermit, Abbot, 356** *Charles Gore, Bishop, Founder of the Community of the Resurrection, 1932* Com. Religious *or* I Sam. 16. 1–13 *esp.* Phil. 3. 7–14 Ps. 89. 19–27 *also* Matt. 19. 16–26 Mark 2. 23–end	Ps. *132*; 147. 1–12 *alt.* Ps. 106† (*or* Ps. 103) Gen. 7. 11–end
	W		Matt. 24. 15–28

18	W	*Amy Carmichael, Founder of the Dohnavur Fellowship, Spiritual Writer, 1951*
		The Week of Prayer for Christian Unity until 25th
		          I Sam. 17. 32–33, 37, 40–51
		          Ps. 144. 1–2, 9–10
		          Mark 3. 1–6
			Ps. *81*; 147. 13–end
			alt. Ps. 110; *111*; 112
			Gen. 8. 1–14

	W		Matt. 24. 29–end
19	Th	**Wulfstan, Bishop of Worcester, 1095** Com. Bishop *or* I Sam. 18. 6–9; 19. 1–7 *esp.* Matt. 24. 42–46 Ps. 56. 1–2, 8–end Mark 3. 7–12	Ps. *76*; 148 *alt.* Ps. 113; *115* Gen. 8.15 – 9.7
	W		Matt. 25. 1–13

20	F	*Richard Rolle of Hampole, Spiritual Writer, 1349*
		          I Sam. 24. 3–22a
		          Ps. 57. 1–2, 8–end
		          Mark 3. 13–19
			Ps. *27*; 149
			alt. Ps. 139
			Gen. 9. 8–19

	W		Matt. 25. 14–30

21	Sa	**Agnes, Child Martyr at Rome, 304**
		Com. Martyr *or* 2 Sam. 1. 1–4, 11–12,
		also Rev. 7. 13–end 17–19, 23–end
		          Ps. 80. 1–6
		          Mark 3. 20–21
			Ps. *122*; 128; 150
			alt. Ps. 120; *121*; 122
			Gen. 11. 1–9

	Wr		Matt. 25. 31–end
22	S	THE THIRD SUNDAY OF EPIPHANY	
		Gen. 14. 17–20 Ps. 128 Rev. 19. 6–10	Ps. 113 Jonah 3. 1–5, 10 John 3. 16–21
	W	John 2. 1–11	
23 DEL 3	M	2 Sam. 5. 1–7, 10 Ps. 89. 19–27 Mark 3. 22–30	Ps. 40; *108* *alt.* Ps. 123; 124; 125; *126* Gen. 11.27 – 12.9
	W		Matt. 26. 1–16
24	Tu	**Francis de Sales, Bishop of Geneva, Teacher, 1622** Com. Teacher *or* 2 Sam. 6. 12–15, 17–19 *also* Prov. 3. 13–18 Ps. 24. 7–end John 3. 17–21 Mark 3. 31–end	Ps. 34; *36* *alt.* Ps. *132*; 133 Gen. 13. 2–end Matt. 26. 17–35
	W		
25	W	THE CONVERSION OF PAUL	
		Jer. 1. 4–10 *or* Acts 9. 1–22 Ps. 67 Acts 9. 1–22 *or* Gal. 1. 11–16a	*MP:* Ps. 66; 147. 13–end Ezek. 3. 22–end Phil. 3. 1–14
	W	Matt. 19. 27–end	

Second Service Evening Prayer	Calendar and Holy Communion	Morning Prayer	Evening Prayer
	THE SECOND SUNDAY AFTER EPIPHANY		
Ps. 96	2 Kings 4. 1–17	Ps. 145. 1–12	Ps. 96
Isa. 60. 9–end	Ps. 107. 13–22	Isa. 62. 1–5	Isa. 60. 9–end
Heb. 6.17 – 7.10	Rom. 12. 6–16a	1 Cor. 6. 11–end	Heb. 6.17 – 7.10
Gospel: Matt. 8. 5–13	John 2. 1–11		
	W or G		
Ps. 71		Gen. 6.11 – 7.10	Amos ch. 6
alt. Ps. 105† (or Ps. 103)		Matt. 24. 1–14	1 Cor. 6. 1–11
Amos ch. 6			
1 Cor. 6. 1–11	W or G		
Ps. 89. 1–37		Gen. 7. 11–end	Amos ch. 7
alt. Ps. 107†		Matt. 24. 15–28	1 Cor. 6. 12–end
Amos ch. 7			
1 Cor. 6. 12–end	W or G		
	Prisca, Martyr at Rome, c. 265		
	For the Week of Prayer for Christian Unity, see *Common Worship* provision.		
Ps. 97; 98	Com. Virgin Martyr	Gen. 8. 1–14	Amos ch. 8
alt. Ps. 119. 129–152		Matt. 24. 29–end	1 Cor. 7. 1–24
Amos ch. 8			
1 Cor. 7. 1–24	Wr or Gr		
Ps. 99; 100; 111		Gen. 8.15 – 9.7	Amos ch. 9
alt. Ps. 114; 116; 117		Matt. 25. 1–13	1 Cor. 7. 25–end
Amos ch. 9			
1 Cor. 7. 25–end	W or G		
	Fabian, Bishop of Rome, Martyr, 250		
Ps. 73	Com. Martyr	Gen. 9. 8–19	Hos. 1.1 – 2.1
alt. Ps. 130; 131; 137		Matt. 25. 14–30	1 Cor. ch. 8
Hos. 1.1 – 2.1			
1 Cor. ch. 8	Wr or Gr		
	Agnes, Child Martyr at Rome, 304		
Ps. 61; 66	Com. Virgin Martyr	Gen. 11. 1–9	Hos. 2. 2–17
alt. Ps. 118		Matt. 25. 31–end	1 Cor. 9. 1–14
Hos. 2. 2–17			
1 Cor. 9. 1–14			
ct	Wr or Gr		ct
	THE THIRD SUNDAY AFTER EPIPHANY		
Ps. 33. 1–12 [13–end]	2 Kings 6. 14b–23	Ps. 113	Ps. 33. 1–12 [13–end]
Jer. 3.21 – 4.2	Ps. 102. 15–22	Jonah 3. 1–5, 10	Jer. 3.21 – 4.2
Titus 2. 1–8, 11–14	Rom. 12. 16b–end	John 3. 16–21	Titus 2. 1–8, 11–14
Gospel: Matt. 4. 12–23	Matt. 8. 1–13		
	W or G		
Ps. 138; 144		Gen. 11.27 – 12.9	Hos. 2.18 – 3.end
alt. Ps. 127; 128; 129		Matt. 26. 1–16	1 Cor. 9. 15–end
Hos. 2.18 – 3.end			
1 Cor. 9. 15–end	W or G		
Ps. 145		Gen. 13. 2–end	Hos. 4. 1–16
alt. Ps. (134); 135		Matt. 26. 17–35	1 Cor. 10. 1–13
Hos. 4. 1–16			or First EP of
1 Cor. 10. 1–13			The Conversion
or First EP of The			of Paul
Conversion of Paul			(Ps. 149)
Ps. 149			Isa. 49. 1–13
Isa. 49. 1–13			Acts 22. 3–16
Acts 22. 3–16			
ct	W or G		W ct
	THE CONVERSION OF PAUL		
EP: Ps. 119. 41–56	Josh. 5. 13–end	(Ps. 66; 147. 13–end)	(Ps. 119. 41–56)
Ecclus. 39. 1–10	Ps. 67	Ezek. 3. 22–end	Ecclus. 39. 1–10
or Isa. 56. 1–8	Acts 9. 1–22	Phil. 3. 1–14	or Isa. 56. 1–8
Col. 1.24 – 2.7	Matt. 19. 27–end		Col. 1.24 – 2.7
	W		

January 2012

			Sunday Principal Service / Weekday Eucharist	Third Service / Morning Prayer

26 Th **Timothy and Titus, Companions of Paul**
Isa. 61. 1–3a   *or* 2 Sam. 7. 18–19, 24–end   Ps. **47**; 48
Ps. 100   Ps. 132. 1–5, 11–15   *alt.* Ps. **143**; 146
2 Tim. 2. 1–8   Mark 4. 21–25   Gen. ch. 15
or Titus 1. 1–5   Matt. 26. 47–56
W Luke 10. 1–9

27 F
2 Sam. 11. 1–10, 13–17   Ps. 61; **65**
Ps. 51. 1–6, 9   *alt.* Ps. 142; **144**
Mark 4. 26–34   Gen. ch. 16
W   Matt. 26. 57–end

28 Sa **Thomas Aquinas, Priest, Philosopher, Teacher, 1274**
Com. Teacher   *or* 2 Sam. 12. 1–7, 10–17   Ps. 68
esp. Wisd. 7. 7–10, 15–16 Ps. 51. 11–16   *alt.* Ps. 147
1 Cor. 2. 9–end   Mark 4. 35–end   Gen. 17. 1–22
John 16. 12–15   Matt. 27. 1–10
W

29 S **THE FOURTH SUNDAY OF EPIPHANY**
*or The Presentation of Christ in the Temple (Candlemas)**
Deut. 18. 15–20   Ps. 71. 1–6, 15–17
Ps. 111   Jer. 1. 4–10
Rev. 12. 1–5a   Mark 1. 40–end
Mark 1. 21–28
W

30 M **Charles, King and Martyr, 1649**
DEL 4 (Ordinary Time starts today if The Presentation is observed on 29 January)**
Com. Martyr   *or* 2 Sam. 15. 13–14, 30;   Ps. **57**; 96
also Ecclus. 2. 12–17   16. 5–13   *alt.* Ps. *1*; 2; 3
1 Tim. 6. 12–16   Ps. 3   Gen. 18. 1–15
                       Mark 5. 1–20   Matt. 27. 11–26
                                                 [Lev. 19. 1–18, 30–end
Wr   1 Tim. 1. 1–17]

31 Tu *John Bosco, Priest, Founder of the Salesian Teaching Order, 1888*
2 Sam. 18.9–10, 14,   Ps. **93**; 97
24–25, 30 – 19.3   *alt.* Ps. **5**; 6; (8)
Ps. 88. 1–6   Gen. 18. 16–end
Mark. 5. 21–end   Matt. 27. 27–44
                         [Lev. 23. 1–22
W   1 Tim. 1. 18 – 2.end]

February 2012

1 W *Brigid, Abbess of Kildare, c. 525*
2 Sam. 24. 2, 9–17   Ps. **95**; 98
Ps. 32. 1–8   *alt.* Ps. 119. 1–32
Mark 6. 1–6a   Gen. 19. 1–3, 12–29
                     Matt. 27. 45–56
                     [Lev. 23. 23–end
                     1 Tim. ch. 3]

W

2 Th **THE PRESENTATION OF CHRIST IN THE TEMPLE (CANDLEMAS)**
Mal. 3. 1–5   *MP:* Ps. **48**; 146
Ps. 24 (or 24. 7–end) Exod. 13. 1–16
Heb. 2. 14–end   Rom. 12. 1–5
Luke 2. 22–40

or, if The Presentation is observed on 29 January:
1 Kings 2. 1–4, 10–12   Ps. 14; **15**; 16
Canticle: 1 Chron. 29. 10–12 Lev. 24. 1–9
or Ps. 145. 1–5   1 Tim. ch. 4
G Mark 6. 7–13

*See provision for First EP on 1 February and throughout the day for The Presentation on 2 February.
**If The Presentation is observed on Sunday 29 January, the readings in square brackets are used this week at Morning and Evening Prayer.

Second Service Evening Prayer	Calendar and Holy Communion	Morning Prayer	Evening Prayer
Ps. *24*; 33 *alt.* Ps. *138*; 140; 141 Hos. 5.8 – 6.6 1 Cor. 11. 2–16 **W** *or* **G**		Gen. ch. 15 Matt. 26. 47–56	Hos. 5.8 – 6.6 1 Cor. 11. 2–16
Ps. *67*; 77 *alt.* Ps. 145 Hos. 6.7 – 7.2 1 Cor. 11. 17–end **W** *or* **G**		Gen. ch. 16 Matt. 26. 57–end	Hos. 6.7 – 7.2 1 Cor. 11. 17–end
Ps. *72*; 76 *alt.* *148*; 149; 150 Hos. ch. 8 1 Cor. 12. 1–11 ct **W** *or* **G**		Gen. 17. 1–22 Matt. 27. 1–10	Hos. ch. 8 1 Cor. 12. 1–11 ct
	THE FOURTH SUNDAY AFTER EPIPHANY		
Ps. 34 (*or* 34. 1–10) 1 Sam. 3. 1–20 1 Cor. 14. 12–20 *Gospel:* Matt. 13. 10–17	1 Sam. 10. 17–24 Ps. 97 Rom. 13. 1–7 Matt. 8. 23–34 **W** *or* **G**	Ps. 71. 1–6, 15–17 Jer. 1. 4–10 Mark 1. 40–end	Ps. 34 (*or* 34. 1–10) 1 Sam. 3. 1–20 1 Cor. 14. 12–20
Ps. 2; *20* *alt.* Ps. *4*; 7 Hos. ch. 9 1 Cor. 12. 12–end [Joel 1. 1–14 John 15. 1–11] **Wr** *or* **Gr**	**Charles, King and Martyr, 1649** Com. Martyr	Gen. 18. 1–15 Matt. 27. 11–26	Hos. ch. 9 1 Cor. 12. 12–end
Ps. *19*; 21 *alt.* Ps. *9*; 10† Hos. ch. 10 1 Cor. ch. 13 [Joel 1. 15–end John 15. 12–17] **W** *or* **G**		Gen. 18. 16–end Matt. 27. 27–44	Hos. ch. 10 1 Cor. ch. 13
First EP of The Presentation Ps. 118 1 Sam. 1. 19b–end Heb. 4. 11–end ℣ ct *or, if The Presentation is kept on 29 January:* Ps. *11*; 12; 13 Joel 2. 1–17 John 15. 18–end **W** *or* **G**		Gen. 19. 1–3, 12–29 Matt. 27. 45–56	*First EP of The Presentation* Ps. 118 1 Sam. 1. 19b–end Heb. 4. 11–end ℣ ct
EP: Ps. 122; *132* Hag. 2. 1–9 John 2. 18–22	**THE PRESENTATION OF CHRIST IN THE TEMPLE** Mal. 3. 1–5 Ps. 48. 1–7 Gal. 4. 1–7 Luke 2. 22–40	Ps. 48; 146 Exod. 13. 1–16 Rom. 12. 1–5	Ps. 122; 132 Hag. 2. 1–9 John 2. 18–22
Ps. 18† Joel 2. 18–27 John 16. 1–15	℣		

February 2012

			Sunday Principal Service Weekday Eucharist	Third Service Morning Prayer
3	F	**Anskar, Archbishop of Hamburg, Missionary in Denmark and Sweden, 865** Ordinary Time starts today (or on 30 January if The Presentation is observed on 29 January)* Com. Missionary　　　　*or* *esp.* Isa. 52. 7–10 *also* Rom. 10. 11–15	Ecclus. 47. 2–11 Ps. 18. 31–36, 50–end Mark 6. 14–29	Ps. 17; *19* Gen. 22. 1–19 Matt. 28. 1–15 [Lev. 25. 1–24
	Gw			1 Tim. 5. 1–16]
4	Sa	*Gilbert of Sempringham, Founder of the Gilbertine Order, 1189* 	1 Kings 3. 4–13 Ps. 119. 9–16 Mark 6. 30–34	Ps. 20; 21; *23* Gen. ch. 23 Matt. 28. 16–end [Num. 6. 1–5, 21–end
	G			1 Tim. 5. 17–end]
5	S	THE THIRD SUNDAY BEFORE LENT **(Proper 1)**	Isa. 40. 21–end Ps. 147. 1–12, 21c (*or* 147. 1–12) 1 Cor. 9. 16–23	Ps. 2; 3 Jer. 26. 1–16 Acts 3. 1–10
	G		Mark 1. 29–39	
6 DEL 5	M	*The Martyrs of Japan, 1597* (The Accession of Queen Elizabeth II may be observed on 6 February, and Collect, Readings and Post-Communion for the Sovereign used.)	1 Kings 8. 1–7, 9–13 Ps. 132. 1–9 Mark 6. 53–end	Ps. 27; *30* Gen. 24. 1–28 1 Tim. 6. 1–10
	G			
7	Tu		1 Kings 8. 22–23, 27–30 Ps. 84. 1–10	Ps. 32; *36* Gen. 24. 29–end
	G		Mark 7. 1–13	1 Tim. 6. 11–end
8	W		1 Kings 10. 1–10 Ps. 37. 3–6, 30–32	Ps. 34 Gen. 25. 7–11, 19–end
	G		Mark 7. 14–23	2 Tim. 1. 1–14
9	Th		1 Kings 11. 4–13 Ps. 106. 3, 35–41	Ps. 37† Gen. 26.34 – 27.40
	G		Mark 7. 24–30	2 Tim. 1.15 – 2.13
10	F	*Scholastica, sister of Benedict, Abbess of Plombariola, c. 543* 	1 Kings 11. 29–32; 12. 19 Ps. 81. 8–14	Ps. 31 Gen. 27.41 – 28.end
	G		Mark 7. 31–end	2 Tim. 2. 14–end
11	Sa		1 Kings 12. 26–32; 13. 33–end Ps. 106. 6–7, 20–23	Ps. 41; *42*; 43 Gen. 29. 1–30 2 Tim. ch. 3
	G		Mark 8. 1–10	
12	S	THE SECOND SUNDAY BEFORE LENT	Prov. 8. 1, 22–31 Ps. 104. 26–end Col. 1. 15–20 John 1. 1–14	Ps. 29; 67 Deut. 8. 1–10 Matt. 6. 25–end
	G			
13 DEL 6	M		James 1. 1–11 Ps. 119. 65–72	Ps. 44 Gen. 29.31 – 30.24
	G		Mark 8. 11–13	2 Tim. 4. 1–8
14	Tu	**Cyril and Methodius, Missionaries to the Slavs, 869 and 885** *Valentine, Martyr at Rome, c. 269* Com. Missionaries　　　　*or* *esp.* Isa. 52. 7–10	James 1. 12–18 Ps. 94. 12–18	Ps. *48*; 52 Gen. 31. 1–24
	Gw	*also* Rom. 10. 11–15	Mark 8. 14–21	2 Tim. 4. 9–end

*The Collect of 5 before Lent is used.

Second Service Evening Prayer	Calendar and Holy Communion	Morning Prayer	Evening Prayer
	Blasius, Bishop of Sebastopol, Martyr, c. 316 Com. Martyr		
Ps. 22 Hos. 13. 1–14 I Cor. 16. 1–9 [Joel 2. 28–end John 16. 16–22]		Gen. 22. 1–19 Matt. 28. 1–15	Hos. 13. 1–14 I Cor. 16. 1–9
	Gr		
Ps. *24*; 25 Hos. ch. 14 I Cor. 16. 10–end [Joel 3. 1–3, 9–end John 16. 23–end] ct		Gen. ch. 23 Matt. 28. 16–end	Hos. ch. 14 I Cor. 16. 10–end ct
	G		
Ps. 5 Num. 13. 1–2, 27–end Phil. 2. 12–28 *Gospel:* Luke 5, 1–11	**SEPTUAGESIMA** Gen. 1. 1–5 Ps. 9. 10–20 I Cor. 9. 24–end Matt. 20. 1–16	Ps. 2; 3 Jer. 26. 1–16 Acts 3. 1–10	Ps. 5 Num 13. 1 2, 27–end Phil. 2. 12–28
	G		
	The Accession of Queen Elizabeth II, 1952		
Ps. 26; *28*; 29 Eccles. ch. 1 John 17. 1–5	*For Accession Service:* Ps. 20; 101; 121; Josh. 1. 1–9; Prov. 8. 1–16; Rom. 13. 1–10; Rev. 21.22 – 22.4 *For The Accession:* I Pet. 2. 11–17	Gen. 24. 1–28 I Tim. 6. 1–10	Eccles. ch. 1 John 17. 1–5
	G Matt. 22. 16–22		
Ps. 33 Eccles. ch. 2 John 17. 6–19	G	Gen. 24. 29–end I Tim. 6. 11–end	Eccles. ch. 2 John 17. 6–19
Ps. 119. 33–56 Eccles. 3. 1–15 John 17. 20–end	G	Gen. 25. 7–11, 19–end 2 Tim. 1. 1–14	Eccles. 3. 1–15 John 17. 20–end
Ps. 39; *40* Eccles. 3.16 – 4.end John 18. 1–11	G	Gen. 26.34 – 27.40 2 Tim. 1.15 – 2.13	Eccles. 3.16 – 4.end John 18. 1–11
Ps. 35 Eccles. ch. 5 John 18. 12–27	G	Gen. 27.41 – 28.end 2 Tim. 2. 14–end	Eccles. ch. 5 John 18. 12–27
Ps. 45; *46* Eccles. ch. 6 John 18. 28–end ct	G	Gen. 29. 1–30 2 Tim. ch. 3	Eccles. ch. 6 John 18. 28–end ct
Ps. 65 Gen. 2. 4b–end Luke 8. 22–35	**SEXAGESIMA** Gen. 3. 9–19 Ps. 83. 1–2, 13–end 2 Cor. 11. 19–31 Luke 8. 4–15	Ps. 29; 67 Deut. 8. 1–10 Matt. 6. 25–end	Ps. 65 Gen. 2. 4b–end Luke 8. 22–35
	G		
Ps. *47*; 49 Eccles. 7. 1–14 John 19. 1–16	G	Gen. 29.31 – 30.24 2 Tim. 4. 1–8	Eccles. 7. 1–14 John 19. 1–16
	Valentine, Martyr at Rome, c. 269 Com. Martyr		
Ps. 50 Eccles. 7. 15–end John 19. 17–30	Gr	Gen. 31. 1–24 2 Tim. 4. 9–end	Eccles. 7. 15–end John 19. 17–30

February 2012

			Sunday Principal Service / Weekday Eucharist	Third Service / Morning Prayer

15 W — *Sigfrid, Bishop, Apostle of Sweden, 1045; Thomas Bray, Priest, Founder of the SPCK and SPG, 1730*

15	W		James 1. 19–end	Ps. 119. 57–80
			Ps. 15	Gen. 31.25 – 32.2
	G		Mark 8. 22–26	Titus ch. 1

16	Th		James 2. 1–9	Ps. 56; *57*; (63†)
			Ps. 34. 1–7	Gen. 32. 3–30
	G		Mark 8. 27–33	Titus ch. 2

17	F	**Janani Luwum, Archbishop of Uganda, Martyr, 1977**		
		Com. Martyr	*or* James 2. 14–24, 26	Ps. *51*; 54
		also Ecclus. 4. 20–28	Ps. 112	Gen. 33. 1–17
	Gr	John 12. 24–32	Mark 8.34 – 9.1	Titus ch. 3

18	Sa		James 3. 1–10	Ps. 68
			Ps. 12. 1–7	Gen. ch. 35
	G		Mark 9. 2–13	Philemon

19	S	THE SUNDAY NEXT BEFORE LENT		
			2 Kings 2. 1–12	Ps. 27; 150
			Ps. 50. 1–6	Exod. 24. 12–end
			2 Cor. 4. 3–6	2 Cor. 3. 12–end
	G		Mark 9. 2–9	

20 DEL 7	M		James 3. 13–end	Ps. 71
			Ps. 19. 7–end	Gen. 37. 1–11
	G		Mark 9. 14–29	Gal. ch. 1

21	Tu		James 4. 1–10	Ps. 73
			Ps. 55. 7–9, 24	Gen. 37. 12–end
	G		Mark 9. 30–37	Gal. 2. 1–10

22	W	**ASH WEDNESDAY**		
			Joel 2. 1–2, 12–17	MP: Ps. 38
			or Isa. 58. 1–12	Dan. 9. 3–6, 17–19
			Ps. 51. 1–18	1 Tim. 6. 6–19
			2 Cor. 5.20b – 6.10	
			Matt. 6. 1–6, 16–21	
	P		*or* John 8. 1–11	

23	Th	**Polycarp, Bishop of Smyrna, Martyr, c. 155**		
		Com. Martyr	*or* Deut. 30. 15–end	Ps. 77
		also Rev. 2. 8–11	Ps. 1	*alt.* Ps. 78. 1–39†
			Luke 9. 22–25	Gen. ch. 39
				Gal. 2. 11–end
	Pr			

24	F*		Isa. 58. 1–9a	Ps. 3; 7
			Ps. 51. 1–5, 17–18	*alt.* Ps. 55
			Matt. 9. 14–15	Gen. ch. 40
	P			Gal. 3. 1–14

25	Sa		Isa. 58. 9b–end	Ps. 71
			Ps. 86. 1–7	*alt.* Ps. *76*; 79
			Luke 5. 27–32	Gen. 41. 1–24
	P			Gal. 3. 15–22

26	S	THE FIRST SUNDAY OF LENT		
			Gen. 9. 8–17	Ps. 77
			Ps. 25. 1–9	Exod. 34. 1–10
			1 Pet. 3. 18–end	Rom. 10. 8b–13
			Mark 1. 9–15	
	P			

*Matthias may be celebrated on 24 February instead of 14 May.

Second Service Evening Prayer		Calendar and Holy Communion	Morning Prayer	Evening Prayer
Ps. *59*; 60; (67) Eccles. ch. 8 John 19. 31–end	G		Gen. 31.25 – 32.2 Titus ch. 1	Eccles. ch. 8 John 19. 31–end
Ps. 61; *62*; 64 Eccles. ch. 9 John 20. 1–10	G		Gen. 32. 3–30 Titus ch. 2	Eccles. ch. 9 John 20. 1–10
Ps. 38 Eccles. 11. 1–8 John 20. 11–18	G		Gen. 33. 1–17 Titus ch. 3	Eccles. 11. 1–8 John 20. 11–18
Ps. 65; *66* Eccles. 11.9 – 12.end John 20. 19–end ct	G		Gen. ch. 35 Philemon	Eccles. 11.9 – 12.end John 20. 19–end ct
Ps. 2 [99] 1 Kings 19. 1–16 2 Pet. 1. 16–end *Gospel:* Mark 9. [2–8] 9–13	G	**QUINQUAGESIMA** Gen 9. 8–17 Ps. 77. 11–end 1 Cor. ch. 13 Luke 18. 31–43	Ps. 41 Exod. 24. 12–end 2 Cor. 3. 12–end	Ps. 2 [99] 1 Kings 19. 1–16 2 Pet. 1. 16–end
Ps. *72*; 75 Jer. ch. 1 John 3. 1–21	G		Gen. 37. 1–11 Gal. ch. 1	Jer. ch. 1 John 3. 1–21
Ps. 74 Jer. 2. 1–13 John 3. 22–end	G		Gen. 37. 12–end Gal. 2. 1–10	Jer. 2. 1–13 John 3. 22–end
EP: Ps. *51* or Ps. 102 (or 102. 1–18) Isa. 1. 10–18 Luke 15. 11–end	P	**ASH WEDNESDAY** Ash Wed. Collect until 7 April Commination Joel 2. 12–17 Ps. 57 James 4. 1–10 Matt. 6. 16–21	Ps. 38 Dan. 9. 3–6, 17–19 1 Tim. 6. 6–19	Ps. 51 or Ps. 102 (or 102. 1–18) Isa. 1. 10–18 Luke 15. 11–end
Ps. 74 alt. Ps. 78. 40–end† Jer. 2. 14–32 John 4. 1–26	P	Exod. 24. 12–end Matt. 8. 5–13	Gen. ch. 39 Gal. 2. 11–end	Jer. 2. 14–32 John 4. 1–26 *or First EP of Matthias* (Ps. 147) Isa. 22. 15–22 Phil. 3.13b – 4.1 R ct
Ps. 31 alt. Ps. 69 Jer. 3. 6–22 John 4. 27–42	R	**MATTHIAS THE APOSTLE** 1 Sam. 2. 27–35 Ps. 16. 1–7 Acts 1. 15–end Matt. 1. 25–end	(Ps. 15) Jonah 1. 1–9 Acts 2. 37–end	(Ps. 80) 1 Sam. 16. 1–13a Matt. 7. 15–27
Ps. 73 alt. Ps. 81; *84* Jer. 4. 1–18 John 4. 43–end ct	P	Isa. 38. 1–6a Mark 6. 45–end	Gen. 41. 1–24 Gal. 3. 15–22	Jer. 4. 1–18 John 4. 43–end ct
Ps. 119. 17–32 Gen. 2. 15–17; 3. 1–7 Rom. 5. 12–19 or Luke 13. 31–end	P	**THE FIRST SUNDAY OF LENT** Collect (1) Lent 1 (2) Ash Wednesday Ember until 3 March Gen. 3. 1–6 Ps. 91. 1–12 2 Cor. 6. 1–10 Matt. 4. 1–11	Ps. 77 Exod. 34. 1–10 Rom. 10. 8b–13	Ps. 119. 17–32 Gen. 2. 15–17; 3. 1–7 Rom. 5. 12–19 or Luke 13. 31–end

February 2012

				Sunday Principal Service Weekday Eucharist	Third Service Morning Prayer
27	M	**George Herbert, Priest, Poet, 1633**			
		Com. Pastor	*or*	Lev. 19. 1–2, 11–18	Ps. 10; *11*
		esp. Mal. 2. 5–7		Ps. 19. 7–end	*alt.* Ps. *80*; 82
		Matt. 11. 25–end		Matt. 25. 31–end	Gen. 41. 25–45
	Pw	*also* Rev. 19. 5–9			Gal. 3.23 – 4.7
28	Tu			Isa. 55. 10–11	Ps. 44
				Ps. 34. 4–6, 21–22	*alt.* Ps. 87; **89. 1–18**
				Matt. 6. 7–15	Gen. 41.46 – 42.5
	P				Gal. 4. 8–20
29	W	Ember Day*			
				Jonah ch. 3	Ps. **6**; 17
				Ps. 51. 1–5, 17–18	*alt.* Ps. 119. 105–128
				Luke 11. 29–32	Gen. 42. 6–17
	P				Gal. 4.21 – 5.1

March 2012

				Sunday Principal Service Weekday Eucharist	Third Service Morning Prayer
1	Th	**David, Bishop of Menevia, Patron of Wales, c. 601**			
		Com. Bishop	*or*	Esther 14. 1–5, 12–14	Ps. **42**; 43
		also 2 Sam. 23. 1–4		*or* Isa. 55. 6–9	*alt.* Ps. 90; **92**
		Ps. 89. 19–22, 24		Ps. 138	Gen. 42. 18–28
	Pw			Matt. 7. 7–12	Gal. 5. 2–15
2	F	**Chad, Bishop of Lichfield, Missionary, 672****			
		Ember Day*			
		Com. Missionary	*or*	Ezek. 18. 21–28	Ps. 22
		also 1 Tim. 6. 11b–16		Ps. 130	*alt.* Ps. **88**; (95)
				Matt. 5. 20–26	Gen. 42. 29–end
	Pw				Gal. 5. 16–end
3	Sa	Ember Day*			
				Deut. 26. 16–end	Ps. 59; **63**
				Ps. 119. 1–8	*alt.* Ps. 96; **97**; 100
				Matt. 5. 43–end	Gen. 43. 1–15
	P				Gal. ch. 6
4	S	THE SECOND SUNDAY OF LENT			
				Gen. 17. 1–7, 15–16	Ps. 105. 1–6, 37–end
				Ps. 22. 23–end	Isa. 51. 1–11
				Rom. 4. 13–end	Gal. 3. 1–9, 23–end
	P			Mark 8. 31–end	
5	M			Dan. 9. 4–10	Ps. 26; **32**
				Ps. 79. 8–9, 12, 14	*alt.* Ps. 98; **99**; 101
				Luke 6. 36–38	Gen. 43. 16–end
	P				Heb. ch. 1
6	Tu			Isa. 1. 10, 16–20	Ps. 50
				Ps. 50. 8, 16–end	*alt.* Ps. **106**† (or 103)
				Matt. 23. 1–12	Gen. 44. 1–17
	P				Heb. 2. 1–9
7	W	**Perpetua, Felicity and their Companions, Martyrs at Carthage, 203**			
		Com. Martyr	*or*	Jer. 18. 18–20	Ps. 35
		esp. Rev. 12. 10–12a		Ps. 31. 4–5, 14–18	*alt.* Ps. 110; *111*; 112
		also Wisd. 3. 1–7		Matt. 20. 17–28	Gen. 44. 18–end
	Pr				Heb. 2. 10–end
8	Th	**Edward King, Bishop of Lincoln, 1910**			
		Felix, Bishop, Apostle to the East Angles, 647; Geoffrey Studdert Kennedy, Priest, Poet, 1929			
		Com. Bishop	*or*	Jer. 17. 5–10	Ps. 34
		also Heb. 13. 1–8		Ps. 1	*alt.* Ps. 113; *115*
				Luke 16. 19–end	Gen. 45. 1–15
	Pw				Heb. 3. 1–6
9	F			Gen. 37. 3–4, 12–13, 17–28	Ps. 40; *41*
				Ps. 105. 16–22	*alt.* Ps. 139
				Matt. 21. 33–43, 45–46	Gen. 45. 16–end
	P				Heb. 3. 7–end

*For Ember Day provision, see p. 11.
**Chad may be celebrated with Cedd on 26 October instead of 2 March.

Second Service Evening Prayer		Calendar and Holy Communion	Morning Prayer	Evening Prayer
Ps. 12; *13*; 14 *alt.* Ps. *85*; 86 Jer. 4. 19—end John 5. 1—18	P	Ezek. 34. 11—16a Matt. 25. 31—end	Gen. 41. 25—45 Gal. 3.23 — 4.7	Jer. 4. 19—end John 5. 1—18
Ps. 46; *49* *alt.* Ps. 89. 19—end Jer. 5. 1—19 John 5. 19—29	P	Isa. 55. 6—11 Matt. 21. 10—16	Gen. 41.46 — 42.5 Gal. 4. 8—20	Jer. 5. 1—19 John 5. 19—29
Ps. 9; *28* *alt.* Ps. *91*; 93 Jer. 5. 20—end John 5. 30—end	P	Ember Day Ember CEG *or* Isa. 58. 1—9a Matt. 12. 38—end	Gen. 42. 6—17 Gal. 4.21 — 5.1	Jer. 5. 20—end John 5. 30—end
Ps. 137; 138; *142* *alt.* Ps. 94 Jer. 6. 9—21 John 6. 1—15	Pw	**David, Bishop of Menevia, Patron of Wales, c. 601** Com. Bishop *or* Isa. 58. 9b—end John 8. 31—45	Gen. 42. 18—28 Gal. 5. 2—15	Jer. 6. 9—21 John 6. 1—15
Ps. 54; *55* *alt.* Ps. 102 Jer. 6. 22—end John 6. 16—27	Pw	**Chad, Bishop of Lichfield, Missionary, 672** Ember Day Com. Bishop *or* Ember CEG *or* Ezek. 18. 20—25 John 5. 2—15	Gen. 42. 29—end Gal. 5. 16—end	Jer. 6. 22—end John 6. 16—27
Ps. *4*; 16 *alt.* Ps. 104 Jer. 7. 1—20 John 6. 27—40 ct	P	Ember Day Ember CEG *or* Ezek. 18. 26—end Matt. 17. 1—9 *or* Luke 4. 16—21 *or* John 10. 1—16	Gen. 43. 1—15 Gal. ch. 6	Jer. 7. 1—20 John 6. 27—40 ct
Ps. 135 (*or* 135. 1—14) Gen. 12. 1—9 Heb. 11. 1—3, 8—16 *Gospel:* John 8. 51—end	P	**THE SECOND SUNDAY OF LENT** Jer. 17. 5—10 Ps. 25. 13—end 1 Thess. 4. 1—8 Matt. 15. 21—28	Ps. 105. 1—6, 37—end Isa. 51. 1—11 Gal. 3. 1—9, 23—end	Ps. 135 (*or* 135. 1—14) Gen. 12. 1—9 Heb. 11. 1—3, 8—16
Ps. 70; *74* *alt.* Ps. *105*† (*or* 103) Jer. 7. 21—end John 6. 41—51	P	Heb. 2. 1—10 John 8. 21—30	Gen. 43. 16—end Heb. ch. 1	Jer. 7. 21—end John 6. 41—51
Ps. *52*; 53; 54 *alt.* Ps. 107† Jer. 8. 1—15 John 6. 52—59	P	Heb. 2. 11—end Matt. 23. 1—12	Gen. 44. 1—17 Heb. 2. 1—9	Jer. 8. 1—15 John 6. 52—59
Ps. *3*; 51 *alt.* Ps. 119. 129—152 Jer. 8.18 — 9.11 John 6. 60—end	Pr	**Perpetua, Martyr at Carthage, 203** Com. Martyr *or* Heb. 3. 1—6 Matt. 20. 17—28	Gen. 44. 18—end Heb. 2. 10—end	Jer. 8.18 — 9.11 John 6. 60—end
Ps. 71 *alt.* Ps. 114; *116*; 117 Jer. 9. 12—24 John 7. 1—13	P	Heb. 3. 7—end John 5. 30—end	Gen. 45. 1—15 Heb. 3. 1—6	Jer. 9. 12—24 John 7. 1—13
Ps. *6*; 38 *alt.* Ps. *130*; 131; 137 Jer. 10. 1—16 John 7. 14—24	P	Heb. ch. 4 Matt. 21. 33—end	Gen. 45. 16—end Heb. 3. 7—end	Jer. 10. 1—16 John 7. 14—24

March 2012

			Sunday Principal Service Weekday Eucharist	Third Service Morning Prayer
10	Sa		Mic. 7. 14–15, 18–20 Ps. 103. 1–4, 9–12 Luke 15. 1–3, 11–end	Ps. 3; **25** *alt.* Ps. 120; **121**; 122 Gen. 46. 1–7, 28–end Heb. 4. 1–13
	P			
11	S	THE THIRD SUNDAY OF LENT	Exod. 20. 1–17 Ps. 19 (*or* 19. 7–end) 1 Cor. 1. 18–25 John 2. 13–22	Ps. 18. 1–25 Jer. ch. 38 Phil. 1. 1–26
	P			
12	M*		2 Kings 5. 1–15 Ps. 42. 1–2; 43. 1–4 Luke 4. 24–30	Ps. **5**; 7 *alt.* Ps. 123; 124; 125; **126** Gen. 47. 1–27 Heb. 4.14 – 5.10
	P			
13	Tu		Song of the Three 2, 11–20 *or* Dan. 2. 20–23 Ps. 25. 3–10 Matt. 18. 21–end	Ps. 6; **9** *alt.* Ps. **132**; 133 Gen. 47.28 – 48.end Heb. 5.11 – 6.12
	P			
14	W		Deut. 4. 1, 5–9 Ps. 147. 13–end Matt. 5. 17–19	Ps. 38 *alt.* Ps. 119. 153–end Gen. 49. 1–32 Heb. 6. 13–end
	P			
15	Th		Jer. 7. 23–28 Ps. 95, 1–2, 6–end Luke 11. 14–23	Ps. **56**; 57 *alt.* Ps. **143**; 146 Gen. 49.33 – 50.end Heb. 7. 1–10
	P			
16	F		Hos. ch. 14 Ps. 81. 6–10, 13, 16 Mark 12. 28–34	Ps. 22 *alt.* Ps. 142; **144** Exod. 1. 1–14 Heb. 7. 11–end
	P			
17	Sa	**Patrick, Bishop, Missionary, Patron of Ireland, c. 460** Com. Missionary *or* *also* Ps. 91. 1–4, 13–end Luke 10. 1–12, 17–20	Hos. 5.15 – 6.6 Ps. 51. 1–2, 17–end Luke 18. 9–14	Ps. 31 *alt.* Ps. 147 Exod. 1.22 – 2.10 Heb. ch. 8
	Pw			
18	S	THE FOURTH SUNDAY OF LENT (Mothering Sunday)	Num. 21. 4–9 Ps. 107. 1–3, 17–22 (*or* 107. 1–9) Eph. 2. 1–10 John 3. 14–21	Ps. 27 1 Sam. 16. 1–13 John 9. 1–25
		or, for Mothering Sunday:	Exod. 2. 1–10 *or* 1 Sam. 1. 20–end Ps. 34. 11–20 *or* Ps. 127. 1–4 2 Cor. 1. 3–7 *or* Col. 3. 12–17 Luke 2. 33–35 *or* John 19. 25b–27	
	P			

*The following readings may replace those provided for Holy Communion on any day during the Third Week of Lent: Exod. 17. 1–7; Ps. 95. 1–2, 6–end; John 4. 5–42.

Second Service Evening Prayer		Calendar and Holy Communion	Morning Prayer	Evening Prayer
Ps. *23*; 27 *alt.* Ps. 118 Jer. 10. 17–24 John 7. 25–36 ct	P	Heb. ch. 5 Luke 15. 11–end	Gen. 46. 1–7, 28–end Heb. 4. 1–13	Jer. 10. 17–24 John 7. 25–36 ct
Ps. 11; 12 Exod. 5.1 – 6.1 Phil. 3. 4b–14 *or* Matt. 10. 16–22	P	**THE THIRD SUNDAY OF LENT** Num. 22. 21–31 Ps. 9. 13–end Eph. 5. 1–14 Luke 11. 14–28	Ps. 18. 1–25 Jer. ch. 38 Phil. 1. 1–26	Ps. 11; 12 Exod. 5.1 – 6.1 Phil. 3. 4b–14 *or* Matt. 10. 16–22
Ps. 11; *17* *alt.* Ps. *127*; 128; 129 Jer. 11. 1–17 John 7. 37–52	Pw	**Gregory the Great, Bishop of Rome, 604** Com. Doctor *or* Heb. 6. 1–10 Luke 4. 23–30	Gen. 47. 1–27 Heb. 4.14 – 5.10	Jer. 11. 1–17 John 7. 37–52
Ps. 61; 62; *64* *alt.* Ps. (*134*); *135* Jer. 11.18 – 12.6 John 7.53 – 8.11	P	Heb. 6. 11–end Matt. 18. 15–22	Gen. 47.28 – 48.end Heb 5 11 – 6.12	Jer. 11.18 – 12.6 John 7.53 – 8.11
Ps. 36; *39* *alt.* Ps. 136 Jer. 13. 1–11 John 8. 12–30	P	Heb. 7. 1–10 Matt. 15. 1–20	Gen. 49. 1–32 Heb. 6. 13–end	Jer. 13. 1–11 John 8. 12–30
Ps. *59*; 60 *alt.* Ps. *138*; 140; 141 Jer. ch. 14 John 8. 31–47	P	Heb. 7. 11–25 John 6. 26–35	Gen. 49.33 – 50.end Heb. 7. 1–10	Jer. ch. 14 John 8. 31–47
Ps. 69 *alt.* Ps. 145 Jer. 15. 10–end John 8. 48–end	P	Heb. 7. 26–end John 4. 5–26	Exod. 1. 1–14 Heb. 7. 11–end	Jer. 15. 10–end John 8. 48–end
Ps. *116*; 130 *alt.* Ps. *148*; 149; 150 Jer. 16.10 – 17.4 John 9. 1–17 ct	P	Heb. 8. 1–6 John 8. 1–11	Exod. 1.22 – 2.10 Heb. ch. 8	Jer. 16.10 – 17.4 John 9. 1–17 ct
Ps. 13; 14 Exod. 6. 2–13 Rom. 5. 1–11 *Gospel:* John 12. 1–8 *If the Principal Service readings for The Fourth Sunday of Lent are displaced by Mothering Sunday provisions, they may be used at the Second Service.* *Or First EP of Joseph* Ps. 132 Hos. 11. 1–9 Luke 2. 41–end **W** ct	P	**THE FOURTH SUNDAY OF LENT** To celebrate Mothering Sunday, see *Common Worship* provision. Exod. 16. 2–7a Ps. 122 Gal. 4. 21–end *or* Heb. 12. 22–24 John 6. 1–14	Ps. 27 1 Sam. 16. 1–13 John 9. 1–25	Ps. 13; 14 Exod. 6. 2–13 Rom. 5. 1–11

March 2012

			Sunday Principal Service / Weekday Eucharist	Third Service / Morning Prayer

19 M* JOSEPH OF NAZARETH

2 Sam. 7. 4–16
Ps. 89. 26–36
Rom. 4. 13–18
W   Matt. 1. 18–end

MP: Ps. 25; 147. 1–12
Isa. 11. 1–10
Matt. 13. 54–end

20 Tu **Cuthbert, Bishop of Lindisfarne, Missionary, 687****
Com. Missionary   *or*   Ezek. 47. 1–9, 12
esp. Ezek. 34. 11–16   Ps. 46. 1–8
also Matt. 18. 12–14   John 5. 1–3, 5–16
Pw

Ps. 54; **79**
alt. Ps. **5**; 6; (8)
Exod. 2.23 – 3.20
Heb. 9. 15–end

21 W **Thomas Cranmer, Archbishop of Canterbury, Reformation Martyr, 1556**
Com. Martyr   *or*   Isa. 49. 8–15
Ps. 145. 8–18
John 5. 17–30
Pr

Ps. 63; **90**
alt. Ps. 119. 1–32
Exod. 4. 1–23
Heb. 10. 1–18

22 Th
Exod. 32. 7–14
Ps. 106. 19–23
John 5. 31–end
P

Ps. 53; **86**
alt. Ps. 14; **15**; 16
Exod. 4.27 – 6.1
Heb. 10. 19–25

23 F
Wisd. 2. 1, 12–22
or Jer. 26. 8–11
Ps. 34. 15–end
John 7. 1–2, 10, 25–30
P

Ps. 102
alt. Ps. 17; **19**
Exod. 6. 2–13
Heb. 10. 26–end

24 Sa *Walter Hilton of Thurgarton, Augustinian Canon, Mystic, 1396; Paul Couturier, Priest, Ecumenist, 1953; Oscar Romero, Archbishop of San Salvador, Martyr, 1980*
Jer. 11. 18–20
Ps. 7. 1–2, 8–10
John 7. 40–52
P

Ps. 32
alt. Ps. 20; 21; **23**
Exod. 7. 8–end
Heb. 11. 1–16

25 S THE FIFTH SUNDAY OF LENT **(Passiontide begins)**
(The Annunciation transferred to 26th)
Jer. 31. 31–34
Ps. 51. 1–13
or Ps. 119. 9–16
Heb. 5. 5–10
John 12. 20–33
P

Ps. 107. 1–22
Exod. 24. 3–8
Heb. 12. 18–end

26 M*** **THE ANNUNCIATION OF OUR LORD TO THE BLESSED VIRGIN MARY**
(transferred from 25th)
Isa. 7. 10–14
Ps. 40. 5–11
Heb. 10. 4–10
𝕎   Luke 1. 26–38

MP: Ps. 111; 113
1 Sam. 2. 1–10
Rom. 5. 12–end

27 Tu
Num. 21. 4–9
Ps. 102. 1–3, 16–23
John 8. 21–30
P

Ps. **35**; 123
alt. Ps. 32; **36**
Exod. 8. 20–end
Heb. 11.32 – 12.2

28 W
Dan. 3. 14–20, 24–25, 28
Canticle: Bless the Lord
John 8. 31–42
P

Ps. **55**; 124
alt. Ps. 34
Exod. 9. 1–12
Heb. 12. 3–13

*The following readings may replace those provided for Holy Communion on any day, except St Joseph's Day, during the Fourth Week of Lent: Mic. 7. 7–9; Ps. 27. 1, 9–10, 16–17; John ch. 9.
**Cuthbert may be celebrated on 4 September instead of 20 March.
***The following readings may replace those provided for Holy Communion on any day, except The Annunciation, during the Fifth Week of Lent: 2 Kings 4. 18–21, 32–37; Ps. 17. 1–8, 16; John 11. 1–45.

Second Service Evening Prayer		Calendar and Holy Communion	Morning Prayer	Evening Prayer
EP: Ps. 1; 112 Gen. 50. 22–end Matt. 2. 13–end		To celebrate Joseph, see *Common Worship* provision. Heb. 11. 1–6 John 2. 13–end	Exod. 2. 11–22 Heb. 9. 1–14	Jer. 17. 5–18 John 9. 18–end
	P			
Ps. *80*; 82 *alt.* Ps. *9*; 10† Jer. 18. 1–12 John 10. 1–10		Heb. 11. 13–16a John 7. 14–24	Exod. 2.23 – 3.20 Heb. 9. 15–end	Jer. 18. 1–12 John 10. 1–10
	P			
Ps. 52; *91* *alt.* Ps. *11*; 12; 13 Jer. 18. 13–end John 10. 11–21		**Benedict, Abbot of Monte Cassino, c. 550** Com. Abbot *or* Heb. 12. 1–11 John 9. 1–17	Exod. 4. 1–23 Heb. 10. 1–18	Jer. 18. 13–end John 10. 11–21
	Pw			
Ps. 94 *alt.* Ps. 18† Jer. 19. 1–13 John 10. 22–end		Heb. 12. 12–17 John 5. 17–27	Exod. 4.27 – 6.1 Heb. 10. 19–25	Jer. 19. 1–13 John 10. 22–end
	P			
Ps. 13; *16* *alt.* Ps. 22 Jer. 19.14 – 20.6 John 11. 1–16		Heb. 12. 22–end John 11. 33–46	Exod. 6. 2–13 Heb. 10. 26–end	Jer. 19.14 – 20.6 John 11. 1–16
	P			
Ps. *140*; 141; 142 *alt.* Ps. *24*; 25 Jer. 20. 7–end John 11. 17–27 ct		Heb. 13. 17–21 John 8. 12–20	Exod. 7. 8–end Heb. 11. 1–16	Jer. 20. 7–end John 11. 17–27 ct
	P			
Ps. 34 (or 34. 1–10) Exod. 7. 8–24 Rom. 5. 12–end *Gospel:* Luke 22. 1–13 *or First EP of* *The Annunciation* Ps. 85 Wisd. 9. 1–12 *or* Gen. 3. 8–15 Gal. 4. 1–5 ℣ ct		**THE FIFTH SUNDAY OF LENT** (*The Annunciation transferred to 26th*) Exod. 24. 4–8 Ps. 143 Heb. 9. 11–15 John 8. 46–end	Ps. 107. 1–22 Jer. 31. 31–34 Heb. 5. 5–10	Ps. 34 (or 34. 1–10) Exod. 7. 8–24 Rom. 5. 12–end *or First EP of* *The Annunciation* Ps. 85 Wisd. 9. 1–12 *or* Gen. 3. 8–15 Gal. 4. 1–5 ℣ ct
	P			
EP: Ps. 131; 146 Isa. 52. 1–12 Heb. 2. 5–end		**THE ANNUNCIATION OF THE BLESSED VIRGIN MARY** (transferred from 25th) Isa. 7. 10–14 [15] Ps. 113 Rom. 5. 12–19 Luke 1. 26–38	Ps. 111 1 Sam. 2. 1–10 Heb. 10. 4–10	Ps. 131; 146 Isa. 52. 1–12 Heb. 2. 5–end
	℣			
Ps. *61*; 64 *alt.* Ps. 33 Jer. 22. 1–5, 13–19 John 11. 45–end		Col. 2. 8–12 John 7. 32–39	Exod. 8. 20–end Heb. 11.32 – 12.2	Jer. 22. 1–5, 13–19 John 11. 45–end
	P			
Ps. 56; *62* *alt.* Ps. 119. 33–56 Jer. 22.20 – 23.8 John 12. 1–11		Col. 2. 13–19 John 7. 40–end	Exod. 9. 1–12 Heb. 12. 3–13	Jer. 22.20 – 23.8 John 12. 1–11
	P			

March 2012

			Sunday Principal Service Weekday Eucharist	Third Service Morning Prayer
29	Th P		Gen. 17. 3–9 Ps. 105. 4–9 John 8. 51–end	Ps. **40**; 125 *alt*. Ps. 37† Exod. 9. 13–end Heb. 12. 14–end
30	F P		Jer. 20. 10–13 Ps. 18. 1–6 John 10. 31–end	Ps. **22**; 126 *alt*. Ps. 31 Exod. ch. 10 Heb. 13. 1–16
31	Sa P	John Donne, Priest, Poet, 1631	Ezek. 37. 21–28 *Canticle:* Jer. 31. 10–13 *or* Ps. 121 John 11. 45–end	Ps. **23**; 127 *alt*. Ps. 41; **42**; 43 Exod. ch. 11 Heb. 13. 17–end

April 2012

			Sunday Principal Service Weekday Eucharist	Third Service Morning Prayer
1	S R	**PALM SUNDAY** *Liturgy of the Palms* Mark 11. 1–11 *or* John 12. 12–16 Ps. 118. 1–2, 19–24 (*or* 118. 19–24)	*Liturgy of the Passion* Isa. 50. 4–9a Ps. 31. 9–16 (*or* 31. 9–18) Phil. 2. 5–11 Mark 14.1 – 15.end *or* Mark 15. 1–39 [40–end]	Ps. 61; 62 Zech. 9. 9–12 1 Cor. 2. 1–12
2	M R	**MONDAY OF HOLY WEEK**	Isa. 42. 1–9 Ps. 36. 5–11 Heb. 9. 11–15 John 12. 1–11	*MP:* Ps. 41 Lam. 1. 1–12a Luke 22. 1–23
3	Tu R	**TUESDAY OF HOLY WEEK**	Isa. 49. 1–7 Ps. 71. 1–14 (*or* 71. 1–8) 1 Cor. 1. 18–31 John 12. 20–36	*MP:* Ps. 27 Lam. 3. 1–18 Luke 22. [24–38] 39–53
4	W R	**WEDNESDAY OF HOLY WEEK**	Isa. 50. 4–9a Ps. 70 Heb. 12. 1–3 John 13. 21–32	*MP:* Ps. 102 (*or* 102. 1–18) Wisd. 1.16 – 2.1, 12–22 *or* Jer. 11. 18–20 Luke 22. 54–end
5	Th W(HC)R	**MAUNDY THURSDAY**	Exod. 12. 1–14 (*or* 12. 1–4, 11–14) Ps. 116. 1, 10–end (*or* 116. 9–end) 1 Cor. 11. 23–26 John 13. 1–17, 31b–35	*MP:* Ps. 42; 43 Lev. 16. 2–24 Luke 23. 1–25
6	F R	**GOOD FRIDAY**	Isa. 52.13 – 53.end Ps. 22 (*or* 22. 1–11 *or* 22. 1–21) Heb. 10. 16–25 *or* Heb. 4. 14–16; 5. 7–9 John 18.1 – 19.end	*MP:* Ps. 69 Gen. 22. 1–18 A part of John 18 – 19 if not read at the Principal Service *or* Heb. 10. 1–10
7	Sa	**EASTER EVE** *These readings are for use at services* *other than the Easter Vigil.*	Job 14. 1–14 *or* Lam. 3. 1–9, 19–24 Ps. 31. 1–4, 15–16 (*or* 31. 1–5) 1 Pet. 4. 1–8 Matt. 27. 57–end *or* John 19. 38–end	Ps. 142 Hos. 6. 1–6 John 2. 18–22

Second Service Evening Prayer		Calendar and Holy Communion	Morning Prayer	Evening Prayer
Ps. 42; *43* *alt.* Ps. 39; *40* Jer. 23. 9–32 John 12. 12–19	P	Col. 3. 8–11 John 10. 22–38	Exod. 9. 13–end Heb. 12. 14–end	Jer. 23. 9–32 John 12. 12–19
Ps. 31 *alt.* Ps. 35 Jer. ch. 24 John 12. 20–36a	P	Col. 3. 12–17 John 11. 47–54	Exod. ch. 10 Heb. 13. 1–16	Jer. ch. 24 John 12. 20–36a
Ps. 128; 129; *130* *alt.* Ps. 45; *46* Jer. 25. 1–14 John 12. 36b–end ct	P	Col. 4. 2–6 John 6. 53–end	Exod. ch. 11 Heb. 13. 17–end	Jer. 25. 1–14 John 12. 36b–end ct
Ps. 69. 1–20 Isa. 5. 1–7 Mark 12. 1–12	R	**PALM SUNDAY** Zech. 9. 9–12 Ps. 73. 22–end Phil. 2. 5–11 Passion acc. to Matthew Matt. 27. 1–54 *or* Matt. 26.1 – 27.61 *or* Matt. 21. 1–13	Ps. 61; 62 Isa. 42. 1–9 1 Cor. 2. 1–12	Ps. 69. 1–20 Isa. 5. 1–7 Mark 12. 1–12
EP: Ps. 25 Lam. 2. 8–19 Col. 1. 18–23	R	**MONDAY OF HOLY WEEK** Isa. 63. 1–19 Ps. 55. 1–8 Gal. 6. 1–11 Mark ch. 14	Ps. 41 Lam. 1. 1–12a John 12. 1–11	Ps. 25 Lam. 2. 8–19 Col. 1. 18–23
EP: Ps. 55. 13–24 Lam. 3. 40–51 Gal. 6. 11–end	R	**TUESDAY OF HOLY WEEK** Isa. 50. 5–11 Ps. 13 Rom. 5. 6–19 Mark 15. 1–39	Ps. 27 Lam. 3. 1–18 John 12. 20–36	Ps. 55. 13–24 Lam. 3. 40–51 Gal. 6. 11–end
EP: Ps. 88 Isa. 63. 1–9 Rev. 14.18 – 15.4	R	**WEDNESDAY OF HOLY WEEK** Isa. 49. 1–9a Ps. 54 Heb. 9. 16–end Luke ch. 22	Ps. 102 (*or* 102. 1–18) Wisd. 1.16 – 2.1, 12–22 *or* Jer. 11. 18–20 John 13. 21–32	Ps. 88 Isa. 63. 1–9 Rev. 14.18 – 15.4
EP: Ps. 39 Exod. ch. 11 Eph. 2. 11–18	W(HC)R	**MAUNDY THURSDAY** Exod. 12. 1–11 Ps. 43 1 Cor. 11. 17–end Luke 23. 1–49	Ps. 42; 43 Lev. 16. 2–24 John 13. 1–17, 31b–35	Ps. 39 Exod. ch. 11 Eph. 2. 11–18
EP: Ps. 130; 143 Lam. 5. 15–end A part of John 18 – 19 if not read at the Principal Service, especially John 19. 38–end *or* Col. 1. 18–23	R	**GOOD FRIDAY** Alt. Collect Passion acc. to John Alt. Gospel, if Passion is read Num. 21. 4–9 Ps. 140. 1–9 Heb. 10. 1–25 John 19. 1–37 *or* John 19. 38–end	Ps. 69 Gen. 22. 1–18 John ch. 18	Ps. 130; 143 Lam. 5. 15–end John 19. 38–end
Ps. 116 Job 19. 21–27 1 John 5. 5–12		**EASTER EVE** Job 14. 1–14 1 Pet. 3. 17–22 Matt. 27. 57–end	Ps. 142 Hos. 6. 1–6 John 2. 18–22	Ps. 116 Job 19. 21–27 1 John 5. 5–12

April 2012

			Sunday Principal Service Weekday Eucharist	Third Service Morning Prayer
8	S	**EASTER DAY** *The following readings and psalms* *(or canticles) are provided for use* *at the Easter Vigil. A minimum of* *three Old Testament readings should* *be chosen. The reading from* Exodus ch. 14 *should always be used.*	Gen. 1.1 – 2.4a & Ps. 136. 1–9, 23–end Gen. 7. 1–5, 11–18; 8. 6–18; 9. 8–13 & Ps. 46 Gen. 22. 1–18 & Ps. 16 Exod. 14. 10–end; 15. 20–21 & Canticle: Exod. 15. 1b–13, 17–18 Isa. 55. 1–11 & *Canticle*: Isa. 12. 2–end Baruch 3.9–15, 32 – 4.4 & Ps. 19 *or* Prov. 8. 1–8, 19–21; 9. 4b–6 & Ps. 19 Ezek. 36. 24–28 & Ps. 42; 43 Ezek. 37. 1–14 & Ps. 143 Zeph. 3. 14–end & Ps. 98 Rom. 6. 3–11 & Ps. 114	
	₩		Mark 16. 1–8	
		Easter Day Services *The reading from Acts must be used* *as either the first or second reading* *at the Principal Service.*	Acts 10. 34–43 *or* Isa. 25. 6–9 Ps. 118. 1–2, 14–24 (*or* 118. 14–24) 1 Cor. 15. 1–11 *or* Acts 10. 34–43 John 20. 1–18	MP: Ps. 114; 117 Gen. 1. 1–5, 26–end 2 Cor. 5.14 – 6.2
	₩		*or* Mark 16. 1–8	
9	M	MONDAY OF EASTER WEEK	Acts 2. 14, 22–32 Ps. 16. 1–2, 6–end Matt. 28. 8–15	Ps. *111*; 117; 146 Exod. 12. 1–14 1 Cor. 15. 1–11
	W			
10	Tu	TUESDAY OF EASTER WEEK	Acts 2. 36–41 Ps. 33. 4–5, 18–end John 20. 11–18	Ps. *112*; 147. 1–12 Exod. 12. 14–36 1 Cor. 15. 12–19
	W			
11	W	WEDNESDAY OF EASTER WEEK	Acts 3. 1–10 Ps. 105. 1–9 Luke 24. 13–35	Ps. *113*; 147. 13–end Exod. 12. 37–end 1 Cor. 15. 20–28
	W			
12	Th	THURSDAY OF EASTER WEEK	Acts 3. 11–end Ps. 8 Luke 24. 35–48	Ps. *114*; 148 Exod. 13. 1–16 1 Cor. 15. 29–34
	W			
13	F	FRIDAY OF EASTER WEEK	Acts 4. 1–12 Ps. 118. 1–4, 22–26 John 21. 1–14	Ps. *115*; 149 Exod. 13.17 – 14.14 1 Cor. 15. 35–50
	W			
14	Sa	SATURDAY OF EASTER WEEK	Acts 4. 13–21 Ps. 118. 1–4, 14–21 Mark 16. 9–15	Ps. *116*; 150 Exod. 14. 15–end 1 Cor. 15. 51–end
	W			
15	S	THE SECOND SUNDAY OF EASTER *The reading from Acts must be used* *as either the first or second reading* *at the Principal Service.*	Acts 4. 32–35 [*or* Exod. 14. 10–end; 15. 20–21] Ps. 133 1 John 1.1 – 2.2 John 20. 19–end	Ps. 22. 20–31 Isa. 53. 6–12 Rom. 4. 13–25
	W			

Second Service Evening Prayer	Calendar and Holy Communion	Morning Prayer	Evening Prayer
	EASTER DAY Exod. 12. 21–28 Ps. 111 Col. 3. 1–7 John 20. 1–10	Ps. 114; 117 Gen. 1. 1–5, 26–end 2 Cor. 5.14 – 6.2	Ps. 105 or Ps. 66 1–11 Isa. 25. 6–9 Luke 24. 13–35
EP: Ps. 105 or Ps. 66. 1–11 Ezek. 37. 1–14 Luke 24. 13–35	℣		
Ps. 135 Song of Sol. 1.9 – 2.7 Mark 16. 1–8	**MONDAY OF EASTER WEEK** Hos. 6. 1–6 Easter Anthems Acts 10. 34–43 W Luke 24. 13–35	Exod. 12. 1–14 1 Cor. 15. 1–11	Song of Sol. 1.9 – 2.7 Mark 16. 1–8
Ps. 136 Song of Sol. 2. 8–end Luke 24. 1–12	**TUESDAY OF EASTER WEEK** 1 Kings 17. 17–end Ps. 16. 9–end Acts 13. 26–41 W Luke 24. 36b–48	Exod. 12. 14–36 1 Cor. 15. 12–19	Song of Sol. 2. 8–end Luke 24. 1–12
Ps. 105 Song of Sol. ch. 3 Matt. 28. 16–end	**WEDNESDAY OF EASTER WEEK** Isa. 42. 10–16 Ps. 111 Acts 3. 12–18 W John 20. 11–18	Exod. 12. 37–end 1 Cor. 15. 20–28	Song of Sol. ch. 3 Matt. 28. 16–end
Ps. 106 Song of Sol. 5.2 – 6.3 Luke 7. 11–17	**THURSDAY OF EASTER WEEK** Isa. 43. 16–21 Ps. 113 Acts 8. 26–end W John 21. 1–14	Exod. 13. 1–16 1 Cor. 15. 29–34	Song of Sol. 5.2 – 6.3 Luke 7. 11–17
Ps. 107 Song of Sol. 7.10 – 8.4 Luke 8. 41–end	**FRIDAY OF EASTER WEEK** Ezek. 37. 1–14 Ps. 116. 1–9 1 Pet. 3. 18–end W Matt. 28. 16–end	Exod. 13.17 – 14.14 1 Cor. 15. 35–50	Song of Sol. 7.10 – 8.4 Luke 8. 41–end
Ps. 145 Song of Sol. 8. 5–7 John 11. 17–44 ct	**SATURDAY OF EASTER WEEK** Zech. 8. 1–8 Ps. 118. 14–21 1 Pet. 2. 1–10 W John 20. 24–end	Exod. 14. 15–end 1 Cor. 15. 51–end	Song of Sol. 8. 5–7 John 11. 17–44 ct
Ps. 143. 1–11 Isa. 26. 1–9, 19 Luke 24. 1–12	**THE FIRST SUNDAY AFTER EASTER** Ezek. 37. 1–10 Ps. 81. 1–4 1 John 5. 4–12 John 20. 19–23 W	Ps. 22. 20–31 Isa. 53. 6–12 Rom. 4. 13–25	Ps. 143. 1–11 Isa. 26. 1–9, 19 Luke 24. 1–12

April 2012

			Sunday Principal Service Weekday Eucharist	Third Service Morning Prayer
16	M	*Isabella Gilmore, Deaconess, 1923*	Acts 4. 23–31 Ps. 2. 1–9 John 3. 1–8	Ps. 2; *19* *alt.* Ps. *1*; 2; 3 Exod. 15. 1–21
	W			Col. 1. 1–14
17	Tu		Acts 4. 32–end Ps. 93 John 3. 7–15	Ps. *8*; 20; 21 *alt.* Ps. *5*; 6; (8) Exod. 15.22 – 16.10
	W			Col. 1. 15–end
18	W		Acts 5. 17–26 Ps. 34. 1–8 John 3. 16–21	Ps. 16; *30* *alt.* Ps. 119. 1–32 Exod. 16. 11–end
	W			Col. 2. 1–15
19	Th	**Alphege, Archbishop of Canterbury, Martyr, 1012** Com. Martyr *or* *also* Heb. 5. 1–4	Acts 5. 27–33 Ps. 34. 1, 15–end John 3. 31–end	Ps. *28*; 29 *alt.* Ps. 14; *15*; 16 Exod. ch. 17
	Wr			Col. 2.16 – 3.11
20	F		Acts 5. 34–42 Ps. 27. 1–5, 16–17 John 6. 1–15	Ps. 57; *61* *alt.* Ps. 17; *19* Exod. 18. 1–12
	W			Col. 3.12 – 4.1
21	Sa	**Anselm, Abbot of Le Bec, Archbishop of Canterbury, Teacher, 1109** Com. Teacher *or* *also* Wisd. 9. 13–end Rom. 5. 8–11	Acts 6. 1–7 Ps. 33. 1–5, 18–19 John 6. 16–21	Ps. 63; *84* *alt.* Ps. 20; 21; *23* Exod. 18. 13–end Col. 4. 2–end
	W			
22	S	THE THIRD SUNDAY OF EASTER *The reading from Acts must be used as either the first or second reading at the Principal Service.*	Acts 3. 12–19 [or Zeph. 3. 14–end] Ps. 4 1 John 3. 1–7 Luke 24. 36b–48	Ps. 77. 11–20 Isa. 63. 7–15 1 Cor. 10. 1–13
	W			
23	M	GEORGE, MARTYR, PATRON OF ENGLAND, c. **304**	1 Macc. 2. 59–64 *or* Rev. 12. 7–12 Ps. 126 2 Tim. 2. 3–13 John 15. 18–21	MP: Ps. 5; 146 Josh. 1. 1–9 Eph. 6. 10–20
	R			
24	Tu	*Mellitus, Bishop of London, first Bishop at St Paul's, 624; The Seven Martyrs of the Melanesian Brotherhood, Solomon Islands, 2003*	Acts 7.51 – 8.1a Ps. 31. 1–5, 16 John 6. 30–35	Ps. *98*; 99; 100 *alt.* Ps. 32; *36* Exod. 20. 1–21 Luke 1. 26–38
	W			
25	W	MARK THE EVANGELIST	Prov. 15. 28–end *or* Acts 15. 35–end Ps. 119. 9–16 Eph. 4. 7–16 Mark 13. 5–13	MP: Ps. 37. 23–end; 148 Isa. 62. 6–10 *or* Ecclus. 51. 13–end Acts 12.25 – 13.13
	R			
26	Th		Acts 8. 26–end Ps. 66. 7–8, 14–end John 6. 44–51	Ps. 136 *alt.* Ps. 37† Exod. 25. 1–22 Luke 1. 57–end
	W			

Second Service Evening Prayer	Calendar and Holy Communion	Morning Prayer	Evening Prayer
Ps. 139 *alt.* Ps. **4**; 7 Deut. 1. 3–18 John 20. 1–10 W		Exod. 15. 1–21 Col. 1. 1–14	Deut. 1. 3–18 John 20. 1–10
Ps. 104 *alt.* Ps. 9; **10**† Deut. 1. 19–40 John 20. 11–18 W		Exod. 15.22 – 16.10 Col. 1. 15–end	Deut. 1. 19–40 John 20. 11–18
Ps. 33 *alt.* Ps. *11*; 12; 13 Deut. 3. 18–end John 20. 19–end W		Exod. 16. 11–end Col. 2. 1–15	Deut. 3. 18–end John 20. 19–end
Ps. 34 *alt.* Ps. 18† Deut. 4. 1–14 John 21. 1–14 Wr	**Alphege, Archbishop of Canterbury, Martyr, 1012** Com. Martyr	Exod. ch. 17 Col. 2.16 – 3.11	Deut. 4. 1–14 John 21. 1–14
Ps. 118 *alt.* Ps. 22 Deut. 4. 15–31 John 21. 15–19 W		Exod. 18. 1–12 Col. 3.12 – 4.1	Deut. 4. 15–31 John 21. 15–19
Ps. 66 *alt.* Ps. **24**; 25 Deut. 4. 32–40 John 21. 20–end ct W		Exod. 18. 13–end Col. 4. 2–end	Deut. 4. 32–40 John 21. 20–end ct
Ps. 142 Deut. 7. 7–13 Rev. 2. 1–11 *Gospel:* Luke 16. 19–end *or First EP of George* Ps. 111; 116 Jer. 15. 15–end Heb. 11.32 – 12.2 **R ct** W	**THE SECOND SUNDAY AFTER EASTER** Ezek. 34. 11–16a Ps. 23 1 Pet. 2. 19–end John 10. 11–16	Ps. 77. 11–20 Isa. 63. 7–15 1 Cor. 10. 1–13	Ps. 142 Deut. 7. 7–13 Rev. 2. 1–11
EP: Ps. 3; 11 Isa. 43. 1–7 John 15. 1–8 Wr	**George, Martyr, Patron of England, c. 304** To celebrate George, see *Common Worship* provision. Com. Martyr	Exod. ch. 19 Luke 1. 1–25	Deut. 5. 1–22 Eph. 1. 1–14
Ps. 71 *alt.* Ps. 33 Deut. 5. 22–end Eph. 1. 15–end *or First EP of Mark* Ps. 19 Isa. 52. 7–10 Mark 1. 1–15 **R ct** W		Exod. 20. 1–21 Luke 1. 26–38	Deut. 5. 22–end Eph. 1. 15–end *or First EP of Mark* (Ps. 19) Isa. 52. 7–10 Mark 1. 1–15 **R ct**
EP: Ps. 45 Ezek. 1. 4–14 2 Tim. 4. 1–11 R	**MARK THE EVANGELIST** Prov. 15. 28–end Ps. 119. 9–16 Eph. 4. 7–16 John 15. 1–11	(Ps. 37. 23–end; 148) Isa. 62. 6–10 *or* Ecclus. 51. 13–end Acts 12.25 – 13.13	(Ps. 45) Ezek. 1. 4–14 2 Tim. 4. 1–11
Ps. 73 *alt.* Ps. 39; **40** Deut. 7. 1–11 Eph. 2. 11–end W		Exod. 25. 1–22 Luke 1. 57–end	Deut. 7. 1–11 Eph. 2. 11–end

April 2012

			Sunday Principal Service Weekday Eucharist	Third Service Morning Prayer
27	F	*Christina Rossetti, Poet, 1894*		
			Acts 9. 1–20	Ps. 107
			Ps. 117	*alt.* Ps. 31
			John 6. 52–59	Exod. 28. 1–4a, 29–38
	W			Luke 2. 1–20
28	Sa	*Peter Chanel, Missionary in the South Pacific, Martyr, 1841*		
			Acts 9. 31–42	Ps. 108; *110*; 111
			Ps. 116. 10–15	*alt.* Ps. 41; *42*; 43
			John 6. 60–69	Exod. 29. 1–9
	W			Luke 2. 21–40
29	S	THE FOURTH SUNDAY OF EASTER *The reading from Acts must be* *used as either the first or second reading* *at the Principal Service.*	Acts 4. 5–12 [Gen. 7. 1–5, 11–18; 8. 6–18; 9. 8–13] Ps. 23 1 John 3. 16–end	Ps. 119. 89–96 Neh. 7.73b – 8.12 Luke 24. 25–32
	W		John 10. 11–18	
30	M	*Pandita Mary Ramabai, Translator of the Scriptures, 1922*		
			Acts 11. 1–18	Ps. 103
			Ps. 42. 1–2; 43. 1–4	*alt.* Ps. 44
			John 10. 1–10 (*or* 10. 11–18)	Exod. 32. 1–14
				Luke 2. 41–end
	W			

May 2012

1	Tu	PHILIP AND JAMES, APOSTLES		
			Isa. 30. 15–21	MP: Ps. 139; 146
			Ps. 119. 1–8	Prov. 4. 10–18
			Eph. 1. 3–10	James 1. 1–12
	R		John 14. 1–14	
2	W	**Athanasius, Bishop of Alexandria, Teacher, 373**		
		Com. Teacher *or*	Acts 12.24 – 13.5	Ps. 135
		also Ecclus. 4. 20–28	Ps. 67	*alt.* Ps. 119. 57–80
		Matt. 10. 24–27	John 12. 44–end	Exod. ch. 33
	W			Luke 3. 15–22
3	Th			
			Acts 13. 13–25	Ps. 118
			Ps. 89. 1–2, 20–26	*alt.* Ps. 56; *57*; (63†)
			John 13. 16–20	Exod. 34. 1–10, 27–end
	W			Luke 4. 1–13
4	F	**English Saints and Martyrs of the Reformation Era**		
		Isa. 43. 1–7	Acts 13. 26–33	Ps. 33
		or Ecclus. 2. 10–17	Ps. 2	*alt.* Ps. *51*; 54
		Ps. 87	John 14. 1–6	Exod. 35.20 – 36.7
		2 Cor. 4. 5–12		Luke 4. 14–30
	W	John 12. 20–26		
5	Sa			
			Acts 13. 44–end	Ps. 34
			Ps. 98. 1–5	*alt.* Ps. 68
			John 14. 7–14	Exod. 40. 17–end
	W			Luke 4. 31–37
6	S	THE FIFTH SUNDAY OF EASTER *The reading from Acts must be* *used as either the first or second reading* *at the Principal Service.*	Acts 8. 26–end [Baruch 3.9–15, 32 – 4.4 *or* Gen. 22. 1–18] Ps. 22. 25–end 1 John 4. 7–end	Ps. 44. 16–end 2 Macc. 7. 7–14 *or* Dan. 3. 16–28 Heb. 11.32 – 12.2
	W		John 15. 1–8	

Second Service Evening Prayer	Calendar and Holy Communion	Morning Prayer	Evening Prayer
Ps. 77 alt. Ps. 35 Deut. 7. 12–end Eph. 3. 1–13 W		Exod. 28. 1–4a, 29–38 Luke 2. 1–20	Deut. 7. 12–end Eph. 3. 1–13
Ps. 23; 27 alt. Ps. 45; 46 Deut. ch. 8 Eph. 3. 14–end ct W		Exod. 29. 1–9 Luke 2. 21–40	Deut. ch. 8 Eph. 3. 14–end ct
Ps. 81. 8–16 Exod. 16. 4–15 Rev. 2. 12–17 Gospel: John 6. 30–40	**THE THIRD SUNDAY AFTER EASTER** Gen. 45. 3–10 Ps. 57 1 Pet. 2. 11–17 John 16. 16–22 W	Ps. 119. 89–96 Neh. 7.73b – 8.12 Luke 24. 25–32	Ps. 81. 8–16 Exod. 16. 4–15 Rev. 2. 12–17
Ps. 112; 113; 114 alt. Ps. 47; 49 Deut. 9. 1–21 Eph. 4. 1–16 or First EP of Philip and James Ps. 25 Isa. 40. 27–end John 12. 20–26 R ct	W	Exod. 32. 1–14 Luke 2. 41–end	Deut. 9. 1–21 Eph. 4. 1–16 or First EP of Philip and James (Ps. 119. 1–8) Isa. 40. 27–end John 12. 20–26 R ct
EP: Ps. 149 Job 23. 1–12 John 1. 43–end	**PHILIP AND JAMES, APOSTLES** Prov. 4. 10–18 Ps. 25. 1–9 James 1. [1] 2–12 John 14. 1–14 R	(Ps. 139; 146) Isa. 30. 1–5 John 12. 20–26	(Ps. 149) Job 23. 1–12 John 1. 43–end
Ps. 47; 48 alt. Ps. 59; 60 (67) Deut. 10. 12–end Eph. 5. 1–14 W		Exod. ch. 33 Luke 3. 15–22	Deut. 10. 12–end Eph. 5. 1–14
Ps. 81; 85 alt. Ps. 61; 62; 64 Deut. 11. 8–end Eph. 5. 15–end Wr	**The Invention of the Cross**	Exod. 34. 1–10, 27–end Luke 4. 1–13	Deut. 11. 8–end Eph. 5. 15–end
Ps. 36; 40 alt. Ps. 38 Deut. 12. 1–14 Eph. 6. 1–9 W		Exod. 35.20 – 36.7 Luke 4. 14–30	Deut. 12. 1–14 Eph. 6. 1–9
Ps. 84; 86 alt. Ps. 65; 66 Deut. 15. 1–18 Eph. 6. 10–end ct W		Exod. 40. 17–end Luke 4. 31–37	Deut. 15. 1–18 Eph. 6. 10–end ct
Ps. 96 Isa. 60. 1–14 Rev. 3. 1–13 Gospel: Mark 16. 9–16	**THE FOURTH SUNDAY AFTER EASTER** Job 19. 21–27a Ps. 66. 14–end James 1. 17–21 John 16. 5–15 W	Ps. 44. 15–end 2 Macc. 7. 7–14 or Dan. 3. 16–28 Heb. 11.32 – 12.2	Ps. 96 Isa. 60. 1–14 Rev. 3. 1–13

May 2012

			Sunday Principal Service Weekday Eucharist	Third Service Morning Prayer
7	M W		Acts 14. 5–18 Ps. 118. 1–3, 14–15 John 14. 21–26	Ps. 145 *alt.* Ps. 71 Num. 9. 15–end; 10. 33–end Luke 4. 38–end
8	Tu W	**Julian of Norwich, Spiritual Writer, c. 1417** Com. Religious *or* *also* 1 Cor. 13. 8–end Matt. 5. 13–16	Acts 14. 19–end Ps. 145. 10–end John 14. 27–end	Ps. *19*; 147. 1–12 *alt.* Ps. 73 Num. 11. 1–33 Luke 5. 1–11
9	W W		Acts 15. 1–6 Ps. 122. 1–5 John 15. 1–8	Ps. *30*; 147. 13–end *alt.* Ps. 77 Num. ch. 12 Luke 5. 12–26
10	Th W		Acts 15. 7–21 Ps. 96. 1–3, 7–10 John 15. 9–11	Ps. *57*; 148 *alt.* Ps. 78. 1–39† Num. 13. 1–3, 17–end Luke 5. 27–end
11	F W		Acts 15. 22–31 Ps. 57. 8–end John 15. 12–17	Ps. *138*; 149 *alt.* Ps. 55 Num. 14. 1–25 Luke 6. 1–11
12	Sa W	*Gregory Dix, Priest, Monk, Scholar, 1952*	Acts 16. 1–10 Ps. 100 John 15. 18–21	Ps. *146*; 150 *alt.* Ps. *76*; 79 Num. 14. 26–end Luke 6. 12–26
13	S W	**THE SIXTH SUNDAY OF EASTER** *The reading from Acts must be used as* *either the first or second reading at the* *Principal Service.*	Acts 10. 44–end [Isa. 55. 1–11] Ps. 98 1 John 5. 1–6 John 15. 9–17	Ps. 104. 26–32 Ezek. 47. 1–12 John 21. 1–19
14	M R W	**MATTHIAS THE APOSTLE*** Rogation Day** *or, if Matthias is celebrated on 24 February:*	Isa. 22. 15–end *or* Acts 1. 15–end Ps. 15 Acts 1. 15–end *or* 1 Cor. 4. 1–7 John 15. 9–17 Acts 16. 11–15 Ps. 149. 1–5 John 15.26 – 16.4	*MP*: Ps. 16; 147. 1–12 1 Sam. 2. 27–35 Acts 2. 37–end Ps. *65*; 67 *alt.* Ps. *80*; 82 Num. 16. 1–35 Luke 6. 27–38
15	Tu W	Rogation Day**	Acts 16. 22–34 Ps. 138 John 16. 5–11	Ps. 124; 125; *126*; 127 *alt.* Ps. 87; *89. 1–18* Num. 16. 36–end Luke 6. 39–end
16	W W	Rogation Day** *Caroline Chisholm, Social Reformer, 1877*	Acts 17.15, 22 – 18.1 Ps. 148. 1–2, 11–end John 16. 12–15	Ps. *132*; 133 *alt.* Ps. 119. 105–128 Num. 17. 1–11 Luke 7. 1–10

*Matthias may be celebrated on 24 February instead of 14 May.
**For Rogation Day provision, see p. 10.

Second Service Evening Prayer	Calendar and Holy Communion	Morning Prayer	Evening Prayer
Ps. 105 alt. Ps. **72**; 75 Deut. 16. 1–20 1 Pet. 1. 1–12	W	Num. 9. 15–end; 10. 33–end Luke 4. 38–end	Deut. 16. 1–20 1 Pet. 1. 1–12
Ps. 96; **97** alt. Ps. 74 Deut. 17. 8–end 1 Pet. 1. 13–end	W	Num. 11. 1–33 Luke 5. 1–11	Deut. 17. 8–end 1 Pet. 1. 13–end
Ps. 98; **99**; 100 alt. Ps. 119. 81–10 Deut. 18. 9–end 1 Pet. 2. 1–10	W	Num. ch. 12 Luke 5. 12–26	Deut. 18. 9–end 1 Pet. 2. 1–10
Ps. 104 alt. Ps. 78. 40–end† Deut. ch. 19 1 Pet. 2. 11–end	W	Num. 13. 1–3, 17–end Luke 5. 27–end	Deut. ch. 19 1 Pet. 2. 11–end
Ps. 66 alt. Ps. 69 Deut. 21.22 – 22.8 1 Pet. 3. 1–12	W	Num. 14. 1–25 Luke 6. 1–11	Deut. 21.22 – 22.8 1 Pet. 3. 1–12
Ps. 118 alt. Ps. 81; **84** Deut. 24. 5–end 1 Pet. 3. 13–end ct	W	Num. 14. 26–end Luke 6. 12–26	Deut. 24. 5–end 1 Pet. 3. 13–end ct
Ps. 45 Song of Sol. 4.16 – 5.2; 8. 6–7 Rev. 3. 14–end Gospel: Luke 22. 24–30 or First EP of Matthias Ps. 147 Isa. 22. 15–22 Phil. 3.13b – 4.1 **R** ct	**THE FIFTH SUNDAY AFTER EASTER** Rogation Sunday Joel 2. 21–26 Ps. 66. 1–8 James 1. 22–end John 16. 23b–end W	Ps. 104. 26–32 Ezek. 47. 1–12 John 21. 1–19	Ps. 45 Song of Sol. 4.16 – 5.2; 8. 6–7 Rev. 3. 14–end
EP: Ps. 80 1 Sam. 16. 1–13a Matt. 7. 15–27	Rogation Day Job 28. 1–11 Ps. 107. 1–9 James 5. 7–11 Luke 6. 36–42	Num. 16. 1–35 Luke 6. 27–38	Deut. ch. 26 1 Pet. 4. 1–11
Ps. **121**; 122; 123 alt. Ps. **85**; 86 Deut. ch. 26 1 Pet. 4. 1–11	W		
Ps. **128**; 129; 130; 131 alt. Ps. 89. 19–end Deut. 28. 1–14 1 Pet. 4. 12–end	Rogation Day Deut. 8. 1–10 Ps. 121 James 5. 16–end W Luke 11. 5–13	Num. 16. 36–end Luke 6. 39–end	Deut. 28. 1–14 1 Pet. 4. 12–end
First EP of Ascension Day Ps. 15; 24 2 Sam. 23. 1–5 Col. 2.20 – 3.4 ℣ ct	Rogation Day Deut. 34. 1–7 Ps. 108. 1–6 Eph. 4. 7–13 W John 17. 1–11	Num. 17. 1–11 Luke 7. 1–10	First EP of Ascension Day Ps. 15; 24 2 Sam. 23. 1–5 Col. 2.20 – 3.4 ℣ ct

May 2012

		Sunday Principal Service Weekday Eucharist	Third Service Morning Prayer
17	Th 🐝	**ASCENSION DAY** *The reading from Acts must be used as either the first or second reading at the Eucharist.*	Acts 1. 1–11 or Dan. 7. 9–14 Ps. 47 *or* Ps. 93 Eph. 1. 15–end *or* Acts 1. 1–11 Luke 24. 44–end	MP: Ps. 110; 150 Isa. 52. 7–end Heb. 7. [11–25] 26–end

18	F W		Acts 18. 9–18 Ps. 47. 1–6 John 16. 20–23	Ps. 20; *81* *alt.* Ps. **88**; (95) Num. 20. 1–13 Luke 7. 11–17 [Exod. 35.30 – 36.1 Gal. 5. 13–end]*

19	Sa W	**Dunstan, Archbishop of Canterbury, Restorer of Monastic Life, 988** Com. Bishop *or* *esp.* Matt. 24. 42–46 *also* Exod. 31. 1–5	Acts 18. 22–end Ps. 47. 1–2, 7–end John 16. 23–28	Ps. 21; *47* *alt.* Ps. 96; **97**; 100 Num. 21. 4–9 Luke 7. 18–35 [Num. 11. 16–17, 24–29 1 Cor. ch. 2]

20	S W	THE SEVENTH SUNDAY OF EASTER (SUNDAY AFTER ASCENSION DAY) *The reading from Acts must be used as either the first or second reading at the Principal Service.*	Acts 1. 15–17, 21–end [Ezek. 36. 24–28] Ps. 1 1 John 5. 9–13 John 17. 6–19	Ps. 76 Isa. 14. 3–15 Rev. 14. 1–13

21	M W	*Helena, Protector of the Holy Places, 330*	Acts 19. 1–8 Ps. 68. 1–6 John 16. 29–end	Ps. **93**; 96; 97 *alt.* Ps. **98**; 99; 101 Num. 22. 1–35 Luke 7. 36–end [Num. 27. 15–end 1 Cor. ch. 3]

22	Tu W		Acts 20. 17–27 Ps. 68. 9–10, 18–19 John 17. 1–11	Ps. 98; *99*; 100 *alt.* Ps. *106*† (or 103) Num. 22.36 – 23.12 Luke 8. 1–15 [1 Sam. 10. 1–10 1 Cor. 12. 1–13]

23	W W		Acts 20. 28–end Ps. 68. 27–28, 32–end John 17. 11–19	Ps. 2; *29* *alt.* Ps. 110; *111*; 112 Num. 23. 13–end Luke 8. 16–25 [1 Kings 19. 1–18 Matt. 3. 13–end]

24	Th W	**John and Charles Wesley, Evangelists, Hymn Writers, 1791 and 1788** Com. Pastor *or* *also* Eph. 5. 15–20	Acts 22. 30; 23. 6–11 Ps. 16. 1, 5–end John 17. 20–end	Ps. *24*; 72 *alt.* Ps. 113; *115* Num. ch. 24 Luke 8. 26–39 [Ezek. 11. 14–20 Matt. 9.35 – 10.20]

25	F W	**The Venerable Bede, Monk at Jarrow, Scholar, Historian, 735** *Aldhelm, Bishop of Sherborne, 709* Com. Religious *or* *also* Ecclus. 39. 1–10	Acts 25. 13–21 Ps. 103. 1–2, 11–12, 19–20 John 21. 15–19	Ps. *28*; 30 *alt.* Ps. 139 Num. 27. 12–end Luke 8. 40–end [Ezek. 36. 22–28 Matt. 12. 22–32]

*The alternative readings in square brackets may be used at one of the offices in preparation for the Day of Pentecost.

Second Service Evening Prayer		Calendar and Holy Communion	Morning Prayer	Evening Prayer
EP: Ps. 8 Song of the Three 29–37 or 2 Kings 2. 1–15 Rev. ch. 5 Gospel: Matt. 28. 16–end	₩	**ASCENSION DAY** Dan. 7. 13–14 Ps. 68. 1–6 Acts 1. 1–11 Mark 16. 14–end or Luke 24. 44–end	Ps. 110; 150 Isa. 52. 7–end Heb. 7. [11–25] 26–end	Ps. 8 Song of the Three 29–37 or 2 Kings 2. 1–15 Rev. ch. 5
Ps. 145 alt. Ps. 102 Deut. 29. 2–15 1 John 1.1 – 2.6	W	Ascension CEG	Num. 20. 1–13 Luke 7. 11–17 [Exod. 35.30 – 36.1 Gal. 5. 13–end]	Deut. 29. 2–15 1 John 1.1 – 2.6
Ps. 84; **85** alt. Ps. 104 Deut. ch. 30 1 John 2. 7–17 ct	W	**Dunstan, Archbishop of Canterbury, Restorer of Monastic Life, 988** Com. Bishop	Num. 21. 4–9 Luke 7. 18–35 [Num. 11. 16–17, 24–29 1 Cor. ch. 2]	Deut. ch. 30 1 John 2. 7–17 ct
Ps. 147. 1–12 Isa. ch. 61 Luke 4. 14–21	W	THE SUNDAY AFTER ASCENSION DAY 2 Kings 2. 9–15 Ps. 68. 32–end 1 Pet. 4. 7–11 John 15.26 – 16.4a	Ps. 76 Isa. 14. 3–15 Rev. 14. 1–13	Ps. 147. 1–12 Isa. ch. 61 Luke 4. 14–21
Ps. 18 alt. Ps. **105**† (or 103) Deut. 31. 1–13 1 John 2. 18–end	W		Num. 22. 1–35 Luke 7. 36–end [Num. 27. 15–end 1 Cor. ch. 3]	Deut. 31. 1–13 1 John 2. 18–end
Ps. 68 alt. Ps. 107† Deut. 31. 14–29 1 John 3. 1–10	W		Num. 22.36 – 23.12 Luke 8. 1–15 [1 Sam. 10. 1–10 1 Cor. 12. 1–13]	Deut. 31. 14–29 1 John 3. 1–10
Ps. 36; **46** alt. Ps. 119. 129–152 Deut. 31.30 – 32.14 1 John 3. 11–end	W		Num. 23. 13–end Luke 8. 16–25 [1 Kings 19. 1–18 Matt. 3. 13–end]	Deut. 31.30 – 32.14 1 John 3. 11–end
Ps. 139 alt. Ps. 114; **116**; 117 Deut. 32. 15–47 1 John 4. 1–6	W		Num. ch. 24 Luke 8. 26–39 [Ezek. 11. 14–20 Matt. 9.35 – 10.20]	Deut. 32. 15–47 1 John 4. 1–6
Ps. 147 alt. Ps. **130**; 131; 137 Deut. ch. 33 1 John 4. 7–end	W		Num. 27. 12–end Luke 8. 40–end [Ezek. 36. 22–28 Matt. 12. 22–32]	Deut. ch. 33 1 John 4. 7–end

May 2012

		Sunday Principal Service / Weekday Eucharist	Third Service / Morning Prayer

26 Sa **Augustine, first Archbishop of Canterbury, 605**
John Calvin, Reformer, 1564; Philip Neri, Founder of the Oratorians, Spiritual Guide, 1595

Com. Bishop   *or*   Acts 28. 16–20, 30–end   Ps. 42; *43*
also I Thess. 2. 2b–8   Ps. 11. 4–end   *alt.* Ps. 120; *121*; 122
Matt. 13. 31–33   John 21. 20–end   Num. 32. 1–27
                 Luke 9. 1–17
                 [Mic. 3. 1–8
W   Eph. 6. 10–20]

27 S **DAY OF PENTECOST (Whit Sunday)**
The reading from Acts must be   Acts 2. 1–21   MP: Ps. 145
used as either the first or second reading   *or* Ezek. 37. 1–14   Isa. 11. 1–9
at the Principal Service.   Ps. 104. 26–36, 37b (*or* 104. 26–end)   *or* Wisd. 7. 15–23 [24–27]
               Rom. 8. 22–27   I Cor. 12. 4–13
               or Acts 2. 1–21
R   John 15. 26–27; 16. 4b–15

28 M *Lanfranc, Prior of Le Bec, Archbishop of Canterbury, Scholar, 1089*
DEL 8   Ordinary Time resumes today
             I Pet. 1. 3–9   Ps. 123; 124; 125; *126*
             Ps. 111   Josh. ch. 1
G   Mark 10. 17–27   Luke 9. 18–27

29 Tu
             I Pet. 1. 10–16   Ps. *132*; 133
             Ps. 98. 1–5   Josh. ch. 2
G   Mark 10. 28–31   Luke 9. 28–36

30 W **Josephine Butler, Social Reformer, 1906**
Joan of Arc, Visionary, 1431; Apolo Kivebulaya, Evangelist in Central Africa, 1933
Com. Saint   *or*   I Pet. 1. 18–end   Ps. 119. 153–end
esp. Isa. 58. 6–11   Ps. 147. 13–end   Josh. ch. 3
also I John 3. 18–23   Mark 10. 32–45   Luke 9. 37–50
Matt. 9. 10–13

Gw

31 Th THE VISIT OF THE BLESSED VIRGIN MARY TO ELIZABETH*
             Zeph. 3. 14–18   MP: Ps. 85; 150
             Ps. 113   I Sam. 2. 1–10
W   Rom. 12. 9–16   Mark 3. 31–end
             Luke 1. 39–49 [50–56]

or, if The Visitation is celebrated on 2 July:
             I Pet. 2. 2–5, 9–12   Ps. *143*; 146
             Ps. 100   Josh. 4.1 – 5.1
G   Mark 10. 46–end   Luke 9. 51–end

June 2012

1 F **Justin, Martyr at Rome, c. 165**

Com. Martyr   *or*   I Pet. 4. 7–13   Ps. *142*; 144
esp. John 15. 18–21   Ps. 96. 10–end   Josh. 5. 2–end
also I Macc. 2. 15–22   Mark 11. 11–26   Luke 10. 1–16
Gr   I Cor. 1. 18–25

2 Sa
             Jude 17, 20–end   Ps. 147
             Ps. 63. 1–6   Josh. 6. 1–20
             Mark 11. 27–end   Luke 10. 17–24
G

*The Visit of the Blessed Virgin Mary to Elizabeth may be celebrated on 2 July instead of 31 May.

Second Service Evening Prayer	Calendar and Holy Communion	Morning Prayer	Evening Prayer
	Augustine, first Archbishop of Canterbury, 605 Com. Bishop		
First EP of Pentecost Ps. 48 Deut. 16. 9–15 John 7. 37–39		Num. 32. 1–27 Luke 9. 1–17 [Mic. 3. 1–8 Eph. 6. 10–20]	First EP of Whit Sunday Ps. 48 Deut. 16. 9–15 John 7. 37–39
R ct	W		R ct
EP: Ps. 139. 1–11, 13–18, 23–24 (or 139. 1–11) Ezek. 36. 22–28 Acts 2. 22–38 Gospel: John 20. 19–23	**WHIT SUNDAY** Deut. 16. 9–12 Ps. 122 Acts 2. 1–11 John 14. 15–31a	Ps. 145 Isa. 11. 1–9 or Wisd. 7. 15–23 [24–27] 1 Cor. 12. 4–13	Ps. 139. 1–11, 13–18, 23–24 (or 139. 1–11) Ezek. 36. 22–28 Acts 2. 22–38
	R		
	Monday in Whitsun Week		
Ps. *127*; 128; 129 Job ch. 1 Rom. 1. 1–17	Acts 10. 34–end John 3. 16–21	Ezek. 11. 14–20 Acts 2. 12–36	Exod. 35.30 – 36.1 Acts 2. 37–end
	R		
	Tuesday in Whitsun Week		
Ps. (134); *135* Job ch. 2 Rom. 1. 18–end	Acts 8. 14–17 John 10. 1–10	Ezek. 37. 1–14 1 Cor. 12. 1–13	2 Sam. 23.1–5 1 Cor. 12.27 – 13.end
	R		
Ps. 136 Job ch. 3 Rom. 2. 1–16 or First EP of the Visit of Mary to Elizabeth Ps. 45 Song of Sol. 2. 8–14 Luke 1. 26–38 W ct	Ember Day Ember CEG or Acts 2. 14–21 John 6. 44–51	Josh. ch. 3 Luke 9. 37–50	Job ch. 3 Rom. 2. 1–16
	R		
EP: Ps. 122; 127; 128 Zech. 2. 10–end John 3. 25–30	Acts 2. 22–28 Luke 9. 1–6	Josh. 4.1 – 5.1 Luke 9. 51–end	Job ch. 4 Rom. 2. 17–end
Ps. *138*; 140; 141 Job ch. 4 Rom. 2. 17–end			
	R		
	Nicomede, Priest and Martyr at Rome (date unknown) Ember Day		
Ps. 145 Job ch. 5 Rom. 3. 1–20	Com. Martyr or Ember CEG or Acts 8. 5–8 Luke 5. 17–26	Josh. 5. 2–end Luke 10. 1–16	Job ch. 5 Rom. 3. 1–20
	R		
First EP of Trinity Sunday Ps. 97; 98 Isa. 40. 12–end Mark 1. 1–13 ₩ ct	Ember Day Ember CEG or Acts 13. 44–end Matt. 20. 29–end	Josh. 6. 1–20 Luke 10. 17–24	First EP of Trinity Sunday Ps. 97; 98 Isa. 40. 12–end Mark 1. 1–13 ₩ ct
	R		

June 2012

			Sunday Principal Service Weekday Eucharist	Third Service Morning Prayer

3 S   TRINITY SUNDAY

	Isa. 6. 1–8	MP: Ps. 33. 1–12
	Ps. 29	Prov. 8. 1–4, 22–31
	Rom. 8. 12–17	2 Cor. 13. [5–10] 11–end
℣℣℣	John 3. 1–17	

4 M   *Petroc, Abbot of Padstow, 6th century*

DEL 9

	2 Pet. 1. 2–7	Ps. *1*; 2; 3
	Ps. 91. 1–2, 14–end	Josh. 7. 1–15
G	Mark 12. 1–12	Luke 10. 25–37

5 Tu   **Boniface (Wynfrith) of Crediton, Bishop, Apostle of Germany, Martyr, 754**

Com. Martyr	*or*	2 Pet. 3. 11–15a, 17–end	Ps. *5*; 6; (8)
also Acts 20. 24–28		Ps. 90. 1–4, 10, 14, 16	Josh. 7. 16–end
Gr		Mark 12. 13–17	Luke 10. 38–end

6 W   *Ini Kopuria, Founder of the Melanesian Brotherhood, 1945*

	2 Tim. 1. 1–3, 6–12	Ps. 119. 1–32
	Ps. 123	Josh. 8. 1–29
	Mark 12. 18–27	Luke 11. 1–13

G

7 Th   DAY OF THANKSGIVING FOR HOLY COMMUNION (CORPUS CHRISTI)

	Gen. 14. 18–20	MP: Ps. 147
	Ps. 116. 10–end	Deut. 8. 2–16
	1 Cor. 11. 23–26	1 Cor. 10. 1–17
W	John 6. 51–58	

or the ferial readings for the day:

	2 Tim. 2. 8–15	Ps. 14; *15*; 16
	Ps. 25. 4–12	Josh. 8. 30–end
G	Mark 12. 28–34	Luke 11. 14–28

8 F   **Thomas Ken, Bishop of Bath and Wells, Nonjuror, Hymn Writer, 1711**

Com. Bishop	*or*	2 Tim. 3. 10–end	Ps. 17; *19*
esp. 2 Cor. 4. 1–10		Ps. 119. 161–168	Josh. 9. 3–26
Gw	Matt. 24. 42–46	Mark 12. 35–37	Luke 11. 29–36

9 Sa   **Columba, Abbot of Iona, Missionary, 597**

Ephrem of Syria, Deacon, Hymn Writer, Teacher, 373

Com. Missionary	*or*	2 Tim. 4. 1–8	Ps. 20; 21; *23*
also Titus 2. 11–end		Ps. 71. 7–16	Josh. 10. 1–15
		Mark 12. 38–end	Luke 11. 37–end
Gw			

10 S   THE FIRST SUNDAY AFTER TRINITY (Proper 5)

Track 1	Track 2	
1 Sam. 8. 4–11[12–15]16–20;	Gen. 3. 8–15	Ps. 36
[11. 14–end]	Ps. 130	Deut. 6. 10–end
Ps. 138	2 Cor. 4. 13 – 5. 1	Acts 22.22 – 23.11
2 Cor. 4. 13 – 5. 1	Mark 3. 20–end	
Mark 3. 20–end		

G

11 M   BARNABAS THE APOSTLE

DEL 10

	Job 29. 11–16	MP: Ps. 100; 101; 117
	or Acts 11. 19–end	Jer. 9. 23–24
	Ps. 112	Acts 4. 32–end
	Acts 11. 19–end	
	or Gal. 2. 1–10	
R	John 15. 12–17	

Second Service Evening Prayer		Calendar and Holy Communion	Morning Prayer	Evening Prayer
EP: Ps. 104. 1–10 Ezek. 1. 4–10, 22–28a Rev. ch. 4 Gospel: Mark 1. 1–13	℣	**TRINITY SUNDAY** Isa. 6. 1–8 Ps. 8 Rev. 4. 1–11 John 3. 1–15	Ps. 33. 1–12 Prov. 8. 1–4, 22–31 2 Cor. 13. [5–10] 11–end	Ps. 104. 1–10 Ezek. 1. 4–10, 22–28a Mark 1. 1–13
Ps. 4; 7 Job ch. 7 Rom. 4. 1–12	G		Josh. 7. 1–15 Luke 10. 25–37	Job ch. 7 Rom. 4. 1–12
Ps. 9; 10† Job ch. 8 Rom. 4. 13–end	Gr	**Boniface (Wynfrith) of Crediton, Bishop, Apostle of Germany, Martyr, 754** Com. Martyr	Josh. 7. 16–end Luke 10. 38–end	Job ch. 8 Rom. 4. 13–end
Ps. 11; 12; 13 Job ch. 9 Rom. 5. 1–11 or First EP of Corpus Christi Ps. 110; 111 Exod. 16. 2–15 John 6. 22–35 **W ct**	G		Josh. 8. 1–29 Luke 11. 1–13	Job ch. 9 Rom. 5. 1–11
EP: Ps. 23; 42; 43 Prov. 9. 1–5 Luke 9. 11–17		To celebrate Corpus Christi, see *Common Worship* provision. Josh. 8. 30–end Luke 11. 14–28	Job. ch. 10 Rom. 5. 12–end	
Ps. 18† Job. ch. 10 Rom. 5. 12–end	G			
Ps. 22 Job ch. 11 Rom. 6. 1–14	G		Josh. 9. 3–26 Luke 11. 29–36	Job ch. 11 Rom. 6. 1–14
Ps. 24; 25 Job ch. 12 Rom. 6. 15–end **ct**	G		Josh. 10. 1–15 Luke 11. 37–end	Job ch. 12 Rom. 6. 15–end **ct**
Ps. 37. 1–17 (or 37. 1–11) Jer. 6. 16–21 Rom. 9. 1–13 Gospel: Luke 7. 11–17 or First EP of Barnabas Ps. 1; 15 Isa. 42. 5–12 Acts 14. 8–end **R ct**	G	**THE FIRST SUNDAY AFTER TRINITY** 2 Sam. 9. 6–end Ps. 41. 1–4 1 John 4. 7–end Luke 16. 19–31	Ps. 36 Deut. 6. 10–end Acts 22.22 – 23.11	Ps. 37. 1–17 (or 37. 1–11) Jer. 6. 16–21 Rom. 9. 1–13 or First EP of Barnabas Ps. 1; 15 Isa. 42. 5–12 Acts 14. 8–end **R ct**
EP: Ps. 147 Eccles. 12. 9–end or Tobit 4. 5–11 Acts 9. 26–31	R	**BARNABAS THE APOSTLE** Job 29. 11–16 Ps. 112 Acts 11. 22–end John 15. 12–16	(Ps. 100; 101; 117) Jer. 9. 23–24 Acts 4. 32–end	(Ps. 147) Eccles. 12. 9–end or Tobit 4. 5–11 Acts 9. 26–31

June 2012

			Sunday Principal Service Weekday Eucharist	Third Service Morning Prayer
12	Tu G		I Kings. 17. 7–16 Ps. 4 Matt. 5. 13–16	Ps. 32; **36** Josh. 21.43 – 22.8 Luke 12. 13–21
13	W G		I Kings 18. 20–39 Ps. 16. 1, 6–end Matt. 5. 17–19	Ps. 34 Josh. 22. 9–end Luke 12. 22–31
14	Th G	*Richard Baxter, Puritan Divine, 1691*	I Kings 18. 41–end Ps. 65. 8–end Matt. 5. 20–26	Ps. 37† Josh. ch. 23 Luke 12. 32–40
15	F G	*Evelyn Underhill, Spiritual Writer, 1941*	I Kings 19. 9, 11–16 Ps. 27. 8–16 Matt. 5. 27–32	Ps. 31 Josh. 24. 1–28 Luke 12. 41–48
16	Sa Gw	**Richard, Bishop of Chichester, 1253** *Joseph Butler, Bishop of Durham, Philosopher, 1752* Com. Bishop *or* *also* John 21. 15–19	I Kings 19. 19–end Ps. 16. 1–7 Matt. 5. 33–37	Ps. 41; **42**; 43 Josh. 24. 29–end Luke 12. 49–end
17	S G	THE SECOND SUNDAY AFTER TRINITY **(Proper 6)** *Track 1* *Track 2* I Sam. 15.34 – 16.13 Ezek. 17. 22–end Ps. 20 Ps. 92. 1–4, 12–end (*or* 19. 1–8) 2 Cor. 5. 6–10 [11–13] 14–17 2 Cor. 5. 6–10 [11–13] 14–17 Mark 4. 26–34 Mark 4. 26–34	Ps. 42; 43 Deut. 10.12 – 11.1 Acts 23. 12–35
18 DEL 11	M G	*Bernard Mizeki, Apostle of the MaShona, Martyr, 1896*	I Kings 21. 1–16 Ps. 5. 1–5 Matt. 5. 38–42	Ps. 44 Judg. ch. 2 Luke 13. 1–9
19	Tu G	*Sundar Singh of India, Sadhu (holy man), Evangelist, Teacher, 1929*	I Kings 21. 17–end Ps. 51. 1–9 Matt. 5. 43–end	Ps. **48**; 52 Judg. 4. 1–23 Luke 13. 10–21
20	W G		2 Kings 2. 1, 6–14 Ps. 31. 21–end Matt. 6. 1–6, 16–18	Ps. 119. 57–80 Judg. ch. 5 Luke 13. 22–end
21	Th G		Ecclus. 48. 1–14 *or* Isa. 63. 7–9 Ps. 97. 1–8 Matt. 6. 7–15	Ps. 56; **57**; (63†) Judg. 6. 1–24 Luke 14. 1–11
22	F Gr	**Alban, first Martyr of Britain, c. 250** Com. Martyr *or* *esp.* 2 Tim. 2. 3–13 John 12. 24–26	2 Kings 11. 1–4, 9–18, 20 Ps. 132. 1–5, 11–13 Matt. 6. 19–23	Ps. **51**; 54 Judg. 6. 25–end Luke 14. 12–24
23	Sa	**Etheldreda, Abbess of Ely, c. 678** Com. Religious *or* *also* Matt. 25. 1–13	2 Chron. 24. 17–25 Ps. 89. 25–33 Matt. 6. 24–end	Ps. 68 Judg. ch. 7 Luke 14. 25–end
	Gw			

Second Service Evening Prayer	Calendar and Holy Communion	Morning Prayer	Evening Prayer
Ps. 33 Job ch. 14 Rom. 7. 7–end	G	Josh. 21.43 – 22.8 Luke 12. 13–21	Job ch. 14 Rom. 7. 7–end
Ps. 119. 33–56 Job ch. 15 Rom. 8. 1–11	G	Josh. 22. 9–end Luke 12. 22–31	Job ch. 15 Rom. 8. 1–11
Ps. 39; **40** Job 16.1 – 17.2 Rom. 8. 12–17	G	Josh. ch. 23 Luke 12. 32–40	Job 16.1 – 17.2 Rom. 8. 12–17
Ps. 35 Job 17. 3–end Rom. 8. 18–30	G	Josh. 24. 1–28 Luke 12. 41–48	Job 17. 3–end Rom. 8. 18–30
Ps. 45; **46** Job ch. 18 Rom. 8. 31–end ct	G	Josh. 24. 29–end Luke 12. 49–end	Job ch. 18 Rom. 8. 31–end ct
	THE SECOND SUNDAY AFTER TRINITY		
Ps. 39 Jer. 7. 1–16 Rom. 9. 14–26 Gospel: Luke 7.36 – 8.3	Gen. 12. 1–4 Ps. 120 1 John 3. 13–end Luke 14. 16–24 G	Ps. 42; 43 Deut. 10.12 – 11.1 Acts 23. 12–35	Ps. 39 Jer. 7. 1–16 Rom. 9. 14–26
Ps. **47**; 49 Job ch. 19 Rom. 9. 1–18	G	Judg. ch. 2 Luke 13. 1–9	Job ch. 19 Rom. 9. 1–18
Ps. 50 Job ch. 21 Rom. 9. 19–end	G	Judg. 4. 1–23 Luke 13. 10–21	Job ch. 21 Rom. 9. 19–end
Ps. **59**; 60; (67) Job ch. 22 Rom. 10. 1–10	**Translation of Edward, King of the West Saxons, 979** Com. Martyr Gr	Judg. ch. 5 Luke 13. 22–end	Job ch. 22 Rom. 10. 1–10
Ps. 61; **62**; 64 Job ch. 23 Rom. 10. 11–end	G	Judg. 6. 1–24 Luke 14. 1–11	Job ch. 23 Rom. 10. 11–end
Ps. 38 Job ch. 24 Rom. 11. 1–12	G	Judg. 6. 25–end Luke 14. 12–24	Job ch. 24 Rom. 11. 1–12
Ps. 65; **66** Job chs 25 & 26 Rom. 11. 13–24 ct or First EP of The Birth of John the Baptist Ps. 71 Judges 13. 2–7, 24–end Luke 1. 5–25 **W** ct	G	Judg. ch. 7 Luke 14. 25–end	Job chs 25 & 26 Rom. 11. 13–24 ct or First EP of The Birth of John the Baptist (Ps. 71) Judges 13. 2–7, 24–end Luke 1. 5–25 **W** ct

June 2012

			Sunday Principal Service / Weekday Eucharist	Third Service / Morning Prayer

24 S   THE BIRTH OF JOHN THE BAPTIST (or transferred to 25th)

Isa. 40. 1–11
Ps. 85. 7–end
Acts 13. 14b–26
or Gal. 3. 23–end
Luke 1. 57–66, 80

MP: Ps. 50; 149
Ecclus. 48. 1–10
or Mal. 3. 1–6
Luke 3. 1–17

W

or, for The Third Sunday after Trinity (Proper 7):
Track 1
1 Sam. 17. [1a, 4–11, 19–23] 32–49
and Ps. 9. 9–end
or 1 Sam. 17.57 – 18.5, 10–16
and Ps. 133
2 Cor. 6. 1–13
Mark 4. 35–end

Track 2
Job 38. 1–11
Ps. 107. 1–3, 23–32
(*or* 107. 23–32)
2 Cor. 6. 1–13
Mark 4. 35–end

Ps. 48
Deut. 11. 1–15
Acts 27. 1–12

G

25   M
DEL 12   G

2 Kings 17. 5–8, 13–15, 18
Ps. 60. 1–5, 11–end
Matt. 7. 1–5

Ps. 71
Judg. 8. 22–end
Luke 15. 1–10

26   Tu

G

2 Kings 19. 9b–11, 14–21, 31–36
Ps. 48. 1–2, 8–end
Matt. 7. 6, 12–14

Ps. 73
Judg. 9. 1–21
Luke 15. 11–end

27   W   Ember Day*
Cyril, Bishop of Alexandria, Teacher, 444

2 Kings 22. 8–13; 23. 1–3
Ps. 119. 33–40
Matt. 7. 15–20

Ps. 77
Judg. 9. 22–end
Luke 16. 1–18

G *or* R

28   Th   **Irenaeus, Bishop of Lyons, Teacher, c. 200**
Com. Teacher   *or*   2 Kings 24. 8–17
also 2 Pet. 1. 16–21   Ps. 79. 1–9, 12
                                    Matt. 7. 21–end

Ps. 78. 1–39†
Judg. 11. 1–11
Luke 16. 19–end

Gw

29   F   PETER AND PAUL, APOSTLES
Ember Day*

Zech. 4. 1–6a, 10b–end
or Acts 12. 1–11
Ps. 125
Acts 12. 1–11
or 2 Tim. 4. 6–8, 17–18
Matt. 16. 13–19

MP: Ps. 71; 113
Isa. 49. 1–6
Acts 11. 1–18

R

or, if Peter is commemorated alone:

Ezek. 3. 22–end
or Acts 12. 1–11
Ps. 125
Acts 12. 1–11
or 1 Pet. 2. 19–end
Matt. 16. 13–19

MP: Ps. 71; 113
Isa. 49. 1–6
Acts 11. 1–18

R

30   Sa   Ember Day*

Lam. 2. 2, 10–14, 18–19
Ps. 74. 1–3, 21–end
Matt. 8. 5–17

Ps. **76**; 79
Judg. 12. 1–7
Luke 17. 11–19

G *or* R

*For Ember Day provision, see p. 11.

Second Service Evening Prayer		Calendar and Holy Communion	Morning Prayer	Evening Prayer
EP: Ps. 80; 82 Mal. ch. 4 Matt. 11. 2–19	W	**THE BIRTH OF JOHN THE BAPTIST** (or transferred to 25th) Isa. 40. 1–11 Ps. 80. 1–7 Acts 13. 22–26 Luke 1. 57–80 *or, for The Third Sunday after Trinity:*	Ps. 50; 149 Ecclus. 48. 1–10 *or* Mal. 3. 1–6 Luke 3. 1–17	Ps. 82 Mal. ch. 4 Matt. 11. 2–19
Ps. 49 Jer. 10. 1–16 Rom. 11. 25–end *Gospel:* Luke 8. 26–39	G	2 Chron. 33. 9–13 Ps. 55. 17–23 1 Pet. 5. 5b–11 Luke 15. 1–10	Ps. 48 Deut. 11. 1–15 Acts 27. 1–12	Ps. 49 Jer. 10. 1–16 Rom. 11. 25–end
Ps. 72; 75 Job ch. 27 Rom. 11. 25–end	G		Judg. 8. 22–end Luke 15. 1–10	Job ch. 27 Rom. 11. 25–end
Ps. 74 Job ch. 28 Rom. 12. 1–8	G		Judg. 9. 1–21 Luke 15. 11–end	Job ch. 28 Rom. 12. 1–8
Ps. 119. 81–104 Job ch. 29 Rom. 12. 9–end	G		Judg. 9. 22–end Luke 16. 1–18	Job ch. 29 Rom. 12. 9–end
Ps. 78. 40–end† Job ch. 30 Rom. 13. 1–7 *or First EP of Peter and Paul* Ps. 66; 67 Ezek. 3. 4–11 Gal. 1.13 – 2.8 *or, for Peter alone:* Acts 9. 32–end **R ct**	G		Judg. 11. 1–11 Luke 16. 19–end	Job ch. 30 Rom. 13. 1–7 *or First EP of Peter* (Ps. 66; 67) Ezek. 3. 4–11 Acts 9. 32–end **R ct**
EP: Ps. 124; 138 Ezek. 34. 11–16 John 21. 15–22 EP: Ps. 124; 138 Ezek. 34. 11–16 John 21. 15–22	R	**PETER THE APOSTLE** Ezek. 3. 4–11 Ps. 125 Acts 12. 1–11 Matt. 16. 13–19	(Ps. 71; 113) Isa. 49. 1–6 Acts 11. 1–18	(Ps. 124; 138) Ezek. 34. 11–16 John 21. 15–22
Ps. 81; 84 Job ch. 32 Rom. 14. 1–12 **ct**	G		Judg. 12. 1–7 Luke 17. 11–19	Job ch. 32 Rom. 14. 1–12 **ct**

July 2012

			Sunday Principal Service Weekday Eucharist	Third Service Morning Prayer
1	S	THE FOURTH SUNDAY AFTER TRINITY **(Proper 8)** *Track 1* 2 Sam. 1. 1, 17–end Ps. 130 2 Cor. 8. 7–end Mark 5. 21–end	*Track 2* Wisd. of Sol. 1. 13–15; 2. 23–24 or Lam. 3. 22–33 *Canticle*: Lam. 3. 22–33 or Ps. 30 2 Cor. 8. 7–end	Ps. 56 Deut. 15. 1–11 Acts 27. [13–32] 33–end
	G		Mark 5. 21–end	
2 DEL 13	M*		Amos 2. 6–10, 13–end Ps. 50. 16–23 Matt. 8. 18–22	Ps. *80*; 82 Judg. 13. 1–24 Luke 17. 20–end
	G			
3	Tu	THOMAS THE APOSTLE***	Hab. 2. 1–4 Ps. 31. 1–6 Eph. 2. 19–end John 20. 24–29	*MP*: Ps. 92; 146 2 Sam. 15. 17–21 or Ecclus. ch. 2 John 11. 1–16
	R	*or, if Thomas is not celebrated:*		
	G		Amos 3. 1–8; 4. 11–12 Ps. 5. 8–end Matt. 8. 23–27	Ps. 87; **89. *1–18*** Judg. ch. 14 Luke 18. 1–14
4	W		Amos 5. 14–15, 21–24 Ps. 50. 7–14 Matt. 8. 28–end	Ps. 119. 105–128 Judg. 15.1 – 16.3 Luke 18. 15–30
	G			
5	Th		Amos 7. 10–end Ps. 19. 7–10 Matt. 9. 1–8	Ps. 90; *92* Judg. 16. 4–end Luke 18. 31–end
	G			
6	F	*Thomas More, Scholar, and John Fisher, Bishop of Rochester, Reformation Martyrs, 1535* Amos 8. 4–6, 9–12 Ps. 119. 1–8 Matt. 9. 9–13		Ps. *88*; (95) Judg. ch. 17 Luke 19. 1–10
	G			
7	Sa****		Amos 9. 11–end Ps. 85. 8–end Matt. 9. 14–17	Ps. 96; *97*; 100 Judg. 18. 1–20, 27–end Luke 19. 11–27
	G			
8	S	THE FIFTH SUNDAY AFTER TRINITY **(Proper 9)** *Track 1* 2 Sam. 5. 1–5, 9–10 Ps. 48 2 Cor. 12. 2–10 Mark 6. 1–13	*Track 2* Ezek. 2. 1–5 Ps. 123 2 Cor. 12. 2–10 Mark 6. 1–13	Ps. 57 Deut. 24. 10–end Acts 28. 1–16
	G			
9 DEL 14	M		Hos. 2. 14–16, 19–20 Ps. 145. 2–9 Matt. 9. 18–26	Ps. *98*; 99; 101 1 Sam. 1. 1–20 Luke 19. 28–40
	G			
10	Tu		Hos. 8. 4–7, 11–13 Ps. 103. 8–12 Matt. 9. 32–end	Ps. *106*† (or 103) 1 Sam. 1.21 – 2.11 Luke 19. 41–end
	G			
11	W	**Benedict of Nursia, Abbot of Monte Cassino, Father of Western Monasticism, c. 550** Com. Religious *also* 1 Cor. 3. 10–11 Luke 18. 18–22	*or* Hos. 10. 1–3, 7–8, 12 Ps. 115. 3–10 Matt. 10. 1–7	Ps. 110; *111*; 112 1 Sam. 2. 12–26 Luke 20. 1–8
	Gw			
12	Th		Hos. 11. 1, 3–4, 8–9 Ps. 105. 1–7 Matt. 10. 7–15	Ps. 113; *115* 1 Sam. 2. 27–end Luke 20. 9–19
	G			

*The Visit of the Blessed Virgin Mary to Elizabeth may be celebrated on 2 July instead of 31 May.
**Common Worship Morning and Evening Prayer provision for 31 May may be used.
***Thomas the Apostle may be celebrated on 21 December instead of 3 July.
****Thomas Becket may be celebrated on 7 July instead of 29 December.

Second Service Evening Prayer	Calendar and Holy Communion	Morning Prayer	Evening Prayer
	THE FOURTH SUNDAY AFTER TRINITY		
Ps. [52]; 53 Jer. 11. 1–14 Rom. 13. 1–10 Gospel: Luke 9. 51–end	Gen. 3. 17–19 Ps. 79. 8–10 Rom. 8. 18–23 Luke 6. 36–42	Ps. 56 Deut. 15. 1–11 Acts 27. [13–32] 33–end	Ps. [52]; 53 Jer. 11. 1–14 Rom. 13. 1–10
	G		
Ps. 85; 86 Job ch. 33 Rom. 14. 13–end or First EP of Thomas Ps. 27 Isa. ch. 35 Heb. 10.35 – 11.1 R ct	The Visitation of the Blessed Virgin Mary** 1 Sam. 2. 1–3 Ps. 113 Gal. 4. 1–5 Luke 1. 39–45 Gw	Judg. 13. 1–24 Luke 17. 20–end	Job ch. 33 Rom. 14. 13–end
EP: Ps. 139 Job 42. 1–6 1 Pet. 1. 3–12		Judg. ch. 14 Luke 18. 1–14	Job ch. 38 Rom. 15. 1–13
Ps. 89. 19–end Job ch. 38 Rom. 15. 1–13	G		
Ps. 91; 93 Job ch. 39 Rom. 15. 14–21	Translation of Martin, Bishop of Tours, c. 397 Com. Bishop Gw	Judg. ch. 14 Luke 18. 1–14	Job ch. 39 Rom. 15. 14–21
Ps. 94 Job ch. 40 Rom. 15. 22–end	G	Judg. 16. 4–end Luke 18. 31–end	Job ch. 40 Rom. 15. 22–end
Ps. 102 Job ch. 41 Rom. 16. 1–16	G	Judg. ch. 17 Luke 19. 1–10	Job ch. 41 Rom. 16. 1–16
Ps. 104 Job ch. 42 Rom. 16. 17–end ct	G	Judg. 18. 1–20, 27–end Luke 19. 11–27	Job ch. 42 Rom. 16. 17–end ct
	THE FIFTH SUNDAY AFTER TRINITY		
Ps. [63]; 64 Jer. 20. 1–11a Rom. 14. 1–17 Gospel: Luke 10. 1–11, 16–20	1 Kings 19. 19–21 Ps. 84. 8–end 1 Pet. 3. 8–15a Luke 5. 1–11	Ps. 57 Deut. 24. 10–end Acts 28. 1–16	Ps. [63]; 64 Jer. 20. 1–11a Rom. 14. 1–17
	G		
Ps. 105† (or 103) Ezek. 1. 1–14 2 Cor. 1. 1–14	G	1 Sam. 1. 1–20 Luke 19. 28–40	Ezek. 1. 1–14 2 Cor. 1. 1–14
Ps. 107† Ezek. 1.15 – 2.2 2 Cor. 1.15 – 2.4	G	1 Sam. 1.21 – 2.11 Luke 19. 41–end	Ezek. 1.15 – 2.2 2 Cor. 1.15 – 2.4
Ps. 119. 129–152 Ezek. 2.3 – 3.11 2 Cor. 2. 5–end	G	1 Sam. 2. 12–26 Luke 20. 1–8	Ezek. 2.3 – 3.11 2 Cor. 2. 5–end
Ps. 114; 116; 117 Ezek. 3. 12–end 2 Cor. ch. 3	G	1 Sam. 2. 27–end Luke 20. 9–19	Ezek. 3. 12–end 2 Cor. ch. 3

July 2012

		Sunday Principal Service Weekday Eucharist	Third Service Morning Prayer
13	F	Hos. 14. 2–end Ps. 80. 1–7	Ps. 139 1 Sam. 3.1 – 4.1a
	G	Matt. 10. 16–23	Luke 20. 20–26
14	Sa	**John Keble, Priest, Tractarian, Poet, 1866** Com. Pastor or Isa. 6. 1–8 also Lam. 3. 19–26 Ps. 51. 1–7 Matt. 5. 1–8 Matt. 10. 24–33	Ps. 120; *121*; 122 1 Sam. 4. 1b–end Luke 20. 27–40
	Gw		
15	S	THE SIXTH SUNDAY AFTER TRINITY **(Proper 10)**	
		Track 1 *Track 2* 2 Sam. 6. 1–5, 12b–19 Amos 7. 7–15 Ps. 24 Ps. 85. 8–end Eph. 1. 3–14 Eph. 1. 3–14 Mark 6. 14–29 Mark 6. 14–29	Ps. 65 Deut. 28. 1–14 Acts 28. 17–end
	G		
16 DEL 15	M	*Osmund, Bishop of Salisbury, 1099* Isa. 1. 11–17 Ps. 50. 7–15	Ps. 123; 124; 125; *126* 1 Sam. ch. 5
	G	Matt. 10.34 – 11.1	Luke 20.41 – 21.4
17	Tu	Isa. 7. 1–9 Ps. 48. 1–7	Ps. *132*; 133 1 Sam. 6. 1–16
	G	Matt. 11. 20–24	Luke 21. 5–19
18	W	*Elizabeth Ferard, first Deaconess of the Church of England, Founder of the Community of St Andrew, 1883* Isa. 10. 5–7, 13–16 Ps. 94. 5–11	Ps. 119. 153–end 1 Sam. ch. 7
	G	Matt. 11. 25–27	Luke 21. 20–28
19	Th	**Gregory, Bishop of Nyssa, and his sister Macrina, Deaconess, Teachers, c. 394 and c. 379** Com. Teacher or Isa. 26. 7–9, 16–19 esp. 1 Cor. 2. 9–13 Ps. 102. 14–21 also Wisd. 9. 13–17 Matt. 11. 28–end	Ps. *143*; 146 1 Sam. ch. 8 Luke 21. 29–end
	Gw		
20	F	*Margaret of Antioch, Martyr, 4th century; Bartolomé de las Casas, Apostle to the Indies, 1566* Isa. 38. 1–6, 21–22, 7–8 Canticle: Isa. 38. 10–16 or Ps. 32. 1–8	Ps. 142; *144* 1 Sam. 9. 1–14 Luke 22. 1–13
	G	Matt. 12. 1–8	
21	Sa	Mic. 2. 1–5 Ps. 10. 1–5a, 12 Matt. 12. 14–21	Ps. 147 1 Sam. 9.15 – 10.1 Luke 22. 14–23
	G		
22	S	MARY MAGDALENE (or transferred to 23rd)	
		Song of Sol. 3. 1–4 Ps. 42. 1–10 2 Cor. 5. 14–17	*MP*: Ps. 30; 32; 150 1 Sam. 16. 14–end Luke 8. 1–3
	W	John 20. 1–2, 11–18	
		or, for The Seventh Sunday after Trinity (Proper 11): *Track 1* *Track 2* 2 Sam. 7. 1–14a Jer. 23. 1–6 Ps. 89. 20–37 Ps. 23 Eph. 2. 11–end Eph. 2. 11–end Mark 6. 30–34, 53–end Mark 6. 30–34, 53–end	Ps. 67; 70 Deut. 30. 1–10 1 Pet. 3. 8–18
	G		
23 DEL 16	M	*Bridget of Sweden, Abbess of Vadstena, 1373* Mic. 6. 1–4, 6–8 Ps. 50. 3–7, 14	Ps. *1*; 2; 3 1 Sam. 10. 1–16
	G	Matt. 12. 38–42	Luke 22. 24–30

Second Service Evening Prayer		Calendar and Holy Communion	Morning Prayer	Evening Prayer
Ps. 130; 131; 137￼ Ezek. ch. 8￼ 2 Cor. ch. 4	G		I Sam. 3.1 – 4.1a￼ Luke 20. 20–26	Ezek. ch. 8￼ 2 Cor. ch. 4
Ps. 118￼ Ezek. ch. 9￼ 2 Cor. ch. 5￼ ct	G		I Sam. 4. 1b–end￼ Luke 20. 27–40	Ezek. ch. 9￼ 2 Cor. ch. 5￼ ct
		THE SIXTH SUNDAY AFTER TRINITY		
Ps. 66 (or 66. 1–8)￼ Job 4. 1; 5. 6–end￼ or Ecclus. 4. 11–end￼ Rom. 15. 14–29￼ Gospel: Luke 10. 25–37	G	Gen. 4. 2b–15￼ Ps. 90. 12–end￼ Rom. 6. 3–11￼ Matt. 5. 20–26	Ps. 65￼ Deut. 28. 1–14￼ Acts 28. 17–end	Ps. 66 (or 66. 1–8)￼ Job 4. 1; 5. 6–end￼ or Ecclus. 4. 11–end￼ Luke 10. 21–24
Ps. 127; 128; 129￼ Ezek. 10. 1–19￼ 2 Cor. 6.1 – 7.1	G		I Sam. ch. 5￼ Luke 20.41 – 21.4	Ezek. 10. 1–19￼ 2 Cor. 6.1 – 7.1
Ps. (134); 135￼ Ezek. 11. 14–end￼ 2 Cor. 7. 2–end	G		I Sam. 6. 1–16￼ Luke 21. 5–19	Ezek. 11. 14–end￼ 2 Cor. 7. 2–end
Ps. 136￼ Ezek. 12. 1–16￼ 2 Cor. 8. 1–15	G		I Sam. ch. 7￼ Luke 21. 20–28	Ezek. 12. 1–16￼ 2 Cor. 8. 1–15
Ps. 138; 140; 141￼ Ezek. 12. 17–end￼ 2 Cor. 8.16 – 9.5	G		I Sam. ch. 8￼ Luke 21. 29–end	Ezek. 12. 17–end￼ 2 Cor. 8.16 – 9.5
Ps. 145￼ Ezek. 13. 1–16￼ 2 Cor. 9. 6–end	Gr	**Margaret of Antioch, Martyr, 4th century**￼ Com. Virgin Martyr	I Sam. 9. 1–14￼ Luke 22. 1–13	Ezek. 13. 1–16￼ 2 Cor. 9. 6–end
Ps. 148; 149; 150￼ Ezek. 14. 1–11￼ 2 Cor. ch. 10￼ ct￼ or First EP of Mary Magdalene￼ Ps. 139￼ Isa. 25. 1–9￼ 2 Cor. 1. 3–7￼ W ct	G		I Sam. 9.15 – 10.1￼ Luke 22. 14–23	Ezek. 14. 1–11￼ 2 Cor. ch. 10￼ ct￼ or First EP of Mary Magdalene￼ (Ps. 139)￼ Isa. 25. 1–9￼ 2 Cor. 1. 3–7￼ W ct
EP: Ps. 63￼ Zeph. 3. 14–end￼ Mark 15.40 – 16.7	W	**MARY MAGDALENE**￼ Zeph. 3. 14–end￼ Ps. 30. 1–5￼ 2 Cor. 5. 14–17￼ John 20. 11–18	Ps. 30; 32; 150￼ I Sam. 16. 14–end￼ Luke 8. 1–3	Ps. 63￼ Song of Sol. 3. 1–4￼ Mark 15.40 – 16.7
		or, for The Seventh Sunday after Trinity:		
Ps. 73 (or 73. 21–end)￼ Job 13.13 – 14.6￼ or Ecclus. 18. 1–14￼ Heb. 2. 5–end￼ Gospel: Luke 10. 38–end	G	I Kings 17. 8–16￼ Ps. 34. 11–end￼ Rom. 6. 19–end￼ Mark 8. 1–10a	Ps. 67; 70￼ Deut. 30. 1–10￼ I Pet. 3. 13–22	Ps. 73 (or 73. 21–end)￼ Job 13.13 – 14.6￼ or Ecclus. 18. 1–14￼ Heb. 2. 5–end
Ps. 4; 7￼ Ezek. 14. 12–end￼ 2 Cor. 11. 1–15	G		I Sam. 10. 1–16￼ Luke 22. 24–30	Ezek. 14. 12–end￼ 2 Cor. 11. 1–15

July 2012

			Sunday Principal Service / Weekday Eucharist	Third Service / Morning Prayer
24	Tu		Mic. 7. 14–15, 18–20 Ps. 85. 1–7 Matt. 12. 46–end	Ps. 5; 6; (8) I Sam. 10. 17–end Luke 22. 31–38
	G			
25	W	JAMES THE APOSTLE	Jer. 45. 1–5 or Acts 11.27 – 12.2 Ps. 126 Acts 11.27 – 12.2 or 2 Cor. 4. 7–15 Matt. 20. 20–28	MP: Ps. 7; 29; 117 2 Kings 1. 9–15 Luke 9. 46–56
	R			
26	Th	**Anne and Joachim, Parents of the Blessed Virgin Mary** Zeph. 3. 14–18a or Ps. 127 Rom. 8. 28–30 Matt. 13. 16–17	Jer. 2. 1–3, 7–8, 12–13 Ps. 36. 5–10 Matt. 13. 10–17	Ps. 14; 15; 16 I Sam. ch. 12 Luke 22. 47–62
	Gw			
27	F	*Brooke Foss Westcott, Bishop of Durham, Teacher, 1901* Jer. 3. 14–17 Ps. 23 *or* *Canticle:* Jer. 31. 10–13 Matt. 13. 18–23		Ps. 17; 19 I Sam. 13. 5–18 Luke 22. 63–end
	G			
28	Sa		Jer. 7. 1–11 Ps. 84. 1–6 Matt. 13. 24–30	Ps. 20; 21; 23 I Sam. 13.19 – 14.15 Luke 23. 1–12
	G			
29	S	THE EIGHTH SUNDAY AFTER TRINITY **(Proper 12)** *Track 1* 2 Sam. 11. 1–15 Ps. 14 Eph. 3. 14–end John 6. 1–21	*Track 2* 2 Kings 4. 42–end Ps. 145. 10–19 Eph. 3. 14–end John 6. 1–21	Ps. 75 Song of Sol. ch. 2 or I Macc. 2. [1–14] 15–22 I Pet. 4. 7–14
	G			
30 DEL 17	M	**William Wilberforce, Social Reformer, Olaudah Equiano and Thomas Clarkson,** **Anti-Slavery Campaigners, 1833, 1797 and 1846** Com. Saint *or* *also* Job 31. 16–23 Gal. 3. 26–end; 4. 6–7 Luke 4. 16–21	Jer. 13. 1–11 Ps. 82 *or* Deut. 32. 18–21 Matt. 13. 31–35	Ps. 27; 30 I Sam. 14. 24–46 Luke 23. 13–25
	Gw			
31	Tu	*Ignatius of Loyola, Founder of the Society of Jesus, 1556* Jer. 14. 17–end Ps. 79. 8–end Matt. 13. 36–43		Ps. 32; 36 I Sam. 15. 1–23 Luke 23. 26–43
	G			

August 2012

1	W		Jer. 15. 10, 16–end Ps. 59. 1–4, 18–end Matt. 13. 44–46	Ps. 34 I Sam. ch. 16 Luke 23. 44–56a
	G			
2	Th		Jer. 18. 1–6 Ps. 146. 1–5 Matt. 13. 47–53	Ps. 37† I Sam. 17. 1–30 Luke 23.56b – 24.12
	G			
3	F		Jer. 26. 1–9 Ps. 69. 4–10 Matt. 13. 54–end	Ps. 31 I Sam. 17. 31–54 Luke 24. 13–35
	G			
4	Sa	*John-Baptiste Vianney, Curé d'Ars, Spiritual Guide, 1859* Jer. 26. 11–16, 24 Ps. 69. 14–20 Matt. 14. 1–12		Ps. 41; 42; 43 I Sam. 17.55 – 18.16 Luke 24. 36–end
	G			

Second Service Evening Prayer	Calendar and Holy Communion	Morning Prayer	Evening Prayer
Ps. **9**; 10† Ezek. 18. 1–20 2 Cor. 11. 16–end or First EP of James Ps. 144 Deut. 30. 11–end Mark 5. 21–end **R ct**	**G**	1 Sam. 10. 17–end Luke 22. 31–38	Ezek. 18. 1–20 2 Cor. 11. 16–end or First EP of James (Ps. 144) Deut. 30. 11–end Mark 5. 21–end **R ct**
EP: Ps. 94 Jer. 26. 1–15 Mark 1. 14–20	**JAMES THE APOSTLE** 2 Kings 1. 9–15 Ps. 15 Acts 11.27 – 12.3a Matt. 20. 20–28 **R**	(Ps. 7; 29; 117) Jer. 45. 1–5 Luke 9. 46–56	(Ps. 94) Jer. 26. 1–15 Mark 1. 14–20
Ps. 18† Ezek. 20. 1–20 2 Cor. ch. 13	**Anne, Mother of the Blessed Virgin Mary** Com. Saint **Gw**	1 Sam. ch. 12 Luke 22. 47–62	Ezek. 20. 1–20 2 Cor. ch. 13
Ps. 22 Ezek. 20. 21–38 James 1. 1–11	**G**	1 Sam. 13. 5–18 Luke 22. 63–end	Ezek. 20. 21–38 James 1. 1–11
Ps. **24**; 25 Ezek. 24. 15–end James 1. 12–end ct	**G**	1 Sam. 13.19 – 14.15 Luke 23. 1–12	Ezek. 24. 15–end James 1. 12–end ct
Ps. 74 (or 74. 11–16) Job 19. 1–27a or Ecclus. 38. 24–end Heb. ch. 8 *Gospel:* Luke 11. 1–13	**THE EIGHTH SUNDAY AFTER TRINITY** Jer. 23. 16–24 Ps. 31. 1–6 Rom. 8. 12–17 Matt. 7. 15–21 **G**	Ps. 75 Song of Sol. ch. 2 or 1 Macc. 2. [1–14] 15–22 1 Pet. 4. 7–14	Ps. 74 (or 74. 11–16) Job 19. 1–27a or Ecclus. 38. 24–end Heb. ch. 8
Ps. 26; **28**; 29 Ezek. 28. 1–19 James 2. 1–13	**G**	1 Sam. 14. 24–46 Luke 23. 13–25	Ezek. 28. 1–19 James 2. 1–13
Ps. 33 Ezek. 33. 1–20 James 2. 14–end	**G**	1 Sam. 15. 1–23 Luke 23. 26–43	Ezek. 33. 1–20 James 2. 14–end
Ps. 119. 33–56 Ezek. 33. 21–end James ch. 3	Lammas Day **G**	1 Sam. ch. 16 Luke 23. 44–56a	Ezek. 33. 21–end James ch. 3
Ps. 39; **40** Ezek. 34. 1–16 James 4. 1–12	**G**	1 Sam. 17. 1–30 Luke 23.56b – 24.12	Ezek. 34. 1–16 James 4. 1–12
Ps. 35 Ezek. 34. 17–end James 4.13 – 5.6	**G**	1 Sam. 17. 31–54 Luke 24. 13–35	Ezek. 34. 17–end James 4.13 – 5.6
Ps. 45; **46** Ezek. 36. 16–36 James 5. 7–end ct	**G**	1 Sam. 17.55 – 18.16 Luke 24. 36–end	Ezek. 36. 16–36 James 5. 7–end ct

August 2012

Sunday Principal Service
Weekday Eucharist

Third Service
Morning Prayer

---

5 S   THE NINTH SUNDAY AFTER TRINITY **(Proper 13)**

Track 1	Track 2	
2 Sam. 11.26 – 12.13a	Exod. 16. 2–4, 9–15	Ps. 86
Ps. 51. 1–13	Ps. 78. 23–29	Song of Sol. 5. 2–end
Eph. 4. 1–16	Eph. 4. 1–16	or 1 Macc. 3. 1–12
John 6. 24–35	John 6. 24–35	2 Pet. 1. 1–15

G

---

6 M   THE TRANSFIGURATION OF OUR LORD

DEL 18

𝖜

Dan. 7. 9–10, 13–14	MP: Ps. 27; 150
Ps. 97	Ecclus. 48. 1–10
2 Pet. 1. 16–19	or 1 Kings 19. 1–16
Luke 9. 28–36	1 John 3. 1–3

---

7 Tu   *John Mason Neale, Priest, Hymn Writer, 1866*

Jer. 30. 1–2, 12–15, 18–22	Ps. **48**; 52
Ps. 102. 16–21	1 Sam. 20. 1–17
Matt. 14. 22–end or 15. 1–2,	Acts 1. 15–end
10–14	

G

---

8 W   **Dominic, Priest, Founder of the Order of Preachers, 1221**

Com. Religious	or	Jer. 31. 1–7	Ps. 119. 57–80
also Ecclus. 39. 1–10		Ps. 121	1 Sam. 20. 18–end

Gw   Matt. 15. 21–28   Acts 2. 1–21

---

9 Th   **Mary Sumner, Founder of the Mothers' Union, 1921**

Com. Saint	or	Jer. 31. 31–34	Ps. 56; **57**; (63†)
also Heb. 13. 1–5		Ps. 51. 11–18	1 Sam. 21.1 – 22.5

Gw   Matt. 16. 13–23   Acts 2. 22–36

---

10 F   **Laurence, Deacon at Rome, Martyr, 258**

Com. Martyr	or	Nahum 2. 1, 3; 3. 1–3, 6–7	Ps. **51**; 54
also 2 Cor. 9. 6–10		Ps. 137. 1–6	1 Sam. 22. 6–end
		or Deut. 32. 35–36, 39, 41	Acts 2. 37–end

Gr   Matt. 16. 24–28

---

11 Sa   **Clare of Assisi, Founder of the Minoresses (Poor Clares), 1253**

John Henry Newman, Priest, Tractarian, 1890

Com. Religious	or	Hab. 1.12 – 2.4	Ps. 68
esp. Song of Sol. 8. 6–7		Ps. 9. 7–11	1 Sam. ch. 23
		Matt. 17. 14–20	Acts 3. 1–10

Gw

---

12 S   THE TENTH SUNDAY AFTER TRINITY **(Proper 14)**

Track 1	Track 2	
2 Sam. 18. 5–9, 15, 31–33	1 Kings 19. 4–8	Ps. 90
Ps. 130	Ps. 34. 1–8	Song of Sol. 8. 5–7
Eph. 4.25 – 5.2	Eph. 4.25 – 5.2	or 1 Macc. 14. 4–15
John 6. 35, 41–51	John 6. 35, 41–51	2 Pet. 3. 8–13

G

---

13 M   **Jeremy Taylor, Bishop of Down and Connor, Teacher, 1667**

DEL 19

Florence Nightingale, Nurse, Social Reformer, 1910; Octavia Hill, Social Reformer, 1912

Com. Teacher	or	Ezek. 1. 2–5, 24–end	Ps. 71
also Titus 2. 7–8, 11–14		Ps. 148. 1–4, 12–13	1 Sam. ch. 24

Gw   Matt. 17. 22–end   Acts 3. 11–end

---

14 Tu   *Maximilian Kolbe, Friar, Martyr, 1941*

Ezek. 2.8 – 3.4	Ps. 73
Ps. 119. 65–72	1 Sam. ch. 26
Matt. 18. 1–5, 10, 12–14	Acts 4. 1–12

G

Second Service Evening Prayer		Calendar and Holy Communion	Morning Prayer	Evening Prayer
		THE NINTH SUNDAY AFTER TRINITY		
Ps. 88 (or 88. 1–10) Job ch. 28 or Ecclus. 42. 15–end Heb. 11. 17–31 Gospel: Luke 12. 13–21 or First EP of The Transfiguration Ps. 99; 110 Exod. 24. 12–end John 12. 27–36a ꝟ ct	G	Num. 10.35 – 11.3 Ps. 95 1 Cor. 10. 1–13 Luke 16. 1–9 or Luke 15. 11–end	Ps. 86 Song of Sol. 5. 2–end or 1 Macc. 3. 1–12 2 Pet. 1. 1–15	Ps. 88 (or 88. 1–10) Job ch. 28 or Ecclus. 42. 15–end Heb. 11. 17–31 or First EP of The Transfiguration Ps. 99; 110 Exod. 24. 12–end John 12. 27–36a ꝟ ct
		THE TRANSFIGURATION OF OUR LORD		
EP: Ps. 72 Exod. 34. 29–end 2 Cor. ch. 3	ꝟ	Exod. 24. 12–end Ps. 84. 1–7 1 John 3. 1–3 Mark 9. 2 7	(Ps. 27; 150) Ecclus. 48. 1–10 or 1 Kings 19. 1–16 2 Pet. 1. 16–19	(Ps. 72) Exod. 34. 29–end 2 Cor. ch. 3
		The Name of Jesus		
Ps. 50 Ezek. 37. 15–end Mark 1. 14–20	Gw	Jer. 14. 7–9 Ps. 8 Acts 4. 8–12 Matt. 1. 20–23	1 Sam. 20. 1–17 Acts 1. 15–end	Ezek. 37. 15–end Mark 1. 14–20
Ps. 59; 60; (67) Ezek. 39. 21–end Mark 1. 21–28	G		1 Sam. 20. 18–end Acts 2. 1–21	Ezek. 39. 21–end Mark 1. 21–28
Ps. 61; 62; 64 Ezek. 43. 1–12 Mark 1. 29–end	G		1 Sam. 21.1 – 22.5 Acts 2. 22–36	Ezek. 43. 1–12 Mark 1. 29–end
		Laurence, Deacon at Rome, Martyr, 258		
Ps. 38 Ezek. 44. 4–16 Mark 2. 1–12	Gr	Com. Martyr	1 Sam. 22. 6–end Acts 2. 37–end	Ezek. 44. 4–16 Mark 2. 1–12
Ps. 65; 66 Ezek. 47. 1–12 Mark 2. 13–22 ct	G		1 Sam. ch. 23 Acts 3. 1–10	Ezek. 47. 1–12 Mark 2. 13–22 ct
		THE TENTH SUNDAY AFTER TRINITY		
Ps. 91 (or 91. 1–12) Job 39.1 – 40.4 or Ecclus. 43. 13–end Heb. 12. 1–17 Gospel: Luke 12. 32–40	G	Jer. 7. 9–15 Ps. 17. 1–8 1 Cor. 12. 1–11 Luke 19. 41–47a	Ps. 89. 1–18 Song of Sol. 8. 5–7 or 1 Macc. 14. 4–15 2 Pet. 3. 8–13	Ps. 91 (or 91. 1–12) Job 39.1 – 40.4 or Ecclus. 43. 13–end Heb. 12. 1–17
Ps. 72; 75 Prov. 1. 1–19 Mark 2.23 – 3.6	G		1 Sam. ch. 24 Acts 3. 11–end	Prov. 1. 1–19 Mark 2.23 – 3.6
Ps. 74 Prov. 1. 20–end Mark 3. 7–19a or First EP of The Blessed Virgin Mary Ps. 72 Prov. 8. 22–31 John 19. 23–27 W ct	G		1 Sam. ch. 26 Acts 4. 1–12	Prov. 1. 20–end Mark 3. 7–19a

August 2012

			Sunday Principal Service / Weekday Eucharist	Third Service / Morning Prayer

15 W — THE BLESSED VIRGIN MARY*

Isa. 61. 10–end	MP: Ps. 98; 138; 147. 1–12
or Rev. 11.19 – 12.6, 10	Isa. 7. 10–15
Ps. 45. 10–end	Luke 11. 27–28
Gal. 4. 4–7	

W   Luke 1. 46–55

or, if The Blessed Virgin Mary is celebrated on 8 September:

Ezek. 9. 1–7; 10. 18–22	Ps. 77
Ps. 113	1 Sam. 28. 3–end
G — Matt. 18. 15–20	Acts 4. 13–31

16 Th

Ezek. 12. 1–12	Ps. 78. 1–39†
Ps. 78. 58–64	1 Sam. ch. 31
G — Matt. 18.21 – 19.1	Acts 4.32 – 5.11

17 F

Ezek. 16. 1–15, 60–end	Ps. 55
Ps. 118. 14–18	2 Sam. ch. 1
or Canticle: Song of Deliverance	Acts 5. 12–26
G — Matt. 19. 3–12	

18 Sa

Ezek. 18. 1–11a, 13b, 30, 32	Ps. 76; 79
Ps. 51. 1–3, 15–17	2 Sam. 2. 1–11
Matt. 19. 13–15	Acts 5. 27–end

G

---

19 S — THE ELEVENTH SUNDAY AFTER TRINITY (Proper 15)

Track 1	Track 2	
1 Kings 2. 10–12; 3. 3–14	Prov. 9. 1–6	Ps. 106. 1–10
Ps. 111	Ps. 34. 9–14	Jonah ch. 1
Eph. 5. 15–20	Eph. 5. 15–20	or Ecclus. 3. 1–15
G — John 6. 51–58	John 6. 51–58	2 Pet. 3. 14–end

20 M — **Bernard, Abbot of Clairvaux, Teacher, 1153**

DEL 20   *William and Catherine Booth, Founders of the Salvation Army, 1912 and 1890*

Com. Religious	or	Ezek. 24. 15–24	Ps. 80; 82
esp. Rev. 19. 5–9		Ps. 78. 1–8	2 Sam. 3. 12–end
Gw		Matt. 19. 16–22	Acts ch. 6

21 Tu

Ezek. 28. 1–10	Ps. 87; 89. 1–18
Ps. 107. 1–3, 40, 43	2 Sam. 5. 1–12
G — Matt. 19. 23–end	Acts 7. 1–16

22 W

Ezek. 34. 1–11	Ps. 119. 105–128
Ps. 23	2 Sam. 6. 1–19
G — Matt. 20. 1–16	Acts 7. 17–43

23 Th

Ezek. 36. 23–28	Ps. 90; 92
Ps. 51. 7–12	2 Sam. 7. 1–17
Matt. 22. 1–14	Acts 7. 44–53

G

---

24 F — BARTHOLOMEW THE APOSTLE

Isa. 43. 8–13	MP: Ps. 86; 117
or Acts 5. 12–16	Gen. 28. 10–17
Ps. 145. 1–7	John 1. 43–end
Acts 5. 12–16	
or 1 Cor. 4. 9–15	
R — Luke 22. 24–30	

25 Sa

Ezek. 43. 1–7	Ps. 96; 97; 100
Ps. 85. 7–end	2 Sam. ch. 9
G — Matt. 23. 1–12	Acts 8. 4–25

---

*The Blessed Virgin Mary may be celebrated on 8 September instead of 15 August.

Second Service Evening Prayer	Calendar and Holy Communion		Morning Prayer	Evening Prayer
	To celebrate The Blessed Virgin Mary, see *Common Worship* provision.			
EP: Ps. 132 Song of Sol. 2. 1–7 Acts 1. 6–14			1 Sam. 28. 3–end Acts 4. 13–31	Prov. ch. 2 Mark 3. 19b–end
Ps. 119. 81–104 Prov. ch. 2 Mark 3. 19b–end	G			
Ps. 78. 40–end† Prov. 3. 1–26 Mark 4. 1–20	G		1 Sam. ch. 31 Acts 4.32 – 5.11	Prov. 3. 1–26 Mark 4. 1–20
Ps. 69 Prov. 3.27 – 4.19 Mark 4. 21–34	G		2 Sam. ch. 1 Acts 5. 12–26	Prov. 3.27 – 4.19 Mark 4. 21–34
Ps. 81; *84* Prov. 6. 1–19 Mark 4. 35–end ct	G		2 Sam. 2. 1–11 Acts 5. 27–end	Prov. 6. 1–19 Mark 4. 35–end ct
	THE ELEVENTH SUNDAY AFTER TRINITY			
Ps. [92]; 100 Exod. 2.23 – 3.10 Heb. 13. 1–15 *Gospel:* Luke 12. 49–56	G	1 Kings 3. 5–15 Ps. 28 1 Cor. 15. 1–11 Luke 18. 9–14	Ps. 106. 1–10 Jonah ch. 1 or Ecclus. 3. 1–15 2 Pet. 3. 14–end	Ps. [92]; 100 Exod. 2.23 – 3.10 Heb. 13. 1–15
Ps. *85*; 86 Prov. 8. 1–21 Mark 5. 1–20	G		2 Sam. 3. 12–end Acts ch. 6	Prov. 8. 1–21 Mark 5. 1–20
Ps. 89. 19–end Prov. 8. 22–end Mark 5. 21–34	G		2 Sam. 5. 1–12 Acts 7. 1–16	Prov. 8. 22–end Mark 5. 21–34
Ps. *91*; 93 Prov. ch. 9 Mark 5. 35–end	G		2 Sam. 6. 1–19 Acts 7. 17–43	Prov. ch. 9 Mark 5. 35–end
Ps. 94 Prov. 10. 1–12 Mark 6. 1–13 or First EP of Bartholomew Ps. 97 Isa. 61. 1–9 2 Cor. 6. 1–10 R ct	G		2 Sam. 7. 1–17 Acts 7. 44–53	Prov. 10. 1–12 Mark 6. 1–13 or First EP of Bartholomew (Ps. 97) Isa. 61. 1–9 2 Cor. 6. 1–10 R ct
EP: Ps. 91; 116 Ecclus. 39. 1–10 or Deut. 18. 15–19 Matt. 10. 1–22	**BARTHOLOMEW THE APOSTLE** Gen. 28. 10–17 Ps. 15 Acts 5. 12–16 Luke 22. 24–30 R		(Ps. 86; 117) Isa. 43. 8–13 John 1. 43–end	(Ps. 91; 116) Ecclus. 39. 1–10 or Deut. 18. 15–19 Matt. 10. 1–22
Ps. 104 Prov. 12. 10–end Mark 6. 30–44 ct	G		2 Sam. ch. 9 Acts 8. 4–25	Prov. 12. 10–end Mark 6. 30–44 ct

August 2012

Sunday Principal Service / Weekday Eucharist
Third Service / Morning Prayer

26 S — THE TWELFTH SUNDAY AFTER TRINITY (Proper 16)
Track 1
1 Kings 8. [1, 6, 10–11] 22–30, 41–43
Ps. 84
Eph. 6. 10–20
G John 6. 56–69
Track 2
Josh. 24. 1–2a, 14–18
Ps. 34. 15–end
Eph. 6. 10–20
John 6. 56–69
Ps. 115
Jonah ch. 2
or Ecclus. 3. 17–29
Rev. ch. 1

27 M — Monica, Mother of Augustine of Hippo, 387
Com. Saint or 2 Thess. 1. 1–5, 11–end
also Ecclus. 26. 1–3, 13–16 Ps. 39. 1–9
Gw Matt. 23. 13–22
DEL 21
Ps. 98; 99; 101
2 Sam. ch. 11
Acts 8. 26–end

28 Tu — Augustine, Bishop of Hippo, Teacher, 430
Com. Teacher or 2 Thess. 2. 1–3a, 14–end
esp. Ecclus. 39. 1–10 Ps. 98
Gw also Rom. 13. 11–13 Matt. 23. 23–26
Ps. 106† (or 103)
2 Sam. 12. 1–25
Acts 9. 1–19a

29 W — The Beheading of John the Baptist
Jer. 1. 4–10 or 2 Thess. 3. 6–10, 16–end
Ps. 11 Ps. 128
Heb. 11.32–12.2 Matt. 23. 27–32
Gr Matt. 14. 1–12
Ps. 110; 111; 112
2 Sam. 15. 1–12
Acts 9. 19b–31

30 Th — John Bunyan, Spiritual Writer, 1688
Com. Teacher or 1 Cor. 1. 1–9
also Heb. 12. 1–2 Ps. 145. 1–7
Gw Luke 21. 21, 34–36 Matt. 24. 42–end
Ps. 113; 115
2 Sam. 15. 13–end
Acts 9. 32–end

31 F — Aidan, Bishop of Lindisfarne, Missionary, 651
Com. Missionary or 1 Cor. 1. 17–25
also 1 Cor. 9. 16–19 Ps. 33. 6–12
Gw Matt. 25. 1–13
Ps. 139
2 Sam. 16. 1–14
Acts 10. 1–16

September 2012

1 Sa — Giles of Provence, Hermit, c. 710
1 Cor. 1. 26–end
Ps. 33. 12–15, 20–end
G Matt. 25. 14–30
Ps. 120; 121; 122
2 Sam. 17. 1–23
Acts 10. 17–33

2 S — THE THIRTEENTH SUNDAY AFTER TRINITY (Proper 17)
Track 1
Song of Sol. 2. 8–13
Ps. 45. 1–2, 6–9 (or 45. 1–7)
James 1. 17–end
G Mark 7. 1–8, 14–15, 21–23
Track 2
Deut. 4. 1–2, 6–9
Ps. 15
James 1. 17–end
Mark 7. 1–8, 14–15, 21–23
Ps. 119. 17–40
Jonah 3. 1–9
or Ecclus. 11. [7–18] 19–28
Rev. 3. 14–end

3 M — Gregory the Great, Bishop of Rome, Teacher, 604
Com. Teacher or 1 Cor. 2. 1–5
also 1 Thess. 2. 3–8 Ps. 33. 12–21
Gw Luke 4. 16–30
DEL 22
Ps. 123; 124; 125; 126
2 Sam. 18. 1–18
Acts 10. 34–end

4 Tu — Birinus, Bishop of Dorchester (Oxon), Apostle of Wessex, 650*
1 Cor. 2. 10b–end
Ps. 145. 10–17
G Luke 4. 31–37
Ps. 132; 133
2 Sam. 18.19 – 19.8a
Acts 11. 1–18

5 W —
1 Cor. 3. 1–9
Ps. 62
G Luke 4. 38–end
Ps. 119. 153–end
2 Sam. 19. 8b–23
Acts 11. 19–end

6 Th — Allen Gardiner, Founder of the South American Mission Society, 1851
1 Cor. 3. 18–end
Ps. 24. 1–6
G Luke 5. 1–11
Ps. 143; 146
2 Sam. 19. 24–end
Acts 12. 1–17

7 F —
1 Cor. 4. 1–5
Ps. 37. 3–8
G Luke 5. 33–end
Ps. 142; 144
2 Sam. 23. 1–7
Acts 12. 18–end

*Cuthbert may be celebrated on 4 September instead of 20 March.

Second Service Evening Prayer		Calendar and Holy Communion	Morning Prayer	Evening Prayer
		THE TWELFTH SUNDAY AFTER TRINITY		
Ps. 116 (or 116. 10–end) Exod. 4.27 – 5.1 Heb. 13. 16–21 Gospel: Luke 13. 10–17	G	Exod. 34. 29–end Ps. 34. 1–10 2 Cor. 3. 4–9 Mark 7. 31–37	Ps. 115 Jonah ch. 2 or Ecclus. 3. 17–29 Rev. ch. 1	Ps. 116 (or 116. 10–end) Exod. 4.27 – 5.1 Heb. 13. 16–21
Ps. 105† (or 103) Prov. 14.31 – 15.17 Mark 6. 45–end	G		2 Sam. ch. 11 Acts 8. 26–end	Prov. 14.31 – 15.17 Mark 6. 45–end
Ps. 107† Prov. 15. 18–end Mark 7. 1–13	Gw	**Augustine, Bishop of Hippo, Teacher, 430** Com. Doctor	2 Sam. 12. 1–25 Acts 9. 1–19a	Prov. 15. 18–end Mark 7. 1–13
Ps. 119. 129–152 Prov. 18. 10–end Mark 7. 14–23	Gr	**The Beheading of John the Baptist** 2 Chron. 24. 17–21 Ps. 92. 11–end Heb. 11.32 –12.2 Matt. 14. 1–12	2 Sam. 15. 1–12 Acts 9. 19b–31	Prov. 18. 10–end Mark 7. 14–23
Ps. 114; 116; 117 Prov. 20. 1–22 Mark 7. 24–30	G		2 Sam. 15. 13–end Acts 9. 32–end	Prov. 20. 1–22 Mark 7. 24–30
Ps. 130; 131; 137 Prov. 22. 1–16 Mark 7. 31–end	G		2 Sam. 16. 1–14 Acts 10. 1–16	Prov. 22. 1–16 Mark 7. 31–end
Ps. 118 Prov. 24. 23–end Mark 8. 1–10 ct	Gw	**Giles of Provence, Hermit, c. 710** Com. Abbot	2 Sam. 17. 1–23 Acts 10. 17–33	Prov. 24. 23–end Mark 8. 1–10 ct
		THE THIRTEENTH SUNDAY AFTER TRINITY		
Ps. 119. 1–16 (or 119. 9–16) Exod. 12. 21–27 Matt. 4.23 – 5.20	G	Lev. 19. 13–18 Ps. 74. 20–end Gal. 3. 16–22 or Heb. 13. 1–6 Luke 10. 23b–37	Ps. 119. 17–40 Jonah 3. 1–9 or Ecclus. 11. [7–18] 19–28 Rev. 3. 14–end	Ps. 119. 1–16 (or 119. 9–16) Exod. 12. 21–27 Matt. 4.23 – 5.20
Ps. 127; 128; 129 Prov. 25. 1–14 Mark 8. 11–21	G		2 Sam. 18. 1–18 Acts 10. 34–end	Prov. 25. 1–14 Mark 8. 11–21
Ps. (134); 135 Prov. 25. 15–end Mark 8. 22–26	G		2 Sam. 18.19 – 19.8a Acts 11. 1–18	Prov. 25. 15–end Mark 8. 22–26
Ps. 136 Prov. 26. 12–end Mark 8.27 – 9.1	G		2 Sam. 19. 8b–23 Acts 11. 19–end	Prov. 26. 12–end Mark 8.27 – 9.1
Ps. 138; 140; 141 Prov. 27. 1–22 Mark 9. 2–13	G		2 Sam. 19. 24–end Acts 12. 1–17	Prov. 27. 1–22 Mark 9. 2–13
Ps. 145 Prov. 30. 1–9, 24–31 Mark 9. 14–29	Gw	**Evurtius, Bishop of Orleans, 4th century** Com. Bishop	2 Sam. 23. 1–7 Acts 12. 18–end	Prov. 30. 1–9, 24–31 Mark 9. 14–29

September 2012

		Sunday Principal Service Weekday Eucharist		Third Service Morning Prayer

8	Sa	**The Birth of the Blessed Virgin Mary*** Com. BVM	*or*	I Cor. 4. 6–15 Ps. 145. 18–end Luke 6. 1–5	Ps. 147 2 Sam. ch. 24 Acts 13. 1–12
	Gw				
9	S	THE FOURTEENTH SUNDAY AFTER TRINITY **(Proper 18)** *Track 1* Prov. 22. 1–2, 8–9, 22–23 Ps. 125 James 2. 1–10 [11–13] 14–17		*Track 2* Isa. 35. 4–7a Ps. 146 James 2. 1–10 [11–13] 14–17	Ps. 119. 57–72 Jonah 3.10 – 4.11 or Ecclus. 27.30 – 28.9
	G	Mark 7. 24–end		Mark 7. 24–end	Rev. 8. 1–5
10 DEL 23	M			I Cor. 5. 1–8 Ps. 5. 5–9a Luke 6. 6–11	Ps. *1*; 2; 3 I Kings 1. 5–31 Acts 13. 13–43
	G				
11	Tu			I Cor. 6. 1–11 Ps. 149. 1–5 Luke 6. 12–19	Ps. *5*; 6; (8) I Kings 1.32 – 2.4, 10–12 Acts 13.44 – 14.7
	G				
12	W			I Cor. 7. 25–31 Ps. 45. 11–end Luke 6. 20–26	Ps. 119. 1–32 I Kings ch. 3 Acts 14. 8–end
	G				
13	Th	**John Chrysostom, Bishop of Constantinople, Teacher, 407** Com. Teacher *esp.* Matt. 5. 13–19 *also* Jer. 1. 4–10	*or*	I Cor. 8. 1–7, 11–end Ps. 139. 1–9 Luke 6. 27–38	Ps. 14; *15*; 16 I Kings 4.29 – 5.12 Acts 15. 1–21
	Gw				
14	F	HOLY CROSS DAY		Num. 21. 4–9 Ps. 22. 23–28 Phil. 2. 6–11	*MP*: Ps. 2; 8; 146 Gen. 3. 1–15 John 12. 27–36a
	R			John 3. 13–17	
15	Sa	**Cyprian, Bishop of Carthage, Martyr, 258** Com. Martyr *esp.* I Pet. 4. 12–end *also* Matt. 18. 18–22	*or*	I Cor. 10. 14–22 Ps. 116. 10–end Luke 6. 43–end	Ps. 20; 21; *23* I Kings 8. 1–30 Acts 15.36 – 16.5
	Gr				
16	S	THE FIFTEENTH SUNDAY AFTER TRINITY **(Proper 19)** *Track 1* Prov. 1. 20–33 Ps. 19 (or 19. 1–6) or *Canticle:* Wisd. 7.26 – 8.1 James 3. 1–12		*Track 2* Isa. 50. 4–9a Ps. 116. 1–8 James 3. 1–12 Mark 8. 27–end	Ps. 119. 105–120 Isa. 44.24 – 45.8 Rev. 12. 1–12
	G	Mark 8. 27–end			
17 DEL 24	M	**Hildegard, Abbess of Bingen, Visionary, 1179** Com. Religious *also* I Cor. 2. 9–13 Luke 10. 21–24	*or*	I Cor. 11. 17–26, 33 Ps. 40. 7–11 Luke 7. 1–10	Ps. 27; *30* I Kings 8. 31–62 Acts 16. 6–24
	Gw				
18	Tu			I Cor. 12. 12–14, 27–end Ps. 100 Luke 7. 11–17	Ps. 32; *36* I Kings 8.63 – 9.9 Acts 16. 25–end
	G				

*The Blessed Virgin Mary may be celebrated on 8 September instead of 15 August.

Second Service Evening Prayer		Calendar and Holy Communion	Morning Prayer	Evening Prayer
		The Birth of the Blessed Virgin Mary		
Ps. *148*; 149; 150		Gen. 3. 9–15	2 Sam. ch. 24	Prov. 31. 10–end
Prov. 31. 10–end		Ps. 45. 11–18	Acts 13. 1–12	Mark 9. 30–37
Mark 9. 30–37		Rom. 5. 12–17		
ct	Gw	Luke 11. 27–28		ct
		THE FOURTEENTH SUNDAY AFTER TRINITY		
Ps. 119. 41–56 (or 119. 49–56)		2 Kings 5. 9–16	Ps. 119. 57–72	Ps. 119. 41–56
Exod. 14. 5–end		Ps. 118. 1–9	Jonah 3.10 – 4.11	(or 119. 49–56)
Matt. 6. 1–18		Gal. 5. 16–24	or Ecclus. 27.30 – 28.9	Exod. 14. 5–end
	G	Luke 17. 11–19	Rev. 8. 1–5	Matt. 6. 1–18
Ps. *4*; 7			I Kings 1. 5–31	Wisd. ch. 1
Wisd. ch. 1			Acts 13. 13–43	or I Chron.
or I Chron. 10.1 – 11.9				10.1 – 11.9
Mark 9. 38–end	G			Mark 9. 38–end
Ps. *9*; 10†			I Kings 1.32 – 2.4, 10–12	Wisd. ch. 2
Wisd. ch. 2			Acts 13.44 – 14.7	or I Chron. ch. 13
or I Chron. ch. 13				Mark 10. 1–16
Mark 10. 1–16	G			
Ps. *11*; 12; 13			I Kings ch. 3	Wisd. 3. 1–9
Wisd. 3. 1–9			Acts 14. 8–end	or I Chron.
or I Chron. 15.1 – 16.3				15.1 – 16.3
Mark 10. 17–31	G			Mark 10. 17–31
Ps. 18†			I Kings 4.29 – 5.12	Wisd. 4. 7–end
Wisd. 4. 7–end			Acts 15. 1–21	or I Chron. ch. 17
or I Chron. ch. 17				Mark 10. 32–34
Mark 10. 32–34				
or *First EP of Holy Cross Day*				
Ps. 66				
Isa. 52.13 – 53.end				
Eph. 2. 11–end				
R ct	G			
		Holy Cross Day		
		To celebrate Holy Cross as a festival, see *Common Worship* provision.		
EP: Ps. 110; 150		Num. 21. 4–9	I Kings 6. 1, 11–28	Wisd. 5. 1–16
Isa. 63. 1–16		Ps. 67	Acts 15. 22–35	or I Chron.
I Cor. 1. 18–25		I Cor. 1. 17–25		21.1 – 22.1
	Gr	John 12. 27–33		Mark 10. 35–45
Ps. *24*; 25			I Kings 8. 1–30	Wisd. 5.17 – 6.11
Wisd. 5.17 – 6.11			Acts 15.36 – 16.5	or I Chron. 22. 2–end
or I Chron. 22. 2–end				Mark 10. 46–end
Mark 10. 46–end				
ct	G			ct
		THE FIFTEENTH SUNDAY AFTER TRINITY		
Ps. 119. 73–88 (or 119. 73–80)		Josh. 24. 14–25	Ps. 119. 105–120	Ps. 119. 73–88
Exod. 18. 13–26		Ps. 92. 1–6	Isa. 44.24 – 45.8	(or 119. 73–80)
Matt. 7. 1–14		Gal. 6. 11–end	Rev. 12. 1–12	Exod. 18. 13–26
	G	Matt. 6. 24–end		Matt. 7. 1–14
		Lambert, Bishop of Maastricht, Martyr, 709		
Ps. 26; *28*; 29		Com. Martyr	I Kings 8. 31–62	Wisd. 6. 12–23
Wisd. 6. 12–23			Acts 16. 6–24	or I Chron. 28. 1–10
or I Chron. 28. 1–10				Mark 11. 1–11
Mark 11. 1–11	Gr			
Ps. 33			I Kings 8.63 – 9.9	Wisd. 7. 1–14
Wisd. 7. 1–14			Acts 16. 25–end	or I Chron. 28. 11–end
or I Chron. 28. 11–end				Mark 11. 12–26
Mark 11. 12–26	G			

September 2012

			Sunday Principal Service Weekday Eucharist	Third Service Morning Prayer
19	W	*Theodore of Tarsus, Archbishop of Canterbury, 690*	I Cor. 12.31b – 13.end Ps. 33. 1–12 Luke 7. 31–35	Ps. 34 I Kings 10. 1–25 Acts 17. 1–15
	G			
20	Th	**John Coleridge Patteson, first Bishop of Melanesia, and his Companions, Martyrs, 1871** Com. Martyr *or* *esp.* 2 Chron. 24. 17–21 *also* Acts 7. 55–end	I Cor. 15. 1–11 Ps. 118. 1–2, 17–20 Luke 7. 36–end	Ps. 37† I Kings 11. 1–13 Acts 17. 16–end
	Gr			
21	F	MATTHEW, APOSTLE AND EVANGELIST	Prov. 3. 13–18 Ps. 119. 65–72 2 Cor. 4. 1–6 Matt. 9. 9–13	*MP:* Ps. 49; 117 I Kings 19. 15–end 2 Tim. 3. 14–end
	R			
22	Sa		I Cor. 15. 35–37, 42–49 Ps. 30. 1–5 Luke 8. 4–15	Ps. 41; *42*; 43 I Kings 12. 1–24 Acts 18.22 – 19.7
	G			
23	S	THE SIXTEENTH SUNDAY AFTER TRINITY **(Proper 20)** *Track 1* Prov. 31. 10–end Ps. 1 James 3.13 – 4.3, 7–8a Mark 9. 30–37	*Track 2* Wisd. 1.16 – 2.1, 12–22 *or* Jer. 11. 18–20 Ps. 54 James 3.13 – 4.3, 7–8a Mark 9. 30–37	Ps. 119. 153–end Isa. 45. 9–22 Rev. 14. 1–5
	G			
24 DEL 25	M		Prov. 3. 27–34 Ps. 15 Luke 8. 16–18	Ps. 44 I Kings 12.25 – 13.10 Acts 19. 8–20
	G			
25	Tu	**Lancelot Andrewes, Bishop of Winchester, Spiritual Writer, 1626** *Sergei of Radonezh, Russian Monastic Reformer, Teacher, 1392* Com. Bishop *or* *esp.* Isa. 6. 1–8	Prov. 21. 1–6, 10–13 Ps. 119. 1–8 Luke 8. 19–21	Ps. *48*; 52 I Kings 13. 11–end Acts 19. 21–end
	Gw			
26	W	Ember Day* *Wilson Carlile, Founder of the Church Army, 1942*	Prov. 30. 5–9 Ps. 119. 105–112 Luke 9. 1–6	Ps. 119. 57–80 I Kings ch. 17 Acts 20. 1–16
	G *or* R			
27	Th	**Vincent de Paul, Founder of the Congregation of the Mission (Lazarists), 1660** Com. Religious *or* *also* I Cor. 1. 25–end Matt. 25. 34–40	Eccles. 1. 2–11 Ps. 90. 1–6 Luke 9. 7–9	Ps. 56; *57*; (63†) I Kings 18. 1–20 Acts 20. 17–end
	Gw			
28	F	Ember Day*	Eccles. 3. 1–11 Ps. 144. 1–4 Luke 9. 18–22	Ps. *51*; 54 I Kings 18. 21–end Acts 21. 1–16
	G *or* R			

Second Service Evening Prayer	Calendar and Holy Communion		Morning Prayer	Evening Prayer
Ps. 119. 33–56 Wisd. 7.15 – 8.4 or 1 Chron. 29. 1–9 Mark 11. 27–end	Ember Day Ember CEG	G	1 Kings 10. 1–25 Acts 17. 1–15	Wisd. 7.15 – 8.4 or 1 Chron. 29. 1–9 Mark 11. 27–end
Ps. 39; *40* Wisd. 8. 5–18 or 1 Chron. 29. 10–20 Mark 12. 1–12 or *First EP of Matthew* Ps. 34 Isa. 33. 13–17 Matt. 6. 19–end **R ct**		G	1 Kings 11. 1–13 Acts 17. 16–end	Wisd. 8. 5–18 or 1 Chron. 29. 10–20 Mark 12. 1–12 or *First EP of Matthew* (Ps. 34) Prov. 3. 3–18 Matt. 6. 19–end **R ct**
EP: Ps. 119. 33–40, 89–96 Eccles. 5. 4–12 Matt. 19. 16–end	**MATTHEW, APOSTLE AND EVANGELIST** Ember Day Isa. 33. 13–17 Ps. 119. 65–72 2 Cor. 4. 1–6 Matt. 9. 9–13	R	(Ps. 49; 117) 1 Kings 19. 15–end 2 Tim. 3. 14–end	(Ps. 119. 33–40, 89–96) Eccles. 5. 4–12 Matt. 19. 16–end
Ps. 45; *46* Wisd. 10.15 – 11.10 or 2 Chron. 1. 1–13 Mark 12. 18–27 **ct**	Ember Day Ember CEG	G	1 Kings 12. 1–24 Acts 18.22 – 19.7	Wisd. 10.15 – 11.10 or 2 Chron. 1. 1–13 Mark 12. 18–27 **ct**
Ps. 119. 137–152 (or 119. 137–144) Exod. 19. 10–end Matt. 8. 23–end	**THE SIXTEENTH SUNDAY AFTER TRINITY** 1 Kings 17. 17–end Ps. 102. 12–17 Eph. 3. 13–end Luke 7. 11–17	G	Ps. 119. 153–end Isa. 45. 9–22 Rev. 14. 1–5	Ps. 119. 137–152 (or 119. 137–144) Exod. 19. 10–end Matt. 8. 23–end
Ps. *47*; 49 Wisd. 11.21 – 12.2 or 2 Chron. 2. 1–16 Mark 12. 28–34		G	1 Kings 12.25 – 13.10 Acts 19. 8–20	Wisd. 11.21 – 12.2 or 2 Chron. 2. 1–16 Mark 12. 28–34
Ps. 50 Wisd. 12. 12–21 or 2 Chron. ch. 3 Mark 12. 35–end		G	1 Kings 13. 11–end Acts 19. 21–end	Wisd. 12. 12–21 or 2 Chron. ch. 3 Mark 12. 35–end
Ps. *59*; 60; (67) Wisd. 13. 1–9 or 2 Chron. ch. 5 Mark 13. 1–13	**Cyprian, Bishop of Carthage, Martyr, 258** Com. Martyr	Gr	1 Kings ch. 17 Acts 20. 1–16	Wisd. 13. 1–9 or 2 Chron. ch. 5 Mark 13. 1–13
Ps. 61; *62*; 64 Wisd. 16.15 – 17.1 or 2 Chron. 6. 1–21 Mark 13. 14–23		G	1 Kings 18. 1–20 Acts 20. 17–end	Wisd. 16.15 – 17.1 or 2 Chron. 6. 1–21 Mark 13. 14–23
Ps. 38 Wisd. 18. 6–19 or 2 Chron. 6. 22–end Mark 13. 24–31 or *First EP of Michael and All Angels* Ps. 91 2 Kings 6. 8–17 Matt. 18. 1–6, 10 **W ct**		G	1 Kings 18. 21–end Acts 21. 1–16	Wisd. 18. 6–19 or 2 Chron. 6. 22–end Mark 13. 24–31 or *First EP of Michael and All Angels* (Ps. 91) 2 Kings 6. 8–17 John 1. 47–51 **W ct**

September 2012

	Sunday Principal Service Weekday Eucharist	Third Service Morning Prayer

29 Sa **MICHAEL AND ALL ANGELS**
Ember Day*

	Sunday Principal Service / Weekday Eucharist	Third Service / Morning Prayer
	Gen. 28. 10–17 or Rev. 12. 7–12 Ps. 103. 19–end Rev. 12. 7–12 or Heb. 1. 5–end	MP: Ps. 34; 150 Tobit 12. 6–end or Dan. 12. 1–4 Acts 12. 1–11
W	John 1. 47–end	

30 S **THE SEVENTEENTH SUNDAY AFTER TRINITY (Proper 21)**

	Track 1	Track 2	
	Esther 7. 1–6, 9–10; 9. 20–22	Num. 11. 4–6, 10–16, 24–29	Ps. 122
	Ps. 124	Ps. 19. 7–end	Isa. 48. 12–end
	James 5. 13–end	James 5. 13–end	Luke 11. 37–end
G	Mark 9. 38–end	Mark 9. 38–end	

October 2012

1 M *Remigius, Bishop of Rheims, Apostle of the Franks, 533; Anthony Ashley Cooper, Earl of Shaftesbury, Social Reformer, 1885*

DEL 26

	Weekday Eucharist	Morning Prayer
	Job 1. 6–end Ps. 17. 1–11 Luke 9. 46–50	Ps. 71 1 Kings ch. 21 Acts 21.37 – 22.21
G		

2 Tu

	Job 3. 1–3, 11–17, 20–23 Ps. 88. 14–19 Luke 9. 51–56	Ps. 73 1 Kings 22. 1–28 Acts 22.22 – 23.11
G		

3 W *George Bell, Bishop of Chichester, Ecumenist, Peacemaker, 1958*

	Job 9. 1–12, 14–16 Ps. 88. 1–6, 11 Luke 9. 57–end	Ps. 77 1 Kings 22. 29–45 Acts 23. 12–end
G		

4 Th **Francis of Assisi, Friar, Founder of the Friars Minor, 1226**

	Com. Religious also Gal. 6. 14–end Luke 12. 22–34	or	Job 19. 21–27a Ps. 27. 13–16 Luke 10. 1–12	Ps. 78. 1–39† 2 Kings 1. 2–17 Acts 24. 1–23
Gw			

5 F

	Job 38. 1, 12–21; 40. 3–5 Ps. 139. 6–11 Luke 10. 13–16	Ps. 55 2 Kings 2. 1–18 Acts 24.24 – 25.12
G		

6 Sa **William Tyndale, Translator of the Scriptures, Reformation Martyr, 1536**

	Com. Martyr also Prov. 8. 4–11 2 Tim. 3. 12–end	or	Job 42. 1–3, 6, 12–end Ps. 119. 169–end Luke 10. 17–24	Ps. 76; 79 2 Kings 4. 1–37 Acts 25. 13–end

Gr

7 S **THE EIGHTEENTH SUNDAY AFTER TRINITY (Proper 22)**

	Track 1	Track 2	
	Job 1. 1; 2. 1–10	Gen. 2. 18–24	Ps. 123; 124
	Ps. 26	Ps. 8	Isa. 49. 13–23
	Heb. 1. 1–4; 2. 5–12	Heb. 1. 1–4; 2. 5–12	Luke 12. 1–12
G	Mark 10. 2–16	Mark 10. 2–16	

or, if observed as Dedication Festival:

	Gen. 28. 11–18 or Rev. 21. 9–14 Ps. 122 1 Pet. 2. 1–10	MP: Ps. 48; 150 Hag. 2. 6–9 Heb. 10. 19–25
₩	John 10. 22–29	

*For Ember Day provision, see p. 11.

Second Service Evening Prayer	Calendar and Holy Communion	Morning Prayer	Evening Prayer
	MICHAEL AND ALL ANGELS		
EP: Ps. 138; 148 Dan. 10. 4–end Rev. ch. 5	Dan. 10. 10–19a Ps. 103. 17–22 Rev. 12. 7–12 Matt. 18. 1–10	(Ps. 34; 150) Tobit 12. 6–end or Dan. 12. 1–4 Acts 12. 1–11	(Ps. 138; 148) Gen. 28. 10–17 Rev. ch. 5
	W		
	THE SEVENTEENTH SUNDAY AFTER TRINITY		
Ps. 120; 121 Exod. ch. 24 Matt. 9. 1–8	Prov. 25. 6–14 Ps. 33. 6–12 Eph. 4. 1–6 Luke 14. 1–11	Ps. 132 Isa. 48. 12–end Luke 11. 37–end	Ps. 120; 121 Exod. ch. 24 Matt. 9. 1–8
	G		
Ps. 72; 75 1 Macc. 1. 1–19 or 2 Chron. 9. 1–12 Mark 14. 1–11	**Remigius, Bishop of Rheims, Apostle of the Franks, 533** Com. Bishop	1 Kings ch. 21 Acts 21.37 – 22.21	1 Macc. 1. 1–19 or 2 Chron. 9. 1–12 Mark 14. 1–11
	Gw		
Ps. 74 1 Macc. 1. 20–40 or 2 Chron. 10.1 – 11.4 Mark 14. 12–25		1 Kings 22. 1–28 Acts 22.22 – 23.11	1 Macc. 1. 20–40 or 2 Chron. 10.1 – 11.4 Mark 14. 12–25
	G		
Ps. 119. 81–104 1 Macc. 1. 41–end or 2 Chron. ch. 12 Mark 14. 26–42		1 Kings 22. 29–45 Acts 23. 12–end	1 Macc. 1. 41–end or 2 Chron. ch. 12 Mark 14. 26–42
	G		
Ps. 78. 40–end† 1 Macc. 2. 1–28 or 2 Chron. 13.1 – 14.1 Mark 14. 43–52		2 Kings 1. 2–17 Acts 24. 1–23	1 Macc. 2. 1–28 or 2 Chron. 13.1 – 14.1 Mark 14. 43–52
	G		
Ps. 69 1 Macc. 2. 29–48 or 2 Chron. 14. 2–end Mark 14. 53–65		2 Kings 2. 1–18 Acts 24.24 – 25.12	1 Macc. 2. 29–48 or 2 Chron. 14. 2–end Mark 14. 53–65
	G		
Ps. 81; 84 1 Macc. 2. 49–end or 2 Chron. 15. 1–15 Mark 14. 66–end ct or First EP of Dedication Festival: Ps. 24 2 Chron. 7. 1–16 John 4. 19–29 ℣ ct	**Faith of Aquitaine, Martyr, c. 304** Com. Virgin Martyr	2 Kings 4. 1–37 Acts 25. 13–end	1 Macc. 2. 49–end or 2 Chron. 15. 1–15 Mark 14. 66–end ct or First EP of Dedication Festival: Ps. 24 2 Chron. 7. 1–16 John 4. 19–29 ℣ ct
	Gr		
	THE EIGHTEENTH SUNDAY AFTER TRINITY		
Ps. 125; 126 Josh. 3. 7–end Matt. 10. 1–22	Deut. 6. 4–9 Ps. 122 1 Cor. 1. 4–8 Matt. 22. 34–end	Ps. 123; 124 Isa. 49. 13–23 Luke 12. 1–12	Ps. 125; 126 Josh. 3. 7–end Matt. 10. 1–22
	G		
EP: Ps. 132 Jer. 7. 1–11 Luke 19. 1–10	or, if observed as Dedication Festival: 2 Chron. 7. 11–16 Ps. 122 1 Cor. 3. 9–17 or 1 Pet. 2. 1–5 Matt. 21. 12–16	Ps. 48; 150 Hag. 2. 6–9 Heb. 10. 19–25	Ps. 132 Jer. 7. 1–11 Luke 19. 1–10
	℣ or John 10. 22–29		

October 2012

		Sunday Principal Service / Weekday Eucharist	Third Service / Morning Prayer

8 M
DEL 27 G
- Gal. 1. 6–12
- Ps. 111. 1–6
- Luke 10. 25–37
- Ps. *80*; 82
- 2 Kings ch. 5
- Acts 26. 1–23

9 Tu / G
Denys, Bishop of Paris, and his Companions, Martyrs, c. 250; Robert Grosseteste, Bishop of Lincoln, Philosopher, Scientist, 1253
- Gal. 1. 13–end
- Ps. 139. 1–9
- Luke 10. 38–end
- Ps. 87; *89. 1–18*
- 2 Kings 6. 1–23
- Acts 26. 24–end

10 W / Gw
Paulinus, Bishop of York, Missionary, 644
Thomas Traherne, Poet, Spiritual Writer, 1674
Com. Missionary *or* Gal. 2. 1–2, 7–14
esp. Matt. 28. 16–end   Ps. 117
              Luke 11. 1–4
- Ps. 119. 105–128
- 2 Kings 9. 1–16
- Acts 27. 1–26

11 Th / G
Ethelburga, Abbess of Barking, 675; James the Deacon, Companion of Paulinus, 7th century
- Gal. 3. 1–5
- Canticle: Benedictus
- Luke 11. 5–13
- Ps. 90; *92*
- 2 Kings 9. 17–end
- Acts 27. 27–end

12 F / Gw
Wilfrid of Ripon, Bishop, Missionary, 709
Elizabeth Fry, Prison Reformer, 1845; Edith Cavell, Nurse, 1915
Com. Missionary *or* Gal. 3. 7–14
esp. Luke 5. 1–11   Ps. 111. 4–end
also 1 Cor. 1. 18–25   Luke 11. 15–26
- Ps. *88*; (95)
- 2 Kings 12. 1–19
- Acts 28. 1–16

13 Sa / Gw
Edward the Confessor, King of England, 1066
Com. Saint *or* Gal. 3. 22–end
also 2 Sam. 23. 1–5   Ps. 105. 1–7
1 John 4. 13–16   Luke 11. 27–28
- Ps. 96; *97*; 100
- 2 Kings 17. 1–23
- Acts 28. 17–end

14 S / G
THE NINETEENTH SUNDAY AFTER TRINITY **(Proper 23)**

Track 1	Track 2	Third Service / Morning Prayer
Job 23. 1–9, 16–end	Amos 5. 6–7, 10–15	Ps. 129; 130
Ps. 22. 1–15	Ps. 90. 12–end	Isa. 50. 4–10
Heb. 4. 12–end	Heb. 4. 12–end	Luke 13. 22–30
Mark 10. 17–31	Mark 10. 17–31	

15 M / Gw
DEL 28
Teresa of Avila, Teacher, 1582
Com. Teacher *or* Gal. 4. 21–24, 26–27, 31; 5. 1
also Rom. 8. 22–27   Ps. 113
              Luke 11. 29–32
- Ps. *98*; 99; 101
- 2 Kings 17. 24–end
- Phil. 1. 1–11

16 Tu / G
Nicholas Ridley, Bishop of London, and Hugh Latimer, Bishop of Worcester, Reformation Martyrs, 1555
- Gal. 5. 1–6
- Ps. 119. 41–48
- Luke 11. 37–41
- Ps. *106*† (or 103)
- 2 Kings 18. 1–12
- Phil. 1. 12–end

17 W / Gr
Ignatius, Bishop of Antioch, Martyr, c. 107
Com. Martyr *or* Gal. 5. 18–end
also Phil. 3. 7–12   Ps. 1
John 6. 52–58   Luke 11. 42–46
- Ps. 110; *111*; 112
- 2 Kings 18. 13–end
- Phil. 2. 1–13

Second Service Evening Prayer		Calendar and Holy Communion	Morning Prayer	Evening Prayer
Ps. *85*; 86 I Macc. 3. 1–26 or 2 Chron. 17. 1–12 Mark 15. 1–15	G		2 Kings ch. 5 Acts 26. 1–23	I Macc. 3. 1–26 or 2 Chron. 17. 1–12 Mark 15. 1–15
Ps. 89. 19–end I Macc. 3. 27–41 or 2 Chron. 18. 1–27 Mark 15. 16–32	Gr	**Denys, Bishop of Paris, Martyr, c. 250** Com. Martyr	2 Kings 6. 1–23 Acts 26. 24–end	I Macc. 3. 27–41 or 2 Chron. 18. 1–27 Mark 15. 16–32
Ps. *91*; 93 I Macc. 3. 42–end or 2 Chron. 18.28 – 19.end Mark 15. 33–41	G		2 Kings 9. 1–16 Acts 27. 1–26	I Macc. 3. 42–end or 2 Chron. 18.28 – 19.end Mark 15. 33–41
Ps. 94 I Macc. 4. 1–25 or 2 Chron. 20. 1–23 Mark 15. 42–end	G		2 Kings 9. 17–end Acts 27. 27–end	I Macc. 4. 1–25 or 2 Chron. 20. 1–23 Mark 15. 42–end
Ps. 102 I Macc. 4. 26–35 or 2 Chron. 22.10 – 23.end Mark 16. 1–8	G		2 Kings 12. 1–19 Acts 28. 1–16	I Macc. 4. 26–35 or 2 Chron. 22.10 – 23.end Mark 16. 1–8
Ps. 104 I Macc. 4. 36–end or 2 Chron. 24. 1–22 Mark 16. 9–end ct	Gw	**Edward the Confessor, King of England, 1066, translated 1163** Com. Saint	2 Kings 17. 1–23 Acts 28. 17–end	I Macc. 4. 36–end or 2 Chron. 24. 1–22 Mark 16. 9–end ct
Ps. 127; [128] Josh. 5.13 – 6.20 Matt. 11. 20–end	G	**THE NINETEENTH SUNDAY AFTER TRINITY** Gen. 18. 23–32 Ps. 141. 1–9 Eph. 4. 17–end Matt. 9. 1–8	Ps. 129; 130 Isa. 50. 4–10 Luke 13. 22–30	Ps. 127; [128] Josh. 5.13 – 6.20 Matt. 11. 20–end
Ps. *105*† (or 103) I Macc. 6. 1–17 or 2 Chron. 26. 1–21 John 13. 1–11	G		2 Kings 17. 24–end Phil. 1. 1–11	I Macc. 6. 1–17 or 2 Chron. 26. 1–21 John 13. 1–11
Ps. 107† I Macc. 6. 18–47 or 2 Chron. ch. 28 John 13. 12–20	G		2 Kings 18. 1–12 Phil. 1. 12–end	I Macc. 6. 18–47 or 2 Chron. ch. 28 John 13. 12–20
Ps. 119. 129–152 I Macc. 7. 1–20 or 2 Chron. 29. 1–19 John 13. 21–30 or First EP of Luke Ps. 33 Hos. 6. 1–3 2 Tim. 3. 10–end **R** ct	Gw	**Etheldreda, Abbess of Ely, 679** Com. Abbess	2 Kings 18. 13–end Phil. 2. 1–13	I Macc. 7. 1–20 or 2 Chron. 29. 1–19 John 13. 21–30 or First EP of Luke (Ps. 33) Hos. 6. 1–3 2 Tim. 3. 10–end **R** ct

October 2012

			Sunday Principal Service / Weekday Eucharist	Third Service / Morning Prayer

18 Th   LUKE THE EVANGELIST

			Isa. 35. 3–6	MP: Ps. 145; 146
			or Acts 16. 6–12a	Isa. ch. 55
			Ps. 147. 1–7	Luke 1. 1–4
			2 Tim. 4. 5–17	
R			Luke 10. 1–9	

19 F   **Henry Martyn, Translator of the Scriptures, Missionary in India and Persia, 1812**

	Com. Missionary	or	Eph. 1. 11–14	Ps. 139
	esp. Mark 16. 15–end		Ps. 33. 1–6, 12	2 Kings 19. 20–36
	also Isa. 55. 6–11		Luke 12. 1–7	Phil. 3.1 – 4.1
Gw				

20 Sa

			Eph. 1. 15–end	Ps. 120; 121; 122
			Ps. 8	2 Kings ch. 20
			Luke 12. 8–12	Phil. 4. 2–end
G				

21 S   THE TWENTIETH SUNDAY AFTER TRINITY (**Proper 24**)

	Track 1	Track 2	
	Job 38. 1–7 [34–end]	Isa. 53. 4–end	Ps. 133; 134; 137. 1–6
	Ps. 104. 1–10, 26, 35c (or 104. 1–10)	Ps. 91. 9–end	Isa. 54. 1–14
	Heb. 5. 1–10	Heb. 5. 1–10	Luke 13. 31–end
G	Mark 10. 35–45	Mark 10. 35–45	

22 M
DEL 29

			Eph. 2. 1–10	Ps. 123; 124; 125; 126
			Ps. 100	2 Kings 21. 1–18
G			Luke 12. 13–21	1 Tim. 1. 1–17

23 Tu

			Eph. 2. 12–end	Ps. 132; 133
			Ps. 85. 7–end	2 Kings 22.1 – 23.3
G			Luke 12. 35–38	1 Tim. 1.18 – 2.end

24 W

			Eph. 3. 2–12	Ps. 119. 153–end
			Ps. 98	2 Kings 23. 4–25
G			Luke 12. 39–48	1 Tim. ch. 3

25 Th   *Crispin and Crispinian, Martyrs at Rome, c. 287*

			Eph. 3. 14–end	Ps. 143; 146
			Ps. 33. 1–6	2 Kings. 23.36 – 24.17
G			Luke 12. 49–53	1 Tim. ch. 4

26 F   **Alfred the Great, King of the West Saxons, Scholar, 899**
Cedd, Abbot of Lastingham, Bishop of the East Saxons, 664*

	Com. Saint	or	Eph. 4. 1–6	Ps. 142; 144
	also 2 Sam. 23. 1–5		Ps. 24. 1–6	2 Kings 24.18 – 25.12
	John 18. 33–37		Luke 12. 54–end	1 Tim. 5. 1–16
Gw				

27 Sa

			Eph. 4. 7–16	Ps. 147
			Ps. 122	2 Kings 25. 22–end
			Luke 13. 1–9	1 Tim. 5. 17–end
G				

*Chad may be celebrated with Cedd on 26 October instead of 2 March.

Second Service Evening Prayer	Calendar and Holy Communion	Morning Prayer	Evening Prayer
	LUKE THE EVANGELIST		
EP: Ps. 103	Isa. 35. 3–6	(Ps. 145; 146)	(Ps. 103)
Ecclus. 38. 1–14	Ps. 147. 1–6	Isa. ch. 55	Ecclus. 38. 1–14
or Isa. 61. 1–6	2 Tim. 4. 5–15	Luke 1. 1–4	or Isa. 61. 1–6
Col. 4. 7–end	Luke 10. 1–9		Col. 4. 7–end
	R or Luke 7. 36–end		
Ps. *130*; 131; 137		2 Kings 19. 20–36	1 Macc. 9. 1–22
1 Macc. 9. 1–22		Phil. 3.1 – 4.1	or 2 Chron. ch. 30
or 2 Chron. ch. 30			John 14. 1–14
John 14. 1–14	**G**		
Ps. 118		2 Kings ch. 20	1 Macc. 13. 41–end;
1 Macc. 13. 41–end; 14. 4–15		Phil. 4. 2–end	14. 4–15
or 2 Chron. 32. 1–22			or 2 Chron. 32. 1–22
John 14. 15–end			John 14. 15–end
ct	**G**		ct
	THE TWENTIETH SUNDAY AFTER TRINITY		
Ps. 141	Prov. 9. 1–6	Ps. 133; 134; 137. 1–6	Ps. 142
Josh. 14. 6–14	Ps. 145. 15–end	Isa. 54. 1–14	Josh. 14. 6–14
Matt. 12. 1–21	Eph. 5. 15–21	Luke 13. 31–end	Matt. 12. 1–21
	G Matt. 22. 1–14		
Ps. *127*; 128; 129		2 Kings 21. 1–18	2 Macc. 4. 7–17
2 Macc. 4. 7–17		1 Tim. 1. 1–17	or 2 Chron. 33. 1–13
or 2 Chron. 33. 1–13			John 15. 1–11
John 15. 1–11	**G**		
Ps. (134); *135*		2 Kings 22.1 – 23.3	2 Macc. 6. 12–end
2 Macc. 6. 12–end		1 Tim. 1.18 – 2.end	or 2 Chron. 34. 1–18
or 2 Chron. 34. 1–18			John 15. 12–17
John 15. 12–17	**G**		
Ps. 136		2 Kings 23. 4–25	2 Macc. 7. 1–19
2 Macc. 7. 1–19		1 Tim. ch. 3	or 2 Chron. 34. 19–end
or 2 Chron. 34. 19–end			John 15. 18–end
John 15. 18–end	**G**		
	Crispin, Martyr at Rome, c. 287		
Ps. *138*; 140; 141	Com. Martyr	2 Kings. 23.36 – 24.17	2 Macc. 7. 20–41
2 Macc. 7. 20–41		1 Tim. ch. 4	or 2 Chron. 35. 1–19
or 2 Chron. 35. 1–19			John 16. 1–15
John 16. 1–15	**Gr**		
Ps. 145		2 Kings 24.18 – 25.12	Tobit ch. 1
Tobit ch. 1		1 Tim. 5. 1–16	or 2 Chron.
or 2 Chron. 35.20 – 36.10			35.20 – 36.10
John 16. 16–22	**G**		John 16. 16–22
Ps. *148*; 149; 150		2 Kings 25. 22–end	Tobit ch. 2
Tobit ch. 2		1 Tim. 5. 17–end	or 2 Chron. 36. 11–end
or 2 Chron. 36. 11–end			John 16. 23–end
John 16. 23–end			
ct			ct
or First EP of Simon and Jude			or First EP of Simon and
Ps. 124; 125; 126			Jude
Deut. 32. 1–4			(Ps. 124; 125; 126)
John 14. 15–26			Deut. 32. 1–4
			John 14. 15–26
R ct	**G**		**R ct**

October 2012

		Sunday Principal Service Weekday Eucharist	Third Service Morning Prayer

28 S   SIMON AND JUDE, APOSTLES* (or transferred to 29th)

	Isa. 28. 14–16	MP: Ps. 116; 117
	Ps. 119. 89–96	Wisd. 5. 1–16
	Eph. 2. 19–end	or Isa. 45. 18–end
	John 15. 17–end	Luke 6. 12–16

R

or, for The Last Sunday after Trinity (Proper 25):

Track 1	Track 2	
Job 42. 1–6, 10–end	Jer. 31. 7–9	Ps. 119. 89–104
Ps. 34. 1–8, 19–end (or 34. 1–8)	Ps. 126	Isa. 59. 9–20
Heb. 7. 23–end	Heb. 7. 23–end	Luke 14. 1–14
G Mark 10. 46–end	Mark 10. 46–end	

or, if being observed as Bible Sunday:

Isa. 55. 1–11	Ps. 119. 89–104
Ps. 19. 7–end	Isa. 45. 22–end
2 Tim. 3.14 – 4.5	Matt. 24. 30–35
G John 5. 36b–end	or Luke 14. 1–14

29 M   **James Hannington, Bishop of Eastern Equatorial Africa, Martyr in Uganda, 1885**
DEL 30

Com. Martyr	or	Eph. 4.32 – 5.8	Ps. 1; 2; 3
esp. Matt. 10. 28–39		Ps. 1	Judith ch. 4
		Luke 13. 10–17	or Exod. 22. 21–27; 23. 1–17
Gr			1 Tim. 6. 1–10

30 Tu

Eph. 5. 21–end	Ps. 5; 6; (8)
Ps. 128	Judith 5.1 – 6.4
Luke 13. 18–21	or Exod. 29.38 – 30.16
G	1 Tim. 6. 11–end

31 W   *Martin Luther, Reformer, 1546*

Eph. 6. 1–9	Ps. 119. 1–32
Ps. 145. 10–20	Judith 6.10 – 7.7
Luke 13. 22–30	or Lev. ch. 8
	2 Tim. 1. 1–14

G

November 2012

1 Th   **ALL SAINTS' DAY**

Wisd. 3. 1–9	MP: Ps. 15; 84; 149
or Isa. 25. 6–9	Isa. ch. 35
Ps. 24. 1–6	Luke 9. 18–27
Rev. 21. 1–6a	
⅏ John 11. 32–44	

or, if the readings above are used on Sunday 4 November:

Isa. 56. 3–8	MP: Ps. 111; 112; 117
or 2 Esdras 2. 42–end	Wisd. 5. 1–16
Ps. 33. 1–5	or Jer. 31. 31–34
Heb. 12. 18–24	2 Cor. 4. 5–12
⅏ Matt. 5. 1–12	

or, if kept as a feria:

Eph. 6. 10–20	Ps. 14; 15; 16
Ps. 144. 1–2, 9–11	Judith 7. 19–end
Luke 13. 31–end	or Lev. ch. 9
G	2 Tim. 1.15 – 2.13

*If the Dedication Festival is kept on this Sunday, use the provision given on 6 and 7 October.

Second Service Evening Prayer		Calendar and Holy Communion	Morning Prayer	Evening Prayer
		SIMON AND JUDE, APOSTLES		
EP: Ps. 119. 1–16		Isa. 28. 9–16	Ps. 119. 89–96	Ps. 119. 1–16
1 Macc. 2. 42–66		Ps. 116. 11–end	Wisd. 5. 1–16	1 Macc. 2. 42–66
or Jer. 3. 11–18		Jude 1–8	or Isa. 45. 18–end	or Jer. 3. 11–18
Jude 1–4, 17–end		or Rev. 21. 9–14	Luke 6. 12–16	Eph. 2. 19–end
	R	John 15. 17–end		
		or, for The Twenty-First Sunday after Trinity:		
Ps. 119. 121–136		Gen. 32. 24–29	Ps. 119. 89–104	Ps. 119. 121–136
Eccles. chs 11 and 12		Ps. 90. 1–12	Isa. 59. 9–20	Eccles. chs 11 and 12
2 Tim. 2. 1–7		Eph. 6. 10–20	Luke 14. 1–14	2 Tim. 2. 1–7
Gospel: Luke 18. 9–14		John 4. 46b–end		
Ps. 119. 1–16				
2 Kings ch. 22				
Col. 3. 12–17				
Gospel: Luke 4. 14–30	G			
Ps. 4; 7			Judith ch. 4	Tobit ch. 3
Tobit ch. 3			or Exod. 22. 21–27;	or Mic. 1. 1–9
or Mic. 1. 1–9			23. 1–17	John 17. 1–5
John 17. 1–5	G		1 Tim. 6. 1–10	
Ps. 9; 10†			Judith 5.1 – 6.4	Tobit ch. 4
Tobit ch. 4			or Exod. 29.38 – 30.16	or Mic. ch. 2
or Mic. ch. 2			1 Tim. 6. 11–end	John 17. 6–19
John 17. 6–19	G			
First EP of All Saints			Judith 6.10 – 7.7	*First EP of All Saints*
Ps. 1; 5			or Lev. ch. 8	Ps. 1; 5
Ecclus. 44. 1–15			2 Tim. 1. 1–14	Ecclus. 44. 1–15
or Isa. 40. 27–end				or Isa. 40. 27–end
Rev. 19. 6–10				Rev. 19. 6–10
ℬ ct				
or, if All Saints is observed				
on 4 November:				
Ps. 11; 12; 13				
Tobit 5.1 – 6.1a				
or Mic. ch. 3				
John 17. 20–end	G			ℬ ct
		ALL SAINTS' DAY		
EP: Ps. 148; 150		Isa. 66. 20–23	Ps. 15; 84; 149	Ps. 148; 150
Isa. 65. 17–end		Ps. 33. 1–5	Isa. ch. 35	Isa. 65. 17–end
Heb. 11.32 – 12.2		Rev. 7. 2–4 [5–8] 9–12	Luke 9. 18–27	Heb. 11.32 – 12.2
		Matt. 5. 1–12		
EP: Ps. 145				
Isa. 66. 20–23				
Col. 1. 9–14				
Ps. 118				
Tobit 6. 1b–end				
or Mic. 4.1 – 5.1				
John 18. 1–11	ℬ			

November 2012

			Sunday Principal Service / Weekday Eucharist	Third Service / Morning Prayer

2   F   **Commemoration of the Faithful Departed (All Souls' Day)**

	Sunday Principal Service / Weekday Eucharist	Third Service / Morning Prayer
Lam. 3. 17–26, 31–33	*or* Phil. 1. 1–11	Ps. 17; *19*
or Wisd. 3. 1–9	Ps. 111	Judith 8. 9–end
Ps. 23	Luke 14. 1–6	*or* Lev. 16. 2–24
or Ps. 27. 1–6, 16–end		2 Tim. 2. 14–end
Rom. 5. 5–11		
or 1 Pet. 1. 3–9		
John 5. 19–25		
or John 6. 37–40		

Rp *or* **Gp**

3   Sa   **Richard Hooker, Priest, Anglican Apologist, Teacher, 1600**
Martin of Porres, Friar, 1639

	Sunday Principal Service / Weekday Eucharist	Third Service / Morning Prayer
Com. Teacher	*or* Phil. 1. 18–26	Ps. 20; 21; *23*
esp. John 16. 12–15	Ps. 42. 1–7	Judith ch. 9
also Ecclus. 44. 10–15	Luke 14. 1, 7–11	*or* Lev. ch. 17
		2 Tim. ch. 3

Rw *or* **Gw**

4   S   THE FOURTH SUNDAY BEFORE ADVENT

	Sunday Principal Service / Weekday Eucharist	Third Service / Morning Prayer
	Deut. 6. 1–9	Ps. 112; 149
	Ps. 119. 1–8	Jer. 31. 31–34
	Heb. 9. 11–14	1 John 3. 1–3
	Mark 12. 28–34	

R *or* **G**

⏏   *or* ALL SAINTS' SUNDAY (see readings for 1 November throughout the day)

5   M   DEL 31

	Sunday Principal Service / Weekday Eucharist	Third Service / Morning Prayer
	Phil. 2. 1–4	Ps. *2*; 146
	Ps. 131	*alt.* Ps. 27; *30*
	Luke 14. 12–14	Dan. ch. 1
		Rev. ch. 1

R *or* **G**

6   Tu   *Leonard, Hermit, 6th century; William Temple, Archbishop of Canterbury, Teacher, 1944*

	Sunday Principal Service / Weekday Eucharist	Third Service / Morning Prayer
	Phil. 2. 5–11	Ps. *5*; 147. 1–12
	Ps. 22. 22–27	*alt.* Ps. 32; *36*
	Luke 14. 15–24	Dan. 2. 1–24
		Rev. 2. 1–11

R *or* **G**

7   W   **Willibrord of York, Bishop, Apostle of Frisia, 739**

	Sunday Principal Service / Weekday Eucharist	Third Service / Morning Prayer
Com. Missionary	*or* Phil. 2. 12–18	Ps. *9*; 147. 13–end
esp. Isa. 52. 7–10	Ps. 27. 1–5	*alt.* Ps. 34
Matt. 28. 16–end	Luke 14. 25–33	Dan. 2. 25–end
		Rev. 2. 12–end

Rw *or* **Gw**

8   Th   **The Saints and Martyrs of England**

	Sunday Principal Service / Weekday Eucharist	Third Service / Morning Prayer
Isa. 61. 4–9	*or* Phil. 3. 3–8a	Ps. 11; *15*; 148
or Ecclus. 44. 1–15	Ps. 105. 1–7	*alt.* Ps. 37†
Ps. 15	Luke 15. 1–10	Dan. 3. 1–18
Rev. 19. 5–10		Rev. 3. 1–13
John 17. 18–23		

Rw *or* **Gw**

9   F   *Margery Kempe, Mystic, c. 1440*

	Sunday Principal Service / Weekday Eucharist	Third Service / Morning Prayer
	Phil. 3.17 – 4.1	Ps. *16*; 149
	Ps. 122	*alt.* Ps. 31
	Luke 16. 1–8	Dan. 3. 19–end
		Rev. 3. 14–end

R *or* **G**

10   Sa   **Leo the Great, Bishop of Rome, Teacher, 461**

	Sunday Principal Service / Weekday Eucharist	Third Service / Morning Prayer
Com. Teacher	*or* Phil. 4. 10–19	Ps. *18. 31–end*; 150
also 1 Pet. 5. 1–11	Ps. 112	*alt.* Ps. 41; *42*; 43
	Luke 16. 9–15	Dan. 4. 1–18
		Rev. ch. 4

Rw *or* **Gw**

11   S   THE THIRD SUNDAY BEFORE ADVENT
(Remembrance Sunday)

	Sunday Principal Service / Weekday Eucharist	Third Service / Morning Prayer
	Jonah 3. 1–5, 10	Ps. 136
	Ps. 62. 5–end	Mic. 4. 1–5
	Heb. 9. 24–end	Phil. 4. 6–9
	Mark 1. 14–20	

R *or* **G**

12   M   DEL 32

	Sunday Principal Service / Weekday Eucharist	Third Service / Morning Prayer
	Titus 1. 1–9	Ps. 19; *20*
	Ps. 24. 1–6	*alt.* Ps. 44
	Luke 17. 1–6	Dan. 4. 19–end
		Rev. ch. 5

R *or* **G**

Second Service Evening Prayer		Calendar and Holy Communion	Morning Prayer	Evening Prayer
		To celebrate All Souls' Day, see *Common Worship* provision.		
Ps. 22 Tobit ch. 7 *or* Mic. 5. 2–end John 18. 12–27			Judith 8. 9–end *or* Lev. 16. 2–24 2 Tim. 2. 14–end	Tobit ch. 7 *or* Mic. 5. 2–end John 18. 12–27
	G			
Ps. *24*; 25 Tobit ch. 8 *or* Mic. ch. 6 John 18. 28–end ct	G		Judith ch. 9 *or* Lev. ch. 17 2 Tim. ch. 3	Tobit ch. 8 *or* Mic. ch. 6 John 18. 28–end ct
		THE TWENTY-SECOND SUNDAY AFTER TRINITY		
Ps. 145 (*or* 145. 1–9) Dan. 2. 1–48 (*or* 2. 1–11, 25–48) Rev. 7. 9–end *Gospel:* Matt. 5. 1–12	G	Gen. 45. 1–7, 15 Ps. 133 Phil. 1. 3–11 Matt. 18. 21–end	Ps. 112; 149 Jer. 31. 31–34 1 John 3. 1–3	Ps. 145 (*or* 145. 1–9) Dan. 2. 1–48 (*or* 2. 1–11, 25–48) Rev. 7. 9–end
Ps. *92*; 96; 97 *alt.* Ps. 26; *28*; 29 Isa. 1. 1–20 Matt. 1. 18–end	G		Dan. ch. 1 Rev. ch. 1	Isa. 1. 1–20 Matt. 1. 18–end
Ps. 98; 99; *100* *alt.* Ps. 33 Isa. 1. 21–end Matt. 2. 1–15	Gw	**Leonard, Hermit, 6th century** Com. Abbot	Dan. 2. 1–24 Rev. 2. 1–11	Isa. 1. 21–end Matt. 2. 1–15
Ps. 111; *112*; 116 *alt.* Ps. 119. 33–56 Isa. 2. 1–11 Matt. 2. 16–end	G		Dan. 2. 25–end Rev. 2. 12–end	Isa. 2. 1–11 Matt. 2. 16–end
Ps. 118 *alt.* Ps. 39; *40* Isa. 2. 12–end Matt. ch. 3	G		Dan. 3. 1–18 Rev. 3. 1–13	Isa. 2. 12–end Matt. ch. 3
Ps. 137; 138; *143* *alt.* Ps. 35 Isa. 3. 1–15 Matt. 4. 1–11	G		Dan. 3. 19–end Rev. 3. 14–end	Isa. 3. 1–15 Matt. 4. 1–11
Ps. 145 *alt.* Ps. 45; *46* Isa. 4.2 – 5.7 Matt. 4. 12–22 ct	G		Dan. 4. 1–18 Rev. ch. 4	Isa. 4.2 – 5.7 Matt. 4. 12–22 ct
		THE TWENTY-THIRD SUNDAY AFTER TRINITY		
Ps. 46; [82] Isa. 10.33 – 11.9 John 14. [1–22] 23–29	G	Isa. 11. 1–10 Ps. 44 1–9 Phil. 3. 17–end Matt. 22. 15–22	Ps. 136 Mic. 4. 1–5 Phil. 4. 6–9	Ps. 144 Isa. 10.33 – 11.9 John 14. [1–22] 23–29
Ps. 34 *alt.* Ps. *47*; 49 Isa. 5. 8–24 Matt. 4.23 – 5.12	G		Dan. 4. 19–end Rev. ch. 5	Isa. 5. 8–24 Matt. 4.23 – 5.12

November 2012

		Sunday Principal Service Weekday Eucharist	Third Service Morning Prayer

13 Tu **Charles Simeon, Priest, Evangelical Divine, 1836**
Com. Pastor   *or* Titus 2. 1–8, 11–14   Ps. *21*; 24
esp. Mal. 2. 5–7   Ps. 37. 3–5, 30–32   *alt.* Ps. *48*; 52
also Col. 1. 3–8   Luke 17. 7–10   Dan. 5. 1–12
Luke 8. 4–8   Rev. ch. 6
Rw *or* Gw

14 W *Samuel Seabury, first Anglican Bishop in North America, 1796*
                                              Titus 3. 1–7   Ps. *23*; 25
                                              Ps. 23   *alt.* Ps. 119. 57–80
                                              Luke 17. 11–19   Dan. 5. 13–end
R *or* G   Rev. 7. 1–4, 9–end

15 Th
                                              Philemon 7–20   Ps. *26*; 27
                                              Ps. 146. 4–end   *alt.* Ps. 56; *57*; (63†)
                                              Luke 17. 20–25   Dan. ch. 6
R *or* G   Rev. ch. 8

16 F **Margaret, Queen of Scotland, Philanthropist, Reformer of the Church, 1093**
Edmund Rich of Abingdon, Archbishop of Canterbury, 1240
Com. Saint   *or* 2 John 4–9   Ps. 28; *32*
also Prov. 3. 31. 10–12, 20, 26–end   Ps. 119. 1–8   *alt.* Ps. *51*; 54
1 Cor. 12.13 – 13.3   Luke 17. 26–end   Dan. 7. 1–14
Matt. 25. 34–end   Rev. 9. 1–12
Rw *or* Gw

17 Sa **Hugh, Bishop of Lincoln, 1200**
Com. Bishop   *or* 3 John 5–8   Ps. 33
also 1 Tim. 6. 11–16   Ps. 112   *alt.* Ps. 68
                                              Luke 18. 1–8   Dan. 7. 15–end
                                                                          Rev. 9. 13–end
Rw *or* Gw

18 S THE SECOND SUNDAY BEFORE ADVENT
                                              Dan. 12. 1–3   Ps. 96
                                              Ps. 16   1 Sam. 9.27 – 10.2a;
                                              Heb. 10. 1–14 [15–18] 19–25   10. 17–26
R *or* G   Mark 13. 1–8   Matt. 13. 31–35

19 M **Hilda, Abbess of Whitby, 680**
DEL 33 *Mechtild, Beguine of Magdeburg, Mystic, 1280*
Com. Religious   *or* Rev. 1. 1–4; 2. 1–5   Ps. 46; *47*
esp. Isa. 61.10 – 62.5   Ps. 1   *alt.* Ps. 71
                                              Luke 18. 35–end   Dan. 8. 1–14
Rw *or* Gw   Rev. ch. 10

20 Tu **Edmund, King of the East Angles, Martyr, 870**
Priscilla Lydia Sellon, a Restorer of the Religious Life in the Church of England, 1876
Com. Martyr   *or* Rev. 3. 1–6, 14–end   Ps. 48; *52*
also Prov. 20. 28; 21. 1–4, 7   Ps. 15   *alt.* Ps. 73
                                              Luke 19. 1–10   Dan. 8. 15–end
R *or* Gr   Rev. 11. 1–14

21 W
                                              Rev. ch. 4   Ps. *56*; 57
                                              Ps. 150   *alt.* Ps. 77
                                              Luke 19. 11–28   Dan. 9. 1–19
R *or* G   Rev. 11. 15–end

22 Th *Cecilia, Martyr at Rome, c. 230*
                                              Rev. 5. 1–10   Ps. 61; *62*
                                              Ps. 149. 1–5   *alt.* Ps. 78. 1–39†
                                              Luke 19. 41–44   Dan. 9. 20–end
R *or* G   Rev. ch. 12

23 F **Clement, Bishop of Rome, Martyr, c. 100**
Com. Martyr   *or* Rev. 10. 8–end   Ps. *63*; 65
also Phil. 3.17 – 4.3   Ps. 119. 65–72   *alt.* Ps. 55
Matt. 16. 13–19   Luke 19. 45–end   Dan. 10.1 – 11.1
R *or* Gr   Rev. 13. 1–10

Second Service Evening Prayer	Calendar and Holy Communion	Morning Prayer	Evening Prayer
Ps. 36; *40* *alt.* Ps. 50 Isa. 5. 25–end Matt. 5. 13–20	**Britius, Bishop of Tours, 444** Com. Bishop Gw	Dan. 5. 1–12 Rev. ch. 6	Isa. 5. 25–end Matt. 5. 13–20
Ps. 37 *alt.* Ps. *59*; 60; (67) Isa. ch. 6 Matt. 5. 21–37	 G	Dan. 5. 13–end Rev. 7. 1–4, 9–end	Isa. ch. 6 Matt. 5. 21–37
Ps. 42; *43* *alt.* Ps. 61; *62*; 64 Isa. 7. 1–17 Matt. 5. 38–end	**Machutus, Bishop, Apostle of Brittany, c. 564** Com. Bishop Gw	Dan. ch. 6 Rev. ch. 8	Isa. 7. 1–17 Matt. 5. 38–end
Ps. 31 *alt.* Ps. 38 Isa. 8. 1–15 Matt. 6. 1–18	 G	Dan. 7. 1–14 Rev. 9. 1–12	Isa. 8. 1–15 Matt. 6. 1–18
Ps. 84; *86* *alt.* Ps. 65; *66* Isa. 8.16 – 9.7 Matt. 6. 19–end ct	**Hugh, Bishop of Lincoln, 1200** Com. Bishop Gw	Dan. 7. 15–end Rev. 9. 13–end	Isa. 8.16 – 9.7 Matt. 6. 19–end ct
Ps. 95 Dan. 3. [1–12] 13–end Matt. 13. 24–30, 36–43	THE TWENTY-FOURTH SUNDAY AFTER TRINITY Isa. 55. 6–11 Ps. 85. 1–7 Col. 1. 3–12 Matt. 9. 18–26 G	Ps. 96 1 Sam. 9.27 – 10.2a; 10. 17–26 Matt. 13. 31–35	Ps. 95 Dan. 3. [1–12] 13–end Matt. 13. 24–30, 36–43
Ps. 70; *71* *alt.* Ps. *72*; 75 Isa. 9.8 – 10.4 Matt. 7. 1–12	 G	Dan. 8. 1–14 Rev. ch. 10	Isa. 9.8 – 10.4 Matt. 7. 1–12
Ps. *67*; 72 *alt.* Ps. 74 Isa. 10. 5–19 Matt. 7. 13–end	**Edmund, King of the East Angles, Martyr, 870** Com. Martyr Gr	Dan. 8. 15–end Rev. 11. 1–14	Isa. 10. 5–19 Matt. 7. 13–end
Ps. 73 *alt.* Ps. 119. 81–104 Isa. 10. 20–32 Matt. 8. 1–13	 G	Dan. 9. 1–19 Rev. 11. 15–end	Isa. 10. 20–32 Matt. 8. 1–13
Ps. 74; *76* *alt.* Ps. 78. 40–end† Isa. 10.33 – 11.9 Matt. 8. 14–22	**Cecilia, Martyr at Rome, c. 230** Com. Virgin Martyr Gr	Dan. 9. 20–end Rev. ch. 12	Isa. 10.33 – 11.9 Matt. 8. 14–22
Ps. 77 *alt.* Ps. 69 Isa. 11.10 – 12.end Matt. 8. 23–end	**Clement, Bishop of Rome, Martyr, c. 100** Com. Martyr Gr	Dan. 10.1 – 11.1 Rev. 13. 1–10	Isa. 11.10 – 12.end Matt. 8. 23–end

November 2012

			Sunday Principal Service Weekday Eucharist	Third Service Morning Prayer
24	Sa		Rev. 11. 4–12 Ps. 144. 1–9 Luke 20. 27–40	Ps. 78. 1–39 *alt.* Ps. 76; 79 Dan. ch. 12 Rev. 13. 11–end
		R *or* G		
25	S	**CHRIST THE KING** The Sunday Next Before Advent	Dan. 7. 9–10, 13–14 Ps. 93 Rev. 1. 4b–8 John 18. 33–37	*MP:* Ps. 29; 110 Isa. 32. 1–8 Rev. 3. 7–end
		R *or* W		
26 DEL 34	M		Rev. 14. 1–5 Ps. 24. 1–6 Luke 21. 1–4	Ps. 92; **96** *alt.* Ps. **80**; 82 Isa. 40. 1–11 Rev. 14. 1–13
		R *or* G		
27	Tu		Rev. 14. 14–19 Ps. 96 Luke 21. 5–11	Ps. **97**; 98; 100 *alt.* Ps. 87; **89. 1–18** Isa. 40. 12–26 Rev. 14.14 – 15.end
		R *or* G		
28	W		Rev. 15. 1–4 Ps. 98 Luke 21. 12–19	Ps. 110; 111; **112** *alt.* Ps. 119. 105–128 Isa. 40.27 – 41.7 Rev. 16. 1–11
		R *or* G		
29	Th		Rev. 18. 1–2, 21–23; 19. 1–3, 9 Ps. 100 Luke 21. 20–28	Ps. **125**; 126; 127; 128 *alt.* Ps. 90; **92** Isa. 41. 8–20 Rev. 16. 12–end
			Day of Intercession and Thanksgiving *for the Missionary Work of the Church* Isa. 49. 1–6; Isa. 52. 7–10; Mic. 4. 1–5 Acts 17. 12–end; 2 Cor. 5.14 – 6.2; Eph. 2. 13–end Ps. 2; 46; 47 Matt. 5. 13–16; Matt. 28. 16–end; John 17. 20–end	
		R *or* G		
30	F	**ANDREW THE APOSTLE**	Isa. 52. 7–10 Ps. 19. 1–6 Rom. 10. 12–18 Matt. 4. 18–22	*MP:* Ps. 47; 147. 1–12 Ezek. 47. 1–12 *or* Ecclus. 14. 20–end John 12. 20–32
		R		

December 2012

1	Sa	*Charles de Foucauld, Hermit in the Sahara, 1916* Rev. 22. 1–7 Ps. 95. 1–7 Luke 21. 34–36		Ps. 145 *alt.* Ps. 96; **97**; 100 Isa. 42. 10–17 Rev. ch. 18
		R *or* G		
2	S	**THE FIRST SUNDAY OF ADVENT** CW Year C begins	Jer. 33. 14–16 Ps. 25. 1–9 1 Thess. 3. 9–end Luke 21. 25–36	Ps. 44 Isa. 51. 4–11 Rom. 13. 11–end
		P		

Second Service Evening Prayer		Calendar and Holy Communion	Morning Prayer	Evening Prayer
Ps. 78. 40–end alt. Ps. 81; *84* Isa. 13. 1–13 Matt. 9. 1–17 ct or First EP of Christ the King Ps. 99; 100 Isa. 10.33 – 11.9 1 Tim. 6. 11–16 **R** or **W** ct	G		Dan. ch. 12 Rev. 13. 11–end	Isa. 13. 1–13 Matt. 9. 1–17 ct
EP: Ps. 72 (or 72. 1–7) Dan. ch. 5 John 6. 1–15	G	THE SUNDAY NEXT BEFORE ADVENT To celebrate Christ the King, see *Common Worship* provision. Jer. 23. 5–8 Ps. 85. 8–end Col. 1. 13–20 John 6. 5–14	Ps. 29; 110 Isa. 32. 1–8 Rev. 3. 7–end	Ps. 72 (or 72. 1–7) Dan. ch. 5 Rev. 1. 4b–8
Ps. *80*; 81 alt. Ps. *85*; 86 Isa. 14. 3–20 Matt. 9. 18–34	G		Isa. 40. 1–11 Rev. 14. 1–13	Isa. 14. 3–20 Matt. 9. 18–34
Ps. 99; *101* alt. Ps. 89. 19–end Isa. ch. 17 Matt. 9.35 – 10.15	G		Isa. 40. 12–26 Rev. 14.14 – 15.end	Isa. ch. 17 Matt. 9.35 – 10.15
Ps. 121; *122*; 123; 124 alt. Ps. *91*; 93 Isa. ch. 19 Matt. 10. 16–33	G		Isa. 40.27 – 41.7 Rev. 16. 1–11	Isa. ch. 19 Matt. 10. 16–33
Ps. 131; 132; *133* alt. Ps. 94 Isa. 21. 1–12 Matt. 10.34 – 11.1 or First EP of Andrew the Apostle Ps. 48 Isa. 49. 1–9a 1 Cor. 4. 9–16 **R** ct	G	To celebrate the Day of Intercession and Thanksgiving for the Missionary Work of the Church, see *Common Worship* provision.	Isa. 41. 8–20 Rev. 16. 12–end	Isa. 21. 1–12 Matt. 10.34 – 11.1 or First EP of Andrew the Apostle (Ps. 48) Isa. 49. 1–9a 1 Cor. 4. 9–16 **R** ct
EP: Ps. 87; 96 Zech. 8. 20–end John 1. 35–42	R	ANDREW THE APOSTLE Zech. 8. 20–end Ps. 92. 1–5 Rom. 10. 9–end Matt. 4. 18–22	(Ps. 47; 147. 1–12) Ezek. 47. 1–12 or Ecclus. 14. 20–end John 12. 20–32	(Ps. 87; 96) Isa. 52. 7–10 John 1. 35–42
Ps. 148; 149; *150* alt. Ps. 104 Isa. ch. 24 Matt. 11. 20–end **P** ct	G		Isa. 42. 10–17 Rev. ch. 18	Isa. ch. 24 Matt. 11. 20–end **P** ct
Ps. 9 (or 9. 1–8) Joel 3. 9–end Rev. 14.13 – 15.4 *Gospel:* John 3. 1–17	P	THE FIRST SUNDAY OF ADVENT Advent 1 Collect until Christmas Eve Mic. 4. 1–4, 6–7 Ps. 25. 1–9 Rom. 13. 8–14 Matt. 21. 1–13	Ps. 44 Isa. 51. 4–11 Rom. 13. 11–end	Ps. 9 (or 9. 1–8) Joel 3. 9–end Rev. 14.13 – 15.4

December 2012

			Sunday Principal Service / Weekday Eucharist	Third Service / Morning Prayer

3 M — *Francis Xavier, Missionary, Apostle of the Indies, 1552*
Daily Eucharistic Lectionary Year 1 begins

	Isa. 2. 1–5	Ps. *50*; 54
	Ps. 122	*alt.* Ps. *1*; 2; 3
	Matt. 8. 5–11	Isa. 42. 18–end
P		Rev. ch. 19

4 Tu — *John of Damascus, Monk, Teacher, c. 749; Nicholas Ferrar, Deacon, Founder of the Little Gidding Community, 1637*

	Isa. 11. 1–10	Ps. *80*; 82
	Ps. 72. 1–4, 18–19	*alt.* Ps. *5*; 6; (8)
	Luke 10. 21–24	Isa. 43. 1–13
P		Rev. ch. 20

5 W

	Isa. 25. 6–10a	Ps. 5; *7*
	Ps. 23	*alt.* Ps. 119. 1–32
	Matt. 15. 29–37	Isa. 43. 14–end
P		Rev. 21. 1–8

6 Th — **Nicholas, Bishop of Myra, c. 326**

Com. Bishop	*or* Isa. 26. 1–6	Ps. *42*; 43
also Isa. 61. 1–3	Ps. 118. 18–27a	*alt.* Ps. 14; *15*; 16
1 Tim. 6. 6–11	Matt. 7. 21, 24–27	Isa. 44. 1–8
Pw Mark 10. 13–16		Rev. 21. 9–21

7 F — **Ambrose, Bishop of Milan, Teacher, 397**

Com. Teacher	*or* Isa. 29. 17–end	Ps. *25*; 26
also Isa. 41. 9b–13	Ps. 27. 1–4, 16–17	*alt.* Ps. 17; *19*
Luke 22. 24–30	Matt. 9. 27–31	Isa. 44. 9–23
Pw		Rev. 21.22 – 22.5

8 Sa — **The Conception of the Blessed Virgin Mary**

Com. BVM	*or* Isa. 30. 19–21, 23–26	Ps. *9*; (10)
	Ps. 146. 4–9	*alt.* Ps. 20; 21; *23*
	Matt. 9.35 – 10.1, 6–8	Isa. 44.24 – 45.13
Pw		Rev. 22. 6–end

9 S — THE SECOND SUNDAY OF ADVENT

	Baruch ch. 5	Ps. 80
	or Mal. 3. 1–4	Isa. 64. 1–7
	Canticle: Benedictus	Matt. 11. 2–11
	Phil. 1. 3–11	
P	Luke 3. 1–6	

10 M

	Isa. ch. 35	Ps. 44
	Ps. 85. 7–end	*alt.* Ps. 27; *30*
	Luke 5. 17–26	Isa. 45. 14–end
P		1 Thess. ch. 1

11 Tu

	Isa. 40. 1–11	Ps. *56*; 57
	Ps. 96. 1, 10–end	*alt.* Ps. 32; *36*
	Matt. 18. 12–14	Isa. ch. 46
P		1 Thess. 2. 1–12

12 W — Ember Day*

	Isa. 40. 25–end	Ps. *62*; 63
	Ps. 103. 8–13	*alt.* Ps. 34
	Matt. 11. 28–end	Isa. ch. 47
P		1 Thess. 2. 13–end

13 Th — **Lucy, Martyr at Syracuse, 304**
Samuel Johnson, Moralist, 1784

Com. Martyr	*or* Isa. 41. 13–20	Ps. 53; *54*; 60
also Wisd. 3. 1–7	Ps. 145. 1, 8–13	*alt.* Ps. 37†
2 Cor. 4. 6–15	Matt. 11. 11–15	Isa. 48. 1–11
Pr		1 Thess. ch. 3

14 F — **John of the Cross, Poet, Teacher, 1591**
Ember Day*

Com. Teacher	*or* Isa. 48. 17–19	Ps. 85; *86*
esp. 1 Cor. 2. 1–10	Ps. 1	*alt.* Ps. 31
also John 14. 18–23	Matt. 11. 16–19	Isa. 48. 12–end
Pw		1 Thess. 4. 1–12

*For Ember Day provision, see p. 11.

Second Service Evening Prayer		Calendar and Holy Communion	Morning Prayer	Evening Prayer
Ps. 70; *71* *alt.* Ps. 4; 7 Isa. 25. 1–9 Matt. 12. 1–21	P		Isa. 42. 18–end Rev. ch. 19	Isa. 25. 1–9 Matt. 12. 1–21
Ps. *74*; 75 *alt.* Ps. 9; 10† Isa. 26. 1–13 Matt. 12. 22–37	P		Isa. 43. 1–13 Rev. ch. 20	Isa. 26. 1–13 Matt. 12. 22–37
Ps. 76; *77* *alt.* Ps. *11*; 12; 13 Isa. 28. 1–13 Matt. 12. 38–end	P		Isa. 43. 14–end Rev. 21. 1–8	Isa. 28. 1–13 Matt. 12. 38–end
Ps. *40*; 46 *alt.* Ps. 18† Isa. 28. 14–end Matt. 13. 1–23	Pw	**Nicholas, Bishop of Myra, c. 326** Com. Bishop	Isa. 44. 1–8 Rev. 21. 9–21	Isa. 20. 11–end Matt. 13. 1–23
Ps. 16; *17* *alt.* Ps. 22 Isa. 29. 1–14 Matt. 13. 24–43	P		Isa. 44. 9–23 Rev. 21.22 – 22.5	Isa. 29. 1–14 Matt. 13. 24–43
Ps. *27*; 28 *alt.* Ps. *24*; 25 Isa. 29. 15–end Matt. 13. 44–end ct	Pw	**The Conception of the Blessed Virgin Mary** Isa. 44.24 – 45.13 Rev. 22. 6–end	Isa. 29. 15–end Matt. 13. 44–end	Isa. 29. 15–end Matt. 13. 44–end ct
Ps. 75; [76] Isa. 40. 1–11 Luke 1. 1–25	P	**THE SECOND SUNDAY OF ADVENT** 2 Kings 22. 8–10; 23. 1–3 Ps. 50. 1–6 Rom. 15. 4–13 Luke 21. 25–33	Ps. 40 Isa. 64. 1–7 Luke 3. 1–6	Ps. 75 [76] Mal. 3. 1–4 Luke 1. 1–25
Ps. *144*; 146 *alt.* Ps. 26; *28*; 29 Isa. 30. 1–18 Matt. 14. 1–12	P		Isa. 45. 14–end 1 Thess. ch. 1	Isa. 30. 1–18 Matt. 14. 1–12
Ps. *11*; 12; 13 *alt.* Ps. 33 Isa. 30. 19–end Matt. 14. 13–end	P		Isa. ch. 46 1 Thess. 2. 1–12	Isa. 30. 19–end Matt. 14. 13–end
Ps. *10*; 14 *alt.* Ps. 119. 33–56 Isa. ch. 31 Matt. 15. 1–20	P		Isa. ch. 47 1 Thess. 2. 13–end	Isa. ch. 31 Matt. 15. 1–20
Ps. 73 *alt.* Ps. 39; *40* Isa. ch. 32 Matt. 15. 21–28	Pr	**Lucy, Martyr at Syracuse, 304** Com. Virgin Martyr	Isa. 48. 1–11 1 Thess. ch. 3	Isa. ch. 32 Matt. 15. 21–28
Ps. 82; *90* *alt.* Ps. 35 Isa. 33. 1–22 Matt. 15. 29–end	P		Isa. 48. 12–end 1 Thess. 4. 1–12	Isa. 33. 1–22 Matt. 15. 29–end

December 2012

			Sunday Principal Service Weekday Eucharist	Third Service Morning Prayer
15	Sa	Ember Day*		
			Ecclus. 48. 1–4, 9–11 or 2 Kings 2. 9–12 Ps. 80. 1–4, 18–19 Matt. 17. 10–13	Ps. 145 *alt.* Ps. 41; *42*; 43 Isa. 49. 1–13 1 Thess. 4. 13–end
	P			
16	S	THE THIRD SUNDAY OF ADVENT		
			Zeph. 3. 14–end *Canticle:* Isa. 12. 2–6 or Ps. 146. 4–end Phil. 4. 4–7	Ps. 12; 14 Isa. 25. 1–9 1 Cor. 4. 1–5
	P		Luke 3. 7–18	
17	M	O Sapientia *Eglantyne Jebb, Social Reformer, Founder of 'Save the Children', 1928*		
			Gen. 49. 2, 8–10 Ps. 72. 1–5, 18–19 Matt. 1. 1–17	Ps. 40 *alt.* Ps. 44 Isa. 49. 14–25 1 Thess. 5. 1–11
	P			
18	Tu		Jer. 23. 5–8 Ps. 72. 1–2, 12–13, 18–end Matt. 1. 18–24	Ps. *70*; 74 *alt.* Ps. *48*; 52 Isa. ch. 50 1 Thess. 5. 12–end
	P			
19	W		Judg. 13. 2–7, 24–end Ps. 71. 3–8 Luke 1. 5–25	Ps. 144; *146* Isa. 51. 1–8 2 Thess. ch. 1
	P			
20	Th		Isa. 7. 10–14 Ps. 24. 1–6 Luke 1. 26–38	Ps. *46*; 95 Isa. 51. 9–16 2 Thess. ch. 2
	P			
21	F**		Zeph. 3. 14–18 Ps. 33. 1–4, 11–12, 20–end Luke 1. 39–45	Ps. *121*; 122; 123 Isa. 51. 17–end 2 Thess. ch. 3
	P			
22	Sa		1 Sam. 1. 24–end Ps. 113 Luke 1. 46–56	Ps. *124*; 125; 126; 127 Isa. 52. 1–12 Jude
	P			
23	S	THE FOURTH SUNDAY OF ADVENT		
			Mic. 5. 2–5a *Canticle:* Magnificat or Ps. 80. 1–8 Heb. 10. 5–10	Ps. 144 Isa. 32. 1–8 Rev. 22. 6–end
	P		Luke 1. 39–45 [46–55]	
24	M	CHRISTMAS EVE		
			Morning Eucharist 2 Sam. 7. 1–5, 8–11, 16 Ps. 89. 2, 19–27 Acts 13. 16–26 Luke 1. 67–79	Ps. *45*; 113 Isa. 52.13 – 53.end 2 Pet. 1. 1–15
	P			

*For Ember Day provision, see p. 11.
**Thomas the Apostle may be celebrated on 21 December instead of 3 July.

Second Service Evening Prayer		Calendar and Holy Communion	Morning Prayer	Evening Prayer
Ps. 93; 94 alt. Ps. 45; 46 Isa. ch. 35 Matt. 16. 1–12 ct	P		Isa. 49. 1–13 1 Thess. 4. 13–end	Isa. ch. 35 Matt. 16. 1–12 ct
Ps. 50. 1–6; [62] Isa. ch. 35 Luke 1. 57–66 [67–end]	P	THE THIRD SUNDAY OF ADVENT O Sapientia Isa. ch. 35 Ps. 80. 1–7 1 Cor. 4. 1–5 Matt. 11. 2–10	Ps. 12; 14 Isa. 25. 1–9 Luke 3. 7–18	Ps. 62 Zeph. 3. 14–end Luke 1. 57–66 [67–end]
Ps. 25; 26 alt. Ps. 47; 49 Isa. 38. 1–8, 21–22 Matt. 16. 13–end	P		Isa. 49. 14–25 1 Thess. 5. 1–11	Isa. 38. 1–8, 21–22 Matt. 16. 13–end
Ps. 50; 54 alt. Ps. 50 Isa. 38. 9–20 Matt. 17. 1–13	P		Isa. ch. 50 1 Thess. 5. 12–end	Isa. 38. 9–20 Matt. 17. 1–13
Ps. 10; 57 Isa. ch. 39 Matt. 17. 14–21	P	Ember Day Ember CEG	Isa. 51. 1–8 2 Thess. ch. 1	Isa. ch. 39 Matt. 17. 14–21
Ps. 4; 9 Zeph. 1.1 – 2.3 Matt. 17. 22–end	P		Isa. 51. 9–16 2 Thess. ch. 2	Zeph. 1.1 – 2.3 Matt. 17. 22–end or First EP of Thomas (Ps. 27) Isa. ch. 35 Heb. 10.35 – 11.1 R ct
Ps. 80; 84 Zeph. 3. 1–13 Matt. 18. 1–20	R	THOMAS THE APOSTLE Ember Day Job 42. 1–6 Ps. 139. 1–11 Eph. 2. 19–end John 20. 24–end	(Ps. 92; 146) 2 Sam. 15. 17–21 or Ecclus. ch. 2 John 11. 1–16	(Ps. 139) Hab. 2. 1–4 1 Pet. 1. 3–12
Ps. 24; 48 Zeph. 3. 14–end Matt. 18. 21–end ct	P	Ember Day Ember CEG	Isa. 52. 1–12 Jude	Zeph. 3. 14–end Matt. 18. 21–end ct
Ps. 123; [131] Isa. 10.33 – 11.10 Matt. 1. 18–end	P	THE FOURTH SUNDAY OF ADVENT Isa. 40. 1–9 Ps. 145. 17–end Phil. 4. 4–7 John 1. 19–28	Ps. 144 Isa. 32. 1–8 Rev. 22. 6–end	Ps. 123; [131] Isa. 10.33 – 11.10 Matt. 1. 18–end
Ps. 85 Zech. ch. 2 Rev. 1. 1–8	P	CHRISTMAS EVE Collect (1) Christmas Eve (2) Advent 1 Mic. 5. 2–5a Ps. 24 Titus 3. 3–7 Luke 2. 1–14	Ps. 45; 113 Isa. 52.13 – 53.end 2 Pet. 1. 1–15	Zech. ch. 2 Rev. 1. 1–8

December 2012

	Sunday Principal Service Weekday Eucharist	Third Service Morning Prayer

25 Tu **CHRISTMAS DAY**

Any of the following sets of readings may be used on the evening of Christmas Eve and on Christmas Day. Set III should be used at some service during the celebration.

I
Isa. 9. 2–7
Ps. 96
Titus 2. 11–14
Luke 2. 1–14 [15–20]

MP: Ps. *110*; 117
Isa. 62. 1–5
Matt. 1. 18–end

II
Isa. 62. 6–end
Ps. 97
Titus 3. 4–7
Luke 2. [1–7] 8–20

III
Isa. 52. 7–10
Ps. 98
Heb. 1. 1–4 [5–12]
₩ John 1. 1–14

---

26 W STEPHEN, DEACON, FIRST MARTYR

2 Chron. 24. 20–22
or Acts 7. 51–end
Ps. 119. 161–168
Acts 7. 51–end
or Gal. 2. 16b–20
Matt. 10. 17–22

MP: Ps. *13*; 31. 1–8; 150
Jer. 26. 12–15
Acts ch. 6

R

---

27 Th JOHN, APOSTLE AND EVANGELIST

Exod. 33. 7–11a
Ps. 117
1 John ch. 1
John 21. 19b–end

MP: Ps. *21*; 147. 13–end
Exod. 33. 12–end
1 John 2. 1–11

W

---

28 F THE HOLY INNOCENTS

Jer. 31. 15–17
Ps. 124
1 Cor. 1. 26–29
Matt. 2. 13–18

MP: Ps. *36*; 146
Baruch 4. 21–27
or Gen. 37. 13–20
Matt. 18. 1–10

R

---

29 Sa **Thomas Becket, Archbishop of Canterbury, Martyr, 1170***
Com. Martyr   *or*   1 John 2. 3–11
esp. Matt. 10. 28–33   Ps. 96. 1–4
also Ecclus. 51. 1–8   Luke 2. 22–35
Wr

Ps. *19*; 20
Isa. 57. 15–end
John 1. 1–18

---

30 S THE FIRST SUNDAY OF CHRISTMAS

1 Sam. 2. 18–20, 26
Ps. 148 (or 148. 1–6)
Col. 3. 12–17
W   Luke 2. 41–end

Ps. 105. 1–11
Isa. 41.21 – 42.1
1 John 1. 1–7

---

31 M *John Wyclif, Reformer, 1384*

1 John 2. 18–21
Ps. 96. 1, 11–end
John 1. 1–18

Ps. 102
Isa. 59. 15b–end
John 1. 29–34

W

---

*Thomas Becket may be celebrated on 7 July instead of 29 December.

Second Service Evening Prayer	Calendar and Holy Communion	Morning Prayer	Evening Prayer
	CHRISTMAS DAY		
EP: Ps. 8	Isa. 9. 2–7	Ps. 110; 117	Ps. 8
Isa. 65. 17–25	Ps. 98	Isa. 62. 1–5	Isa. 65. 17–25
Phil. 2. 5–11	Heb. 1. 1–12	Matt. 1. 18–end	Phil. 2. 5–11
or Luke 2. 1–20	John 1. 1–14		*or Luke 2. 1–20*
if it has not been used at the principal service of the day			
	𝔚		
	STEPHEN, DEACON, FIRST MARTYR		
EP: Ps. 57; **86**	Collect	(Ps. 13; 31. 1–8; 150)	(Ps. 57; 86)
Gen. 4. 1–10	(1) Stephen	Jer. 26. 12–15	Gen. 4. 1–10
Matt. 23. 34–end	(2) Christmas	Acts ch. 6	Matt. 10. 17–22
	2 Chron. 24. 20–22		
	Ps. 119. 161–168		
	Acts 7. 55–end		
	R Matt. 23. 34–end		
	JOHN, APOSTLE AND EVANGELIST		
EP: Ps. 97	Collect	(Ps. 21; 147. 13–end)	(Ps. 97)
Isa. 6. 1–8	(1) John	Exod. 33. 7–11a	Isa. 6. 1–8
1 John 5. 1–12	(2) Christmas	1 John 2. 1–11	1 John 5. 1–12
	Exod. 33. 18–end		
	Ps. 92. 11–end		
	1 John ch. 1		
	W John 21. 19b–end		
	THE HOLY INNOCENTS		
EP: Ps. 123; **128**	Collect	(Ps. 36; 146)	(Ps. 124; 128)
Isa. 49. 14–25	(1) Innocents	Baruch 4. 21–27	Isa. 49. 14–25
Mark 10. 13–16	(2) Christmas	*or Gen. 37. 13–20*	Mark 10. 13–16
	Jer. 31. 10–17	Matt. 18. 1–10	
	Ps. 123		
	Rev. 14. 1–5		
	R Matt. 2. 13–18		
Ps. 131; **132**		Isa. 57. 15–end	Jonah ch. 1
Jonah ch. 1		John 1. 1–18	Col. 1. 1–14
Col. 1. 1–14			
ct	W		ct
	THE SUNDAY AFTER CHRISTMAS DAY		
Ps. 132	Isa. 62. 10–12	Ps. 105. 1–11	Ps. 132
Isa. ch. 61	Ps. 45. 1–7	Isa. 41.21 – 42.1	Isa. ch. 61
Gal. 3.27 – 4.7	Gal. 4. 1–7	1 John 1. 1–7	Luke 2. 15–21
Gospel: Luke 2. 15–21	W Matt. 1. 18–end		
	Silvester, Bishop of Rome, 335		
Ps. **90**; 148	Com. Bishop	Isa. 59. 15b–end	Jonah chs 3 & 4
Jonah chs 3 & 4		John 1. 29–34	Col. 1.24 – 2.7
Col. 1.24 – 2.7			*or First EP of*
or First EP of The Naming			*The Circumcision*
of Jesus			*of Christ*
Ps. 148			(Ps. 148)
Jer. 23. 1–6			Jer. 23. 1–6
Col. 2. 8–15			Col. 2. 8–15
ct	W		ct

The *Common Worship* Additional Weekday Lectionary

The Additional Weekday Lectionary provides two readings on a one-year cycle for each day (except for Sundays, Principal Feasts and Holy Days, Festivals and Holy Week). They 'stand alone' and are intended particularly for use in those churches and cathedrals that attract occasional rather than regular congregations. The Additional Weekday Lectionary has been designed to complement rather than replace the existing Weekday Lectionary. Thus a church with a regular congregation in the morning and a congregation made up mainly of visitors in the evening would continue to use the Weekday Lectionary in the morning but might choose to use this Additional Weekday Lectionary for Evening Prayer.

Psalms are not provided, since the Weekday Lectionary already offers a variety of approaches with regard to psalmody. This Lectionary is not intended for use at the Eucharist; the Daily Eucharistic Lectionary is already authorized for that purpose.

On Sundays, Principal Feasts, other Principal Holy Days, Festivals, and in Holy Week, where no readings are provided in this table, the lectionary provision in the main part of this volume should be used, including the optional first Evening Prayer on the eve of a Principal Feast or Festival.

Date		Old Testament	New Testament
November 2011			
27	S	THE FIRST SUNDAY OF ADVENT	
28	M	Mal. 3. 1–6	Matt. 3. 1–6
29	Tu	Zeph. 3. 14–end	1 Thess. 4. 13–end
30	W	ANDREW THE APOSTLE	
December 2011			
1	Th	Mic. 5. 2–5a	John 3. 16–21
2	F	Isa. 66. 18–end	Luke 13. 22–30
3	Sa	Mic. 7. 8–15	Rom. 15.30 – 16.7, 25–end
4	S	THE SECOND SUNDAY OF ADVENT	
5	M	Jer. 7. 1–11	Phil. 4. 4–9
6	Tu	Dan. 7. 9–14	Matt. 24. 15–28
7	W	Amos 9. 11–end	Rom. 13. 8–14
8	Th	Jer. 23. 5–8	Mark 11. 1–11
9	F	Jer. 33. 14–22	Luke 21. 25–36
10	Sa	Zech. 14. 4–11	Rev. 22. 1–7
11	S	THE THIRD SUNDAY OF ADVENT	
12	M	Isa. 40. 1–11	Matt. 3. 1–12
13	Tu	Lam. 3. 22–33	1 Cor. 1. 1–9
14	W	Joel 3. 9–16	Matt. 24. 29–35
15	Th	Isa. ch. 62	1 Thess. 3. 6–13
16	F	Isa. 2. 1–5	Acts 11. 1–18
17	Sa	Ecclus. 24. 1–9 *or* Prov. 8. 22–31	1 Cor. 2. 1–13
18	S	THE FOURTH SUNDAY OF ADVENT	
19	M	Isa. 11. 1–9	Rom. 15. 7–13
20	Tu	Isa. 22. 21–23	Rev. 3. 7–13
21	W	Num. 24. 15b–19	Rev. 22. 10–21
22	Th	Jer. 30. 7–11a	Acts 4. 1–12
23	F	Isa. 7. 10–15	Matt. 1. 18–23
24	Sa	*At Evening Prayer the readings for Christmas Eve are used. At other services, the following readings are used:*	
		Isa. 29. 13–18	1 John 4. 7–16
25	S	**CHRISTMAS DAY**	
26	M	STEPHEN	
27	Tu	JOHN THE EVANGELIST	
28	W	THE HOLY INNOCENTS	
29	Th	Mic. 1. 1–4; 2. 12–13	Luke 2. 1–7
30	F	Isa. 9. 2–7	John 8. 12–20
31	Sa	Eccles. 3. 1–13	Rev. 21. 1–8
January 2012			
1	S	**NAMING AND CIRCUMCISION OF JESUS** (THE FIRST SUNDAY OF CHRISTMAS) *In years in which 6 January is not a Sunday, if, for pastoral reasons, The Epiphany is celebrated on the Sunday between 2 and 8 January, the readings appointed for 2–8 January are read in order on the days other than the Saturday and Sunday in that period.*	
2	M	Isa. 66. 6–14 *or Naming and Circumcision of Jesus*	Matt. 12. 46–50
3	Tu	Deut. 6. 4–15	John 10. 31–end
4	W	Isa. 63. 7–16	Gal. 3.23 – 4.7
5	Th	*At Evening Prayer the readings for the Eve of The Epiphany are used. At other services, or, where, for pastoral reasons, The Epiphany is celebrated on Sunday 8 January, the following readings are used:*	
		Isa. ch. 12	2 Cor. 2, 12–end
6	F	**THE EPIPHANY** *Where, for pastoral reasons, The Epiphany is celebrated on Sunday 8 January, the following readings are used:*	
		Gen. 25. 19–end	Eph. 1. 1–6
7	Sa	*Where The Baptism of Christ is celebrated on Sunday 8 January, the readings for the Eve of The Baptism of Christ are used at Evening Prayer. At other services, the following readings are used:*	
		Gen. 25. 19–end	Eph. 1. 1–6
		Where The Epiphany is celebrated on Sunday 8 January, the readings for the Eve of The Epiphany are used at Evening Prayer. At other services, the following readings are used:	
		Joel 2. 28–end	Eph. 1. 7–14
8	S	THE BAPTISM OF CHRIST (The First Sunday of Epiphany) *or The Epiphany*	
9	M	*Where The Epiphany is celebrated on Friday 6 January and The Baptism of Christ on Sunday 8 January, these readings are used on Monday 9 January:*	
		Isa. 41. 14–20	John 1. 29–34
		Where The Epiphany is celebrated on Sunday 8 January, The Baptism of Christ is transferred to Monday 9 January.	
10	Tu	Exod. 17. 1–7	Acts 8. 26–end
11	W	Exod. 15. 1–19	Col. 2. 8–15
12	Th	Zech. 6. 9–15	1 Pet. 2. 4–10
13	F	Isa. 51. 7–16	Gal. 6. 14–18
14	Sa	Lev. 16. 11–22	Heb. 10. 19–25
15	S	THE SECOND SUNDAY OF EPIPHANY	
16	M	1 Kings 17. 8–16	Mark 8. 1–10
17	Tu	1 Kings 19. 1–9a	Mark 1. 9–15
18	W	1 Kings 19. 9b–18	Mark 9. 2–13
19	Th	Lev. 11. 1–8, 13–19, 41–45	Acts 10. 9–16
20	F	Isa. 49. 8–13	Acts 10. 34–43
21	Sa	Gen. 35. 1–15	Acts 10. 44–end
22	S	THE THIRD SUNDAY OF EPIPHANY	
23	M	Ezek. 37. 15–end	John 17. 1–19
24	Tu	Ezek. 20. 39–44	John 17. 20–end
25	W	THE CONVERSION OF PAUL	
26	Th	Deut. 26. 16–end	Rom. 14. 1–9
27	F	Lev. 19. 9–28	Rom. 15. 1–7
28	Sa	Jer. 33. 1–11	1 Pet. 5. 5b–end
		or, where The Presentation is celebrated on Sunday 29 January, First EP of Presentation of Christ	
29	S	THE FOURTH SUNDAY OF EPIPHANY (or The Presentation)	

Date	Old Testament	New Testament
	The readings appointed for the week of the Fourth Sunday of Epiphany are not used after The Presentation of Christ in the Temple. The alternative readings for Monday to Wednesday are used if The Presentation is observed on Sunday 29 January.	
30 M	Jonah ch. 3	2 Cor. 5. 11–21 *or*
	Gen. 1. 26–end	Matt. 10. 1–16
31 Tu	Prov. 4. 10–end	Matt. 5. 13–20 *or*
	Ruth 1. 1–18	1 John 3. 14–end

February 2012

Date	Old Testament	New Testament
1 W	Isa. 61. 1–9	Luke 7. 18–30 *or*
	1 Sam. 1. 19b–end	Luke 2. 41–end
2 Th	THE PRESENTATION *or*	
	Gen. 47. 1–12	Eph. 3. 14–end
3 F	2 Sam. 1. 17–end	Rom. 8. 28–end
4 Sa	Song of Sol. 2. 8–end	1 Cor. ch. 13
5 S	THE THIRD SUNDAY BEFORE LENT	
6 M	Exod. 23. 1–13	James 2. 1–13
7 Tu	Deut. 10. 12–end	Heb. 13. 1–16
8 W	Isa. 58. 6–end	Matt. 25. 31–end
9 Th	Isa. 42. 1–9	Luke 4. 14–21
10 F	Amos 5. 6–15	Eph. 4. 25–end
11 Sa	Amos 5. 18–24	John 2. 13–22
12 S	THE SECOND SUNDAY BEFORE LENT	
13 M	Isa. 61. 1–9	Mark 6. 1–13
14 Tu	Isa. 52. 1–10	Rom. 10. 5–21
15 W	Isa. 52.13 – 53.6	Rom. 15. 14–21
16 Th	Isa. 53. 4–12	2 Cor. 4. 1–10
17 F	Zech. 8. 16–end	Matt. 10. 1–15
18 Sa	Jer. 1. 4–10	Matt. 10. 16–22
19 S	THE SUNDAY NEXT BEFORE LENT	
20 M	2 Kings 2. 13–22	3 John
21 Tu	Judg. 14. 5–17	Rev. 10. 4–11
22 W	ASH WEDNESDAY	
23 Th	Gen. 2. 7–end	Heb. 2. 5–end
24 F	Gen. 4. 1–12	Heb. 4. 12–end
25 Sa	2 Kings 22. 11–end	Heb. 5. 1–10
26 S	THE FIRST SUNDAY OF LENT	
27 M	Gen. 6. 11–end; 7. 11–16	Luke 4. 14–21
28 Tu	Deut. 31. 7–13	1 John 3. 1–10
29 W	Gen. 11. 1–9	Matt. 24. 15–28

March 2012

Date	Old Testament	New Testament
1 Th	Gen. 13. 1–13	1 Pet. 2. 13–end
2 F	Gen. 21. 1–8	Luke 9. 18–27
3 Sa	Gen. 32. 22–32	2 Pet. 1. 10–end
4 S	THE SECOND SUNDAY OF LENT	
5 M	1 Chron. 21. 1–17	1 John 2. 1–8
6 Tu	Zech. ch. 3	2 Pet. 2. 1–10a
7 W	Job. 1. 1–22	Luke 21. 34 – 22.6
8 Th	2 Chron. 29. 1–11	Mark 11. 15–19
9 F	Exod. 19. 1–9a	1 Pet. 1. 1–9
10 Sa	Exod. 19. 9b–19	Acts 7. 44–50
11 S	THE THIRD SUNDAY OF LENT	
12 M	Josh. 4. 1–13	Luke 9. 1–11
13 Tu	Exod. 15. 2–27	Heb. 10. 32–end
14 W	Gen. 9. 8–17	1 Pet. 3. 18–end
15 Th	Dan. 12. 5–end	Mark 13. 21–end
16 F	Num. 20. 1–13	1 Cor. 10. 23–end
17 Sa	Isa. 43. 14–end	Heb. 3. 1–15
18 S	THE FOURTH SUNDAY OF LENT (Mothering Sunday)	
19 M	JOSEPH OF NAZARETH	
20 Tu	Jer. 13. 12–19	Acts 13. 26–35
21 W	Jer. 13. 20–27	1 Pet. 1.17 – 2.3
22 Th	Jer. 22. 11–19	Luke 11. 37–52
23 F	Jer. 17. 1–14	Luke 6. 17–26
24 Sa	Ezra ch. 1	2 Cor. 1. 12–19

Date	Old Testament	New Testament
25 S	THE FIFTH SUNDAY OF LENT (Passiontide begins)	
26 M	THE ANNUNCIATION (transferred from 25th)	
27 Tu	Isa. 58. 1–14	Mark 10. 32–45
28 W	Joel 36. 1–12	John 14. 1–14
29 Th	Jer. 9. 17–22	Luke 13. 31–35
30 F	Lam. 5. 1–3, 19–22	John 12. 20–26
31 Sa	Job 17. 6–end	John 12. 27–36

April 2012

Date	Old Testament	New Testament
1 S	PALM SUNDAY	
	HOLY WEEK	
8 S	EASTER DAY	
9 M	Isa. 54. 1–14	Rom. 1. 1–7
10 Tu	Isa. 51. 1–11	John 5. 19–29
11 W	Isa. 26. 1–19	John 20. 1–10
12 Th	Isa. 43. 14–21	Rev. 1. 4–end
13 F	Isa. 42. 10–17	1 Thess. 5. 1–11
14 Sa	Job 14. 1–14	John 21. 1–14
15 S	THE SECOND SUNDAY OF EASTER	
16 M	Ezek. 1. 22–end	Rev. ch. 4
17 Tu	Prov. 8. 1–11	Acts 16. 6–15
18 W	Hos. 5.15 – 6.6	1 Cor. 15. 1–11
19 Th	Jonah ch. 2	Mark 4. 35–end
20 F	Gen. 6. 9–end	1 Pet. 3. 8–end
21 Sa	1 Sam. 2. 1–8	Matt. 28. 8–15
22 S	THE THIRD SUNDAY OF EASTER	
23 M	GEORGE	
24 Tu	Lev. 19. 9–18, 32–end	Matt. 5. 38–end
25 W	MARK	
26 Th	Isa. 33. 13–22	Mark 6. 47–end
27 F	Neh. 9. 6–17	Rom. 5. 12–end
28 Sa	Isa. 61.10 – 62.5	Luke 24. 1–12
29 S	THE FOURTH SUNDAY OF EASTER	
30 M	Jer. 31. 10–17	Rev. 7. 9–end

May 2012

Date	Old Testament	New Testament
1 Tu	PHILIP AND JAMES	
2 W	Gen. 2. 4b–9	1 Cor. 15. 35–49
3 Th	Prov. 28. 3–end	Mark 10. 17–31
4 F	Eccles. 12. 1–8	Rom. 6. 1–11
5 Sa	1 Chron. 29. 10–13	Luke 24. 13–35
6 S	THE FIFTH SUNDAY OF EASTER	
7 M	Gen. 15. 1–18	Rom. 4. 13–end
8 Tu	Deut. 8. 1–10	Matt. 6. 19–end
9 W	Hos. 13. 4–14	1 Cor. 15. 50–end
10 Th	Exod. 3. 1–15	Mark 12. 18–27
11 F	Ezek. 36. 33–end	Rom. 8. 1–11
12 Sa	Isa. 38. 9–20	Luke 24. 33–end
13 S	THE SIXTH SUNDAY OF EASTER	
14 M	MATTHIAS	
15 Tu	Isa. 32. 12–end	Rom. 5. 1–11
16 W	At Evening Prayer the readings for the Eve of Ascension Day are used. At other services, the following readings are used:	
	Isa. 43. 1–13	Titus 2.11 – 3.8
17 Th	ASCENSION DAY	
18 F	Exod. 35.30 – 36.1	Gal. 5. 13–end
19 Sa	Num. 11. 16–17, 24–29	1 Cor. ch. 2
20 S	THE SEVENTH SUNDAY OF EASTER (Sunday after Ascension Day)	
21 M	Num. 27. 15–end	1 Cor. ch. 3
22 Tu	1 Sam. 10. 1–10	1 Cor. 12. 1–13
23 W	1 Kings 19. 1–18	Matt. 3. 13–end
24 Th	Ezek. 11. 14–20	Matt. 9.35 – 10.20
25 F	Ezek. 36. 22–28	Matt. 12. 22–32
26 Sa	At Evening Prayer the readings for the Eve of Pentecost are used. At other services, the following readings are used:	
	Mic. 3. 1–8	Eph. 6. 10–20

Date		Old Testament	New Testament
27	S	**PENTECOST** (Whit Sunday)	
28	M	Gen. 12. 1–9	Rom. 4. 13–end
29	Tu	Gen. 13. 1–12	Rom. 12. 9–end
30	W	Gen. ch. 15	Rom. 4. 1–8
31	Th	THE VISITATION	

June 2012

Date		Old Testament	New Testament
1	F	Isa. 51. 1–8	John 8. 48–end
2	Sa	At Evening Prayer the readings for the Eve of Trinity Sunday are used. At other services, the following readings are used:	
		Ecclus. 44. 19–23 or	
		Josh. 2. 1–15	James 2. 14–26
3	S	**TRINITY SUNDAY**	
4	M	Exod. 2. 1–10	Heb. 11. 23–31
5	Tu	Exod. 2. 11–end	Acts 7. 17–29
6	W	Exod. 3. 1–12	Acts 7. 30–38
7	Th	Day of Thanksgiving for the Institution of the Holy Communion (Corpus Christi) or, where Corpus Christi is celebrated as a Lesser Festival:	
		Exod. 6. 1–13	John 9. 24–38
8	F	Exod. 34. 1–10	Mark 7. 1–13
9	Sa	Exod. 34. 27–end	2 Cor. 3. 7–end
10	S	THE FIRST SUNDAY AFTER TRINITY	
11	M	BARNABAS	
12	Tu	Gen. 41. 15–40	Mark 13. 1–13
13	W	Gen. 42. 17–end	Matt. 18. 1–14
14	Th	Gen. 45. 1–15	Acts 7. 9–16
15	F	Gen. 47. 1–12	1 Thess. 5. 12–end
16	Sa	Gen. 50. 4–21	Luke 15. 11–end
17	S	THE SECOND SUNDAY AFTER TRINITY	
18	M	Isa. ch. 32	James 3. 13–end
19	Tu	Prov. 3. 1–18	Matt. 5. 1–12
20	W	Judg. 6. 1–16	Matt. 5. 13–24
21	Th	Jer. 6. 9–15	1 Tim. 2. 1–6
22	F	1 Sam. 16. 14–end	John 14. 15–end
23	Sa	Isa. 6. 1–9	Rev. 19. 9–end
24	S	THE BIRTH OF JOHN THE BAPTIST (THE THIRD SUNDAY AFTER TRINITY)	
25	M	Where The Birth of John the Baptist is celebrated on Sunday 24 June:	
		Exod. 13. 13b–end	Luke 15. 1–10
		or The Birth of John the Baptist	
26	Tu	Prov. 1. 20–end	James 5. 13–end
27	W	Isa. 5. 8–24	James 1. 17–25
28	Th	Isa. 57. 14–end	John 13. 1–17
29	F	PETER AND PAUL	
30	Sa	Isa. 25. 1–9	Acts 2. 22–33

July 2012

Date		Old Testament	New Testament
1	S	THE FOURTH SUNDAY AFTER TRINITY	
2	M	Exod. 20. 1–17	Matt. 6. 1–15
3	Tu	THOMAS	
4	W	Isa. 24. 1–15	1 Cor. 6. 1–11
5	Th	Job ch. 7	Matt. 7. 21–29
6	F	Jer. 20. 7–end	Matt. 27. 27–44
7	Sa	Job ch. 28	Heb. 11.32 – 12.2
8	S	THE FIFTH SUNDAY AFTER TRINITY	
9	M	Exod. 32. 1–14	Col. 3. 1–11
10	Tu	Prov. 9. 1–12	2 Thess. 2.13 – 3.5
11	W	Isa. 26. 1–9	Rom. 8. 12–27
12	Th	Jer. 8.18 – 9.6	John 13. 21–35
13	F	2 Sam. 5. 1–12	Matt. 27. 45–56
14	Sa	Hos. 11. 1–11	Matt. 28. 1–7
15	S	THE SIXTH SUNDAY AFTER TRINITY	
16	M	Exod. 40. 1–16	Luke 14. 15–24
17	Tu	Prov. 11. 1–12	Mark 12. 38–44
18	W	Isa. 33. 2–10	Phil. 1. 1–11

Date		Old Testament	New Testament
19	Th	Job ch. 38	Luke 18. 1–14
20	F	Job 42. 1–6	John 3. 1–15
21	Sa	Eccles. 9. 1–11	Heb. 1. 1–9
22	S	MARY MAGDALENE (THE SEVENTH SUNDAY AFTER TRINITY)	
23	M	Where Mary Magdalene is celebrated on Sunday 22 July:	
		Num. 23. 1–12	1 Cor. 1. 10–17
		or Mary Magdalene	
24	Tu	Prov. 12. 1–12	Gal. 3. 1–14
25	W	JAMES	
26	Th	Hos. ch. 14	John 15. 1–17
27	F	2 Sam. 18. 18–end	Matt. 27. 57–66
28	Sa	Isa. 55. 1–7	Mark 6. 1–8
29	S	THE EIGHTH SUNDAY AFTER TRINITY	
30	M	Joel 3. 16–21	Mark 4. 21–34
31	Tu	Prov. 12. 13–end	John 1. 43–51

August 2012

Date		Old Testament	New Testament
1	W	Isa. 55. 8–end	2 Tim. 2. 8–19
2	Th	Isa. 38. 1–8	Mark 5. 21–43
3	F	Jer. 14. 1–9	Luke 8. 4–15
4	Sa	Eccles. 5. 10–19	1 Tim. 6. 6–16
5	S	THE NINTH SUNDAY AFTER TRINITY	
6	M	THE TRANSFIGURATION	
7	Tu	Prov. 15. 1–11	Gal. 2. 15–end
8	W	Isa. 49. 1–7	1 John 1
9	Th	Prov. 27. 1–12	John 15. 12–27
10	F	Isa. 59. 8–end	Mark 15. 6–20
11	Sa	Zech. 7.8 – 8.8	Luke 20. 27–40
12	S	THE TENTH SUNDAY AFTER TRINITY	
13	M	Judg. 13. 1–23	Luke 10. 38–42
14	Tu	Prov. 15. 15–end	Matt. 15. 21–28
15	W	THE BLESSED VIRGIN MARY	
16	Th	Jer. 16. 1–5	Luke 12. 35–48
17	F	Jer. 18. 1–11	Heb. 1. 1–9
18	Sa	Jer. 26. 1–19	Eph. 3. 1–13
19	S	THE ELEVENTH SUNDAY AFTER TRINITY	
20	M	Ruth 2. 1–13	Luke 10. 25–37
21	Tu	Prov. 16. 1–11	Phil. 3. 4b–end
22	W	Deut. 11. 1–21	2 Cor. 9. 6–end
23	Th	Ecclus. ch. 2 or	
		Eccles. 2. 12–25	John 16. 1–15
24	F	BARTHOLOMEW	
25	Sa	2 Kings 2. 11–14	Luke 24. 36–end
26	S	THE TWELFTH SUNDAY AFTER TRINITY	
27	M	1 Sam. 17. 32–50	Matt. 8. 14–22
28	Tu	Prov. 17. 1–15	Luke 7. 1–17
29	W	Jer. 5. 20–end	2 Pet. 3. 8–end
30	Th	Dan. 2. 1–23	Luke 10. 1–20
31	F	Dan. 3. 1–28	Rev. ch. 15

September 2012

Date		Old Testament	New Testament
1	Sa	Dan. ch. 6	Phil. 2. 14–24
2	S	THE THIRTEENTH SUNDAY AFTER TRINITY	
3	M	2 Sam. 7. 4–17	2 Cor. 5. 1–10
4	Tu	Prov. 18. 10–21	Rom. 14. 10–end
5	W	Judg. 4. 1–10	Rom. 1. 8–17
6	Th	Isa. 49. 14–end	John 16. 16–24
7	F	Job 9. 1–24	Mark 15. 21–32
8	Sa	Exod. 19. 1–9	John 20. 11–18
9	S	THE FOURTEENTH SUNDAY AFTER TRINITY	
10	M	Hag. ch. 1	Mark 7. 9–23
11	Tu	Prov. 21. 1–18	Mark 6. 30–44
12	W	Hos. 11. 1–11	1 John 4. 9–end
13	Th	Lam. 3. 34–48	Rom. 7. 14–end
14	F	HOLY CROSS DAY	
15	Sa	Ecclus. 4. 1–28 or	
		Deut. 29. 2–15	2 Tim. 3. 10–end
16	S	THE FIFTEENTH SUNDAY AFTER TRINITY	

Date		Old Testament	New Testament
17	M	Wisd. 6. 12–21 *or*	
		Job 12. 1–16	Matt. 15. 1–9
18	Tu	Prov. 8. 1–11	Luke 6. 39–end
19	W	Prov. 2. 1–15	Col. 1. 9–20
20	Th	Baruch 3. 14–end *or*	
		Gen. 1. 1–13	John 1. 1–18
21	F	MATTHEW	
22	Sa	Wisd. 9. 1–12 *or*	
		Jer. 1. 4–10	Luke 2. 41–end
23	S	THE SIXTEENTH SUNDAY AFTER TRINITY	
24	M	Gen. 21. 1–13	Luke 1. 26–38
25	Tu	Ruth 4. 7–17	Luke 2. 25–38
26	W	2 Kings 4. 1–7	John 2. 1–11
27	Th	2 Kings 4. 25b–37	Mark 3. 19b–35
28	F	Judith 8. 9–17, 28–36 *or*	
		Ruth 1. 1–18	John 19. 25b–30
29	Sa	MICHAEL AND ALL ANGELS	
30	S	THE SEVENTEENTH SUNDAY AFTER TRINITY	

October 2012

Date		Old Testament	New Testament
1	M	Exod. 19. 16–end	Heb. 12. 18–end
2	Tu	1 Chron. 16. 1–13	Rev. 11. 15–end
3	W	1 Chron. 29. 10–19	Col. 3. 12–17
4	Th	Neh. 8. 1–12	1 Cor. 14. 1–12
5	F	Isa. 1. 10–17	Mark 12. 28–34
6	Sa	Dan. 6. 6–23	Rev. 12. 7–12
7	S	THE EIGHTEENTH SUNDAY AFTER TRINITY	
8	M	2 Sam. 22. 4–7, 17–20	Heb. 7.26 – 8.6
9	Tu	Prov. 22. 17–end	2 Cor. 12. 1–10
10	W	Hos. ch. 14	James 2. 14–26
11	Th	Isa. 24. 1–15	John 16. 25–33
12	F	Jer. 14. 1–9	Luke 23. 44–56
13	Sa	Zech. 8. 14–end	John 20. 19–end
14	S	THE NINETEENTH SUNDAY AFTER TRINITY	
15	M	1 Kings 3. 3–14	1 Tim. 3.13 – 4.8
16	Tu	Prov. 27. 11–end	Gal. 6. 1–10
17	W	Isa. 51. 1–6	2 Cor. 1. 1–11
18	Th	LUKE	
19	F	Ecclus. 28. 2–12 *or* Job	
		19. 21–end	Mark 15. 33–37
20	Sa	Isa. 44. 21–end	John 21. 15–end
21	S	THE TWENTIETH SUNDAY AFTER TRINITY	
22	M	1 Kings 6. 2–10	John 12. 1–11
23	Tu	Prov. 31. 10–end	Luke 10. 38–42
24	W	Jonah ch. 1	Luke 5. 1–11
25	Th	Exod. 12. 1–20	1 Thess. 4. 1–12
26	F	Isa. ch. 64	Matt. 27. 45–56
27	Sa	2 Sam. 7. 18–end	Acts 2. 22–33
28	S	SIMON AND JUDE, APOSTLES (THE LAST SUNDAY AFTER TRINITY)	
29	M	*Where Simon and Jude is celebrated on Sunday 28 October:*	
		Isa. 42. 14–21	Luke 1. 5–25
		or Simon and Jude	
30	Tu	1 Sam. 4. 12–end	Luke 1. 57–80
31	W	*At Evening Prayer the readings for the Eve of All Saints are used. At other services, the following readings are used:*	
		Baruch ch. 5 *or*	Mark 1. 1–11
		Hag. 1. 1–11	

November 2012

Date		Old Testament	New Testament
1	Th	**ALL SAINTS' DAY**	
		or, where All Saints' Day is celebrated on Sunday 4 November only:	
		Isa. ch. 35	Matt. 11. 2–19
2	F	2 Sam. 11. 1–17	Matt. 14. 1–12
3	Sa	Isa. 43. 15–21	Acts 19. 1–10

Date		Old Testament	New Testament
4	S	THE FOURTH SUNDAY BEFORE ADVENT	
5	M	Esther 3. 1–11; 4. 7–17	Matt. 18. 1–10
6	Tu	Ezek. 18. 21–end	Matt. 18. 12–20
7	W	Prov. 3. 27–end	Matt. 18. 21–end
8	Th	Exod. 23. 1–9	Matt. 19. 1–15
9	F	Prov. 3. 13–18	Matt. 19. 16–end
10	Sa	Deut. 28. 1–6	Matt. 20. 1–16
11	S	THE THIRD SUNDAY BEFORE ADVENT	
12	M	Isa. 40. 21–end	Rom. 11. 25–end
13	Tu	Ezek. 34. 20–end	John 10. 1–18
14	W	Lev. 26. 3–13	Titus 2. 1–10
15	Th	Hos. 6. 1–6	Matt. 9. 9–13
16	F	Mal. ch. 4	John 4. 5–26
17	Sa	Mic. 6. 6–8	Col. 3. 12–17
18	S	THE SECOND SUNDAY BEFORE ADVENT	
19	M	Mic. 7. 1–7	Matt. 10. 24–39
20	Tu	Hab. 3. 1–19a	1 Cor. 4. 9–16
21	W	Zech. 8. 1–13	Mark 13. 3–8
22	Th	Zech. 10. 6–end	1 Pet. 5. 1–11
23	F	Mic. 4. 1–5	Luke 9. 28–36
24	Sa	*At Evening Prayer the readings for the Eve of Christ the King are used. At other services, the following readings are used:*	
		Exod. 16. 1–21	John 6. 3–15
25	S	CHRIST THE KING (The Sunday next before Advent)	
26	M	Jer. 30. 1–3, 10–17	Rom. 12. 9–21
27	Tu	Jer. 30. 18–24	John 10. 22–30
28	W	Jer. 31. 1–9	Matt. 15. 21–31
29	Th	Jer. 31. 10–17	Matt. 16. 13–end
30	F	ANDREW	

December 2012

Date		Old Testament	New Testament
1	Sa	Isa. 51.17 – 52.2	Eph. 5. 1–20
2	S	THE FIRST SUNDAY OF ADVENT	
3	M	Mal. 3. 1–6	Matt. 3. 1–6
4	Tu	Zeph. 3. 14–end	1 Thess. 4. 13–end
5	W	Isa. 65.17 – 66.2	Matt. 24. 1–14
6	Th	Mic. 5. 2–5a	John 3. 16–21
7	F	Isa. 66. 18–end	Luke 13. 22–30
8	Sa	Mic. 7. 8–15	Rom. 15.30 – 16.7, 25–end
9	S	THE SECOND SUNDAY OF ADVENT	
10	M	Jer. 7. 1–11	Phil. 4. 4–9
11	Tu	Dan. 7. 9–14	Matt. 24. 15–28
12	W	Amos 9. 11–end	Rom. 13. 8–14
13	Th	Jer. 23. 5–8	Mark 11. 1–11
14	F	Jer. 33. 14–22	Luke 21. 25–36
15	Sa	Zech. 14. 4–11	Rev. 22. 1–7
16	S	THE THIRD SUNDAY OF ADVENT	
17	M	Ecclus. 24. 1–9 *or*	
		Prov. 6. 22–31	1 Cor. 2. 1–13
18	Tu	Exod. 3. 1–6	Acts 7. 20–36
19	W	Isa. 11. 1–9	Rom. 15. 7–13
20	Th	Isa. 22. 21–23	Rev. 3. 7–13
21	F	Num. 24. 15b–19	Rev. 22. 10–21
22	Sa	Jer. 30. 7–11a	Acts 4. 1–12
23	S	THE FOURTH SUNDAY OF ADVENT	
24	M	*At Evening Prayer the readings for Christmas Eve are used. At other services, the following readings are used:*	
		Isa. 29. 13–18	1 John 4. 7–16
25	Tu	**CHRISTMAS DAY**	
26	W	STEPHEN	
27	Th	JOHN THE EVANGELIST	
28	F	THE HOLY INNOCENTS	
29	Sa	Mic. 1. 1–4; 2. 12–13	Luke 2. 1–7
30	S	THE FIRST SUNDAY OF CHRISTMAS	
31	M	Eccles. 3. 1–13	Rev. 21. 1–8

CALENDAR 2013

JANUARY
Su	M	Tu	W	Th	F	Sa
		B	E²	E³	.	E⁴
.	.	1	2	3	4	5
6	7	8	9	10	11	12
13	14	15	16	17	18	19
20	21	22	23	24	25	26
27	28	29	30	31	.	.

FEBRUARY
Su	M	Tu	W	Th	F	Sa
.	.	.	.	.	Pr	L²
L³	L⁴	L⁵	.	.	1	2
3	4	5	6	7	8	9
10	11	12	13	14	15	16
17	18	19	20	21	22	23
24	25	26	27	28	.	.

MARCH
Su	M	Tu	W	Th	F	Sa
.	.	.	.	.	P	E
L³	L⁴	L⁵	.	1	18	2
3	4	5	6	7	8	9
10	11	12	13	14	15	16
17	18	19	20	21	22	23
24	25	26	27	28	29	30

APRIL
Su	M	Tu	W	Th	F	Sa
.	.	.	.	.	.	E⁵
.	1	An	2	3	4	5
6	7	8	9	10	11	12
13	14	15	16	17	18	19
E²	E³	E⁴	22	23	24	25

MAY
Su	M	Tu	W	Th	F	Sa
.	.	.	.	E⁴	W	T
E⁵	6	13	20	27	.	.
.	7	14	21	28	.	.
.	8	15	22	29	.	.
A	9	16	23	30	.	.
11	18	25	.			

JUNE
Su	M	Tu	W	Th	F	Sa
.	.	.	.	.	.	T⁵
T¹	T²	T³	17	18	19	24
3	10	11	12	13	20	25
4	5	12	13	20	21	26
6	7	14	21	22	27	.
8	15	22	29			

JULY
Su	M	Tu	W	Th	F	Sa
.	.	.	.	.	T⁸	.
T⁶	T⁷	15	22	29	.	.
8	16	23	30	.	.	.
9	10	17	24	31	.	.
11	18	25	.			
12	19	26	.			
13	20	27				

AUGUST
Su	M	Tu	W	Th	F	Sa
.	.	.	.	1	2	T⁹
T¹⁰	T¹¹	T¹²	19	26	.	.
5	12	13	20	27	.	.
6	7	14	21	28	.	.
7	8	15	22	29	.	.
9	16	23	30			
17	24	31				

SEPTEMBER
Su	M	Tu	W	Th	F	Sa
.	.	.	.	.	.	T¹⁸
T¹⁵	T¹⁶	T¹⁷	23	24	25	30
2	9	10	17	18	26	.
4	11	12	19	20	27	.
6	13	14	21	28	.	.
8	15	22	29			

OCTOBER
Su	M	Tu	W	Th	F	Sa
.	.	1	2	3	4	T⁹
T¹⁹	T²⁰	T²¹	16	23	24	25
7	8	15	22	29	30	26
9	10	17	24	31	.	.
11	18	25	.			
12	19	26				

NOVEMBER
Su	M	Tu	W	Th	F	Sa
.	.	.	.	.	1	AS
A⁻⁴	A⁻³	A⁻²	A⁻¹	21	28	2
4	5	12	19	26	.	.
6	13	20	27	.	.	.
8	15	22	29	.	.	.
9	16	23	30			

DECEMBER
Su	M	Tu	W	Th	F	Sa
.	.	.	.	.	.	T⁻⁸
A⁻¹	A²	A³	A⁴	23	30	.
2	9	16	17	24	31	.
4	5	11	18	X	.	.
6	13	20	27	.	.	.
7	14	21	28			

Legend (2013)
P = Palm Sunday
Pr = Presentation
T = Trinity
(T³ = also Birth of John the Baptist, 2012)
(T⁷ = also Mary Magdalene, 2012)
(T¹⁸ = also Michael and All Angels, 2013)
Tᴸ = Last Sunday after Trinity
(Tᴸ = also Simon and Jude, 2012)
W = Pentecost (Whit Sunday)
X = Christmas

CALENDAR 2012

JANUARY
Su	M	Tu	W	Th	F	Sa
X²	B	E²	E³	E⁴	.	.
2	3	16	17	24	25	30
3	10	17	24	31	.	.
4	11	18	25	.	.	.
5	12	19	26	.	.	.
E	13	20	27	.	.	.
7	14	21	28			

FEBRUARY
Su	M	Tu	W	Th	F	Sa
.	.	.	.	.	Pr	L²
L³	L⁴	L⁻¹	L⁻	27	28	.
6	13	20	21	A	29	.
7	14	15	22	23	.	.
8	9	16	17	24	25	.
10	11	18				

MARCH
Su	M	Tu	W	Th	F	Sa
.	.	.	.	.	L²	L⁴	5
L³	5	12	19	20	27	28
6	7	13	20	21	28	29
7	8	14	21	22	23	30
An	9	16	17	24	31	.
3	10	17	24			

APRIL
Su	M	Tu	W	Th	F	Sa
.	.	.	.	.	.	E⁵
P	2	9	16	23	24	30
2	3	10	17	18	25	.
4	11	12	19	26	.	.
G	5	13	20	27	.	.
7	14	21	28			

MAY
Su	M	Tu	W	Th	F	Sa
.	.	1	2	3	W	T
E⁵	7	14	21	28	.	.
6	13	15	22	29	.	.
8	9	16	23	30	.	.
10	A	17	24	31	.	.
12	19					

JUNE
Su	M	Tu	W	Th	F	Sa
.	.	.	.	.	1	T³
T¹	4	11	18	25	.	.
3	5	12	19	26	.	.
6	13	20	27	.	.	.
7	14	21	28	.	.	.
8	9	16	23	30	.	.

JULY
Su	M	Tu	W	Th	F	Sa
.	.	.	.	.	T⁷	T⁹
T⁵	2	9	16	23	30	.
2	3	10	17	24	31	.
4	11	18	25	.	.	.
5	12	19	26	.	.	.
6	13	20	27			

AUGUST
Su	M	Tu	W	Th	F	Sa
.	.	.	1	2	3	T⁹
T¹⁰	T¹¹	T¹²	20	27	.	.
5	6	13	20	28	.	.
7	8	15	22	29	.	.
9	16	23	30	.	.	.
11	18	25	.			

SEPTEMBER
Su	M	Tu	W	Th	F	Sa
.	.	.	.	.	.	T¹⁶
T¹³	T¹⁴	T¹⁵	17	24	.	.
3	10	11	18	25	26	.
5	12	19	20	27	.	.
6	13	14	21	28	.	.
8	15	22	29			

OCTOBER
Su	M	Tu	W	Th	F	Sa
T¹⁸	T¹⁹	T²⁰	17	24	25	X¹
1	8	15	22	23	30	31
2	9	16	17	24	31	.
3	10	17	24	31	.	.
5	12	19	26	.	.	.
6	13	20	27			

NOVEMBER
Su	M	Tu	W	Th	F	Sa
.	.	.	.	AS	A⁻²	A⁻¹
A⁻⁴	A⁻³	5	12	19	26	.
4	5	13	20	27	.	.
6	7	14	21	28	.	.
8	9	16	23	30	.	.
3	10	17	24			

DECEMBER
Su	M	Tu	W	Th	F	Sa
.	.	.	.	.	.	A¹
A⁻¹	A²	A³	17	24	25	22
3	4	10	17	18	X	29
4	11	12	19	26	.	.
6	13	20	27	.	.	.
8	15	22	1			

Legend (2012)
A = Ash Wednesday, Ascension, Advent
A⁻ = Before Advent
A⁻¹ = also All Saints (if trans.)
A⁻¹ = Christ the King
An = Annunciation
AS = All Saints
B = Baptism
E = Epiphany, Easter
E⁴ = also Presentation (if trans.)
G = Good Friday
L = Lent
L⁻ = Before Lent
M = Maundy Thursday